STRAND ANNEX

What's My Name?

Black Vernacular Intellectuals

Grant Farred

University of Minnesota Press
Minneapolis • London

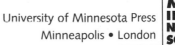

D0720260

See pages 297–98 for permission information.

Copyright 2003 by the Regents of the University of Minnesota

All rights reserved. No part of this publication may be reproduced, stored in a retrieval system, or trans-mitted, in any form or by any means, electronic, mechanical, photocopying, recording, or otherwise, without the prior written permission of the publisher.

Published by the University of Minnesota Press
111 Third Avenue South, Suite 290
Minneapolis, MN 55401-2520
http://www.upress.umn.edu

Library of Congress Cataloging-in-Publication Data

Farred, Grant.
    What's my name? : Black vernacular intellectuals / Grant Farred.
        p. cm.
Includes bibliographical references (p.) and index.
    ISBN 0-8166-3316-9 (alk. paper)—ISBN 0-8166-3317-7 (pbk. : alk. paper)
    1. Intellectuals. 2. Ali, Muhammad, 1942—Political and social
views. 3. James, C. L. R. (Cyril Lionel Robert), 1901—Political and
social views. 4. Hall, Stuart—Political and social views. 5. Marley,
Bob—Political and social views. 6. Race relations—Political aspects.
I. Title.
HM728 .F37 2003
305.5′52—dc21

2003006543

Printed in the United States of America on acid-free paper

The University of Minnesota is an equal-opportunity educator and employer.

12 11 10 09 08 07 06 05 04 03   10 9 8 7 6 5 4 3 2 1

To my daughter,
Andrea Farred:
with love, Bug,
for you,
always.

Contents

Acknowledgments

This project began a while ago, in a very different form, in a restaurant that no longer exists. What has endured throughout the process is a series of conversations with Andrew Ross, a rare intellectual and friend. *What's My Name?* could not have been conceived without Andrew's continued support (in this and so many other ventures), his vision, and his generosity. He was astute on C. L. R. James, gave me keen insight into Stuart Hall, and brought no small amount of joie de vivre to the Muhammad Ali and Bob Marley chapters. He cajoled and, most important, challenged me to think assiduously about my category of the vernacular intellectual. Through it all he never stopped believing in the book, and his advice was sage, sane, and always inflected with his most endearing quality: a sense of fun and perspective about the academy and the work we do in and outside of it. I owe Andrew a great many debts.

My editors at the University of Minnesota Press, William Murphy and Richard Morrison, lent their different strengths and personalities to the project. William brought a focus, seriousness, and intensity that I deeply appreciate. Richard pushed and probed, always making encouraging noises, always insisting not so subtly on deadlines, always pushing me to think about the issue one more time. I seldom met the deadlines but the sound of his voice seemed most resonant when I was pursuing other writings. He kept me on track. My thanks to William and Richard and the Press for their faith in *What's My Name?*.

I am grateful to Stuart Hall for answering my queries with his inimitable generosity. In encounters from London to Kingston, he listened to me good naturedly about the project though I have little doubt that he would, typical of his modesty, rather not have discussed himself. Like many cultural studies and postcolonial theory scholars, I have benefited immensely from the vast Hall corpus, conversations with him, and, most important, the intellectual and political example that Stuart sets for all of us. So much work in both these fields would be unimaginable without the foundation he provided and the ongoing contributions he makes to this and several disciplines.

To my friends: Ian Balfour, for his wry advice, his impeccable taste in music, and his love of the popular, the profane, and the sublime. Tess Chakkalakal, for her persistent intelligence, her unquenchable interest in sport, and her humor. Wahneema Lubiano, for being a remarkable teacher and colleague and for a mind that never fails to amaze. Jan Radway, a serious scholar whose work in cultural studies offers an example to so many in the field. Thanks to Rebecca Ohm, librarian with a smile, and Tammi Brooks, who guided me through the editing. To Prabha Jerrybandan, who provided humor in the final stages. To all these folks, my thanks for reading various versions of the manuscript, offering incisive comments and suggestions, and bibliographic help. The final product would have been poorer without their input.

And finally, to my daughter Andrea Farred: for your irascibility, your capacity for fun and ringing laughter, your remarkable courage and fortitude, your immersion in popular culture, and the joy you bring me in every exchange, this book is dedicated to you. With love.

Durham, July 2003

Thinking in the Vernacular

Who knows but that on the lower frequencies, I speak for you?

—Ralph Ellison, *Invisible Man*

Vernacularize. Explore and explicate the links between the popular and the political. Never underestimate the capacity of the popular to elucidate the ideological, to animate the political, never overlook the vernacular as a means of producing a subaltern or postcolonial voice that resists, subverts, disrupts, reconfigures, or impacts the dominant discourse. For disempowered constituencies, resistance against the domination is extremely difficult without a vernacular component. Challenging or overcoming subjugation frequently depends on those expressions of disenfranchised life that articulate ideological oppositionality and the pleasures that are contained within—and extraneous to—acts of political resistance. The political is not always pleasurable; but the pleasurable, within the vernacular, is always potentially political. Within the terms of the vernacular, no minority or anticolonial struggle can be sustained if it does not contain in it a cultural element; an element, moreover, that has popular purchase. In the vernacular conception of politics, popular culture constitutes a singular practice. It represents that mode in which the political and the popular conjoin identificatory pleasure with ideological resistance.

In order for a black or marginalized intellectual (more so than for other figures) to be politically efficacious, the historical injunction is overdetermined: vernacularity is an absolute prerequisite. From W. E. B. DuBois's *The Souls of Black Folk*, a study of black life in the Reconstruction

1

South, to Stuart Hall's writing on cultural studies, from C. L. R. James's treatise on cricket *(Beyond a Boundary)* to Angela Davis's theorization of the black woman's condition, black public thinkers of the twentieth century have been at their most incisive and effective when they adopt vernacularity as the dominant intellectual mode.[1]

The vernacular, I argue in *What's My Name?*, is a distinct definition of—and a way of being—the intellectual. Deeply grounded in the ways in which the cultural shapes and reshapes the political impact of four black thinkers, Cyril Lionel Robert (C. L. R.) James, Stuart Hall, Muhammad Ali, and Bob Marley, this study reconsiders the post- and anticolonial figure as an intellectual. In setting Ali and Marley alongside James and Hall, I offer a conceptualization beyond the existing categorizations of the intellectual. This book rethinks the most fundamental tenet of what is accepted as "intellectual" by asking, Who is an intellectual? And, why? This study is an exploration of how these four different figures, from different parts and classes of the Caribbean and the United States, are understood as intellectuals; it refigures the public interventions they made (and are all, in their various ways, still making) and explicates how their various articulations, their different engagements with the dominant culture, register as intellectual labor.

In conceptualizing the vernacular intellectual, I draw on and develop, and then distinguish the category from, Antonio Gramsci's organic or traditional model. The Italian Marxist's construction of the intellectual (which turns on his famously egalitarian definition, "All men are intellectuals, one could therefore say: but not all men have in society the function of intellectuals") provides the groundwork for the vernacular intellectual.[2] Gramsci's democratization of the role of public thinkers (gendered as it is)—"All men are intellectuals"—provides the basis for conceiving of the African-American boxer, the Trinidadian-born Marxist, the Jamaican-born New Lefter, and the Jamaican reggae star as political and cultural figures who perform, in their different societies, distinct "functions" as "intellectuals." Gramsci's definition allows for (re)configuring a paradigm in which the articulations of a Marley (the various critiques of race, class, and ideology contained in his lyrics) and a James (using cricket to inveigh against colonialism, racism, and economic exploitation) can both be understood as culturally based intellectual interventions; following Gramsci, it is possible to think of Ali and James simultaneously as antiracist black intellectuals, to imagine Hall and Marley as postcolonial figures who have as much resonance (more, until recently, in Hall's case) in the metropolis as they do in their peripheral Caribbean.[3]

However, if everyone can categorically be named an intellectual, it requires more than a reconceptualization of the "function" deemed intellectual to redefine the intellectual. *What's My Name?* rethinks what constitutes intellectual articulation and, in distinguishing itself from Gramsci's work, posits that what counts as intellectual labor extends beyond the framework of *The Prison Notebooks*—Gramsci's egalitarian terms in which he constructs intellectuals as those figures who represent more than the printed or spoken word of the educated middle classes, the bourgeoisie, or the formally trained working-class intellectual. The vernacular is a critique of the traditional/organic intellectual, at once a recognition of Gramsci's inadequacies and a model that exceeds by incorporating within its framework, without eliding difference, the work of scholars such as Hall and James and cultural figures such as Ali and Marley. Vernacularity allows for the thinking together of James and Marley, understanding how their intellectual influences derive from a similar locale: the recognition of popular culture as a primary site of politics. The popular is the social conjuncture that marks the complicated nexus between pleasure and resistance; the Marxist immersion in and critique of cricket intersects, overlaps, and coincides with a musician's socially conscious lyrics. In the terms of the vernacular, James's and Marley's oeuvres can be read as discrete articulations of the same sociopolitical process; James and Marley both speak, in their different registers and in their different historical moments, in the vernacular; they both grasp the popular as the most efficacious language and mode of resistance. However, as the later discussion of the crisis of Hall and James as organic intellectuals demonstrates, if for Marley the popular is the (only) political (modality), then for James the vernacular is the acquired discourse; Marley is the organic vernacular, James represents the process by which the traditional organic intellectual conceives of, integrates, and writes himself into vernacularity.

In *The Prison Notebooks*, Gramsci's conception of the organic intellectual differs from that of the traditional intellectual in that they represent both distinct historical moments and modes of being a thinker; temporality and modality are equally important in distinguishing the traditional from the organic. The traditional intellectual belongs primarily to the ecclesiastical class (the landed aristocracy) while the organic intellectual represents new economic and political modes—the increasing bureaucratization of the state and its need to produce thinkers, a managerial class, who originate from within this new class and are therefore committed to this class, its interests, and its future within the state and its machinery. Every political constituency, as Gramsci points out in a discussion of the working class, can give birth to spokespersons or functionaries innate to it—every class has a cadre of thinkers dedicated to voicing its positions, organic to itself: "The working class, like the bourgeoisie before it, is capable of developing from within its ranks its own organic intellectuals, and the function of the political party, whether mass or vanguard, is that of channeling the activity of these organic intellectuals and providing a link between the class and certain sections of the traditional intelligentsia" (4). Organic intellectuals of early-twentieth-century capitalism represent, according to Gramsci, a new intellectual tradition in which class affiliation determines the role—or the function—of the well-schooled activist. Phrased in a Leninist vocabulary ("mass" or "vanguard"), it is clear from his meditation that Gramsci conceives of the intellectual as primarily a conventional political actor—as the working-class spokesperson who negotiates between his constituency of origin and the dominant classes.

While acknowledging the political impact and the import of the organic intellectual, *What's My Name?* offers a reading of the anti- and postcolonial figure that understands political intervention beyond the scope of the party, the trade union, and the "traditional bourgeoisie." This book redefines what we understand an intellectual to be. However, it is not only, though it is that too, an interrogation of the functions intellectuals perform; it rethinks *who* is an intellectual—as in, paradigmatically phrased, who an intellectual is. It is not simply a cataloging of who an intellectual is and what an intellectual does; it is a renovation of the category so that Ali, Jimi Hendrix, Grace Jones, Janis Joplin, and Martina Navratilova can, inter alia, be conceived as intellectuals, not simply as sportspersons or musicians.

Located at the intersection of cultural studies and postcolonial theory, and motivated by both, *What's My Name?* pivots on the importance of the "intellectualized popular"—the practices and the producers of that culture—to both these disciplines. The anti- and postcolonial struggle included more than simply the armed revolutionary movement; the independent Third World state's existence is inextricably linked to cultural campaigns for self-determination and respect for black and brown cultural practices denigrated, appropriated, or dismissed from official history by European colonial powers. Cultural studies, which is founded on the refutation of the high/low hierarchy and the reading of popular culture, can be said to take the engagement with these cultural practices seriously only if it acknowledges the variegated and layered intellectual process involved in producing the popular—and its multiple pleasures. To recast Gramsci, "All men and women who participate in the production of popular cultural practices are intellectuals": the production of popular culture is a profoundly intellectual process. Marley, Eartha Kitt, Billie Holiday are particular kinds of intellectuals: they are iconic figures in large measure because they are producers, articulators, and disseminators of cultural knowledge; they are public figures who contribute and create new forms of knowledge; they think carefully about what they say (as much as any conventional intellectual), how they say it, why they are moved to say it; and they understand how their rhetorical interventions connect to their originary constituency. They recognize how, in Ellisonian terms, they are heard—or misheard or misrepresented—by the dominant culture.

In their turn, James and Hall are integrated into—and assume the status of—the vernacular through their grasp of the signality of the cultural popular. By understanding cricket rather than formal political independence as *the* social practice that marks, and indeed precedes, West Indian sovereignty, James establishes himself as a vernacular intellectual. For this reason *Beyond a Boundary* together with *The Black Jacobins*, his treatise on the struggle for Haitian independence, stand as his major works: in *Beyond a Boundary* James demonstrates how the cultural is always political; how the cultural encodes, complicates, and sometimes anticipates the ideological; how culture is, in short, a series of inscribed political articulations; how culture can sometimes in and of itself constitute an instructive politics. In Hall's case, his several returnings to culture enable him to resituate himself within the vernacular—in his first turning to culture as a young member of the British New Left, in his later rethinking as one of the leading figures in the Birmingham Centre for Contemporary Cultural Studies where popular culture is first properly made an object of scholarly investigation, in his mediated turn to race through the popular (and denigrated, oppressive) experience of black migrants in Britain during the tail end of his time in Birmingham (the mid- to late 1970s), and in his 1980s work on identity politics and the postcolonial condition.

James and Hall share, in their vernacularity, a transgressiveness with Ali and Marley. Much like Ali transgresses established codes—quiescence, African-American acquiescence, the stereotype of the mute, rarely verbal, and, by extension, largely unthinking fighter—of his sport, so *Beyond a Boundary* marks James's reinterpretation of Marxist-Trotskyist intellectual production. In this work James privileges culture over class analysis and he suggests that social revolutions, while they may depend upon the laboring classes, can take political forms all too frequently ignored or dismissed (as "opiates of the masses") by Marxist critics. In this text James is transgressing philosophically, marking not only a break within his own oeuvre but with the tradition in which he produced *The Black Jacobins* and his other main works.

Much like Marley creates reggae as musical genre to articulate the experience of the Trenchtown sufferer (most often cast as a Rastafarian subject), weaving together religion, politics, and culture, so Hall's various intellectual modalities—especially from the Birmingham years on, though that is clearly grounded in the New Left years—speak of an intellectual transgression. Hall's work transforms itself into, is repeatedly drawn toward, the vernacular. The vernacular is crucial for Hall because existing intellectual and ideological formations cannot adequately accommodate the issues he is addressing, the questions he is posing, the landscapes he seeks to reimagine. Hall and James have to transgress intellectually (they have work against the dominant traditions in which they have operated and are committed to), they have to act "improperly" in relation to their disciplines by questioning its efficacy, they have to move outside, alongside, disjunctively in relation to their various disciplines in order to conduct their inquiries.[4] The vernacular represents, for all these figures for this reason, a singular phenomenon: transgression as an intellectually generative mode. Through their various transgressions, through breaking with and giving offense to their traditions and the dominant public(s), and through setting themselves in opposition to various hegemonies, James, Marley, Hall, and Ali construct themselves as vernacular intellectuals. The vernacular is the transcription of the popular (subaltern) experience into political oppositionality.

What's My Name? is, in this way, a double-edged project. As much as Marley and Ali are thrown into sharp relief through the implicit comparison with Hall and James, considered disjunctively as I later argue, so this book also argues for the continuity and contiguity of vernacularity. Marley and Hall can at once stand alongside each other and their vernacularity can abut each other's. Their vernacularities share certain intellectual traits, such as a preoccupation with the popular, but also speaks from different locales, to different publics that seldom overlap, and in different vernacular registers. The vernacular is a shared intellectual paradigm for these figures, but it is a framework in which various differences cannot be overlooked or disregarded. The vernacular is a variegated, complex construct, and it requires a keen attentiveness to difference—the different kinds of work that James and Ali do, the different kinds of interventions Hall and Marley can make, considering where they speak from, to whom they speak, who hears them, and how they are heard—if it is to function as an efficacious political category. Most important, however, in *What's My Name?*—the vernacular is not the exceptional. It constitutes the normative and most efficacious political modality for all of these figures.

The specific kind of historical, political, and ideological work that these figures, these vernacular intellectuals, perform, makes it necessary to think beyond the Gramscian paradigm. Gramsci insists that the distinction "between intellectuals and non-intellectuals" is simply a "reference" to the "immediate social function of the professional category of the intellectuals, that is, one has in mind the direction in which their specific professional activity is weighted, whether towards intellectual elaboration or towards muscular-nervous effort" (9). While James and Hall can easily be claimed by the "professional category," Ali (especially) and Marley offer a conundrum that Gramsci does not address: they combine "intellectual elaboration" with their "muscular-nervous effort." In fact, in Ali's case especially—and more mutedly so for Marley—his physical actions, his skills as a boxer, are indistinguishable from his cerebral contemplations. Ali was, not to put too fine a point on it, a deeply intellectual fighter: a pugilist who thought strategically, assiduously, and craftily about his approach to boxing, about how not only to beat but to outwit his opponents. Ali's "muscular-nervous effort"—his skill as a boxer—was an articulation of his "intellectual elaboration"—the ways in which he conceived himself not only as a fighter but as a black boxer who understood the ideological demands of his historical moment. Ali's vernacular "intellectuality" is integral to, and indistinguishable from, his fistic armory, and, as importantly, his insistence on his right to rename himself. In Derrida's *"Khora,"* the final essay in a three-part series of contemplations on naming, the name is conceived of as inscribing both social hierarchy and a rare physicality and geographical locality. *"Khora* means," in Derrida's terms, "place occupied by someone, country, inhabited place, marked place, rank, post, assigned position, territory or region."[5] Ali and Marley both rejected the "places" their different societies assigned them; they resisted the ways in which America and the Caribbean marked their bodies, their histories, and circumscribed their sense(s) of themselves. Ali and Marley also, through their vernacular articulations, transcended—through cultural and ideological transgression—the restrictions placed upon their names. Moreover, they not only exceeded the "marked" (and marred) place in their own countries, but also achieved for (and through) their names a resonance that enabled them to speak at once oppositionally in and beyond their original sites of habitation. For Ali the significance attached to his name was also achieved through the process of renaming (the major transition that transformed Cassius Marcellus Clay into Muhammad Ali), of metaphorically occupying the same "place"—and other places—as a reconstructed, ideologically (religiously) different person. This was a process that Marley, who adopted Rastafarianism as a faith, also undertook, though his conversion was less dramatic than Ali's. Marley expended a great deal of time and effort both on his guitar-playing and in producing lyrics and music that integrated his Rastafarian faith, popular appeal, his belief in racial equality, and his commitment to social transformation. Ali and Marley complicate Gramsci's contemplations on the intellectuals by demonstrating how vernacular figures occupy a number of different places and by elucidating how cultural figures demand a reconsideration of even the most accommodating, expansive, and intellectually democratic of paradigms.

The ways in which Ali spoke (and, sometimes, still speaks now, as his post–September 11 public pronouncements demonstrate) and Marley sang (and continues to be heard) have long required, considering how they responded to the pressures of their (sometimes similar) historical conjunctures and their commitments to fashioning themselves as representatives of their (differently) oppressed constituencies, that they be conceptualized as more than simply cultural icons—articulate, highly public figures who belonged only to the world of sport or entertainment. The careers of Ali and Marley, however, have long exceeded such an understanding of their cultural and political work—or, their politicized cultural interventions—because they have affected the thinking, the actions, the public utterances of constituencies well beyond the packed arenas and stadiums of sports and popular music. What Marley's lyrics and Ali's witty rhymes speak to, for, and about constituencies and issues can only be grasped in its full complexity transgressively. Marley and Ali intervene(d) in and provoke(d) public debates far beyond the ordinary purview of the reggae star (or rock star, since the Jamaican was the first of his genre) or the athlete.

The chapters on Ali and Marley, and, to a lesser extent, the chapters on James and Hall, reexamine the public role and the public utterances of the intellectual, and the public locations—beyond the university, parliamentary debate, the anticolonial resistance movement, the editorial column, café society, the organized (and unorganized) political rally or protest—in which public figures function. *What's My Name?* posits previously unrecognized localities, the music concert, the press conference, the boxing ring, the popular music lyric, as intellectual sites by and for cultural figures who speak as vernacular intellectuals. Ali and Marley, and James and Hall, in their different ways, hold forth in the vernacular to a range of constituencies, some fluent in the vernacular, others acquiring it through the dissemination of the subaltern popular. Vernacular intellectuals are, as the process of bringing them to public prominence demonstrates, a complex representation of the voices from below or the margins speaking at once to, within, and against the hegemonic order.

Reading Disjunctively

What's My Name? maps the various trajectories that produce James, Hall, Marley, and Ali as intellectuals and enunciates—and illuminates—the disjunctures that mark their vernacularity. Recognizing that James and Hall are conventionally defined as intellectuals and that Ali and Marley are not, mapping the different paths by which these four figures come to construct themselves as intellectuals, this project utilizes disjuncture to interrogate the concept of the intellectual. *What's My Name?* explores and challenges notions of intellectual difference: How is James's status of intellectual distinct from Ali's, how is Hall's different from Marley's, or Ali's from Marley's, how is the conventional understanding of the intellectual reconfigured in the juxtaposition between Hall and Marley? What happens to the category of the intellectual when it is interrupted, dislocated, and vernacularized? How is the icon of popular culture transformed when he or she is represented as an intellectual, of the vernacular or other variety? At the core of *What's My Name?* are the following questions: How expansive, incorporative, and complex is the category of the intellectual? How is the category of the intellectual reconfigured by vernacularity? How is this category complicated by contours of vernacularity since all vernacularities are clearly not the same? What happens in the process of vernacular cross-referencing, in which Hall and Marley are thought of in continuous relation to each other?

Ali and Marley represent, in this disjuncture, the grounded vernacular intellectual. These popular figures are thinkers, spokespersons, cultural articulators who emerge autochthonously from within the ranks of the popular classes, the working classes, or the underclasses within the minority or disenfranchised constituency. James and Hall, on the other hand, mark the more circuitous trajectory, the more protracted process, by which the conventionally trained—and institutionalized—intellectuals become vernacular thinkers.

Vernacularity marks that sociopolitical occasion when the conventional intellectual speaks less as a product of a hegemonic cultural-economic system than as a thinker capable of translating the disenfranchised experience of subjugation as an oppositional, ideologically recognizable, vernacularized discourse. Vernacularity represents the moment of a significant, palimpsestic transformation. Vernacularity signals the discursive turning away from the accepted, dominant intellectual modality and vocabulary and the adoption of a new positioning and idiomatic language. It also signals a turning toward, not in a nostalgic but in a considered and deliberate fashion, and (re)connection to an originary—but not necessary umbilical—community: it marks the initiation of that process when the conventionally trained intellectual is ideologically remade through culture—the culture of the subjugated, diasporic community, those cultural practices that signify an intersection between the dominant and the subjugated, those practices that, while being marked as Other, have transformed both the periphery and the metropolis, that have affected relations between the (erstwhile) colonizer and the colonized, those practices that have reconstituted the diasporized constituencies and the metropolis as a whole.

The vernacular intellectual is distinguished from the Gramscian organic by a situatedness within the popular, frequently racialized experience of disempowered constituencies. While the organic is rooted in communities, the vernacular articulates an equivocal relationship to hegemony, a complex negotiation with the dominant group that is characterized by a self-conscious difference and defiance. The vernacular is defined by its immersion in the language of the popular, the particularities, idiosyncrasies, and distinctness of vernacular speech; the vernacular is marked by its ability to speak popular resistance and popular culture to power. Here vernacular is discrete from the organic, which is intensely preoccupied with disarticulating existing formations of power without attending to how power is located within and articulated through the popular. Vernacular intellectuals, of the grounded (Marley) or "protracted" (James) mien, are those figures who understand, utilize, and deploy vernacularity as a discourse within and against the dominant sphere—though not always from the same vantage point.

In considering how the vernacular functions, firmly rooted in race and the popular as it is here, it is important to recognize that issues such as gender and sexual orientation add further complexity, nuance, limitations, and possibilities to the model of the postcolonial vernacular intellectual. Historically, like most other modes of struggle and recorded in works that range from sub-Saharan fictions to sub-(Asian) continental histories, resistance to colonialism was a series of profoundly misogynistic practices. Anticolonial forces, as much as independent postcolonial societies, denied women access to public spheres, curtailing their capacity to give voice to their particular vernacularity. Female athletes such as Althea Gibson, the openly gay Navratilova, or the Williams sisters (women who have certainly not been afraid to either challenge accepted images of tennis players or raise the issue of racism as it continues to obtain in the still predominantly lily-white world of tennis) had—and have—to engage a great deal more than racial discrimination. These women have had to confront the ways in which the sport's public and the media are so indelibly shaped by patriarchy, the cultural disenfranchisement of women, and heteronormativity. The same applies to black female artists such as Aretha Franklin and Eartha Kitt who had and have to work within paradigms that are markedly different from those of their male counterparts.

The largely male-dominated world of sport and popular music reveals how embedded the vernacular is in suppressing its own "female unconscious," how the subaltern is in part constituted by its own oppressive treatment of women and gays as underclasses, how it is marked by its own silences. The vernacular's history is, as regards the struggles of women or gays and lesbians, marked by incompletions. The vernacular provides only a partial accounting of resistance, a construction of the intellectual that is at once deeply oppositional and radical and yet bound by the patriarchal constraints of its historical modality. Ali and Marley speak an incendiary but deficient vernacular truth to power, offering a postcolonial narrative that is less inadequate—though it is that too—than marked by historical partiality. Oppositional figures such as Janis Joplin or the androgynous Grace Jones (who complicates gender identity in a very distinct way) speak from decidedly different, and significantly less empowered, public locales. Sometimes, more disturbingly, they are not allowed to speak at all. Even when these women do secure public voice, they are, consequently, sometimes heard—if and when they are listened to—on the lowest of the Ellisonian frequencies, rendering them invisible women. For women the vernacular, even as it seeks to create new possibilities for subaltern articulation, serves as a reminder of how female alienation by the patriarchal/racist complex impacts and manifests itself in the vernacular.

The critical reception afforded the Czech-born Navratilova demonstrates how inveterately heteronormative our various popular cultures remain—despite the struggles and gains around the politics of identity—and how difficult it is for the lesbian or gay sportsperson to craft her- or himself as a vernacular figure. Although Navratilova's sexual orientation is now largely accepted by the sport's media and its public, when she first revealed her homosexuality she met with considerable opposition—the women's tennis tour is still (much like women's golf), from time to time, branded as a hotbed of sport's lesbianism. Deeply eroticized as the vernacular is, it is always a pronouncedly heterosexual desire—regardless of whether or not it is xenotropic. In delineating the vernacular, the specificities, peculiarities, and effects of gender and sexual orientation have to be closely attended to if this conception of intellectuals is to have any efficacy.

Even as it proposes a categorical difference, the vernacular requires critical vigilance: an awareness of Other differences that have to be accounted for, other social forces that impact the construction and identity of the intellectual. How does the sexual ambiguity of Grace Jones or Prince affect the paradigm of the vernacular? How would a gay football player or baseball player reconfigure the category? Would Marley signify differently as a vernacular intellectual if he were bisexual? I do not take up these interrogations in *What's My Name?* but they are inquiries that have great salience for the conception of other popular figures as vernacular intellectuals.

The issue of difference, however, does resonate in this project because, as the discussions of the grounded and "achieved" vernacular will show, vernacularity can be derived from remarkably variegated locales, from unexpected histories and contradictory relationships to hegemony. The vernacular is a mobile and flexible experience, accommodating of different trajectories, and is a theoretically supple category: it derives from a keen understanding of and engagement with the popular, but it is—like the popular cultural producers and cultural theorists critiqued in this book—neither narrow nor prescriptive in its conception. The four figures under study here are four versions of the postcolonial intellectual. *What's My Name?* charts how they become vernacular in their own way. The project recognizes that the vernacular is a particularized experience that has specific purchase in various sites, and the intellectual is shaped by the workings of that (local) context.

By delineating the advantages and limitations of that "traditional" construction and the ways in which political conjunctures intervene to compel a rethinking of their position, the chapters on James and Hall both demonstrate how historical—and epistemological—crises produce the recasting of the cosmopolitan, metropolitan, diasporic, and organic intellectual into a vernacular mold. The key issue in these chapters is transition: How does the organic intellectual become a vernacular figure? What marks the point of transition? What accounts for the transformation? How does the intellectual's work change in the process? In the Ali chapter, from which the project takes its title, and the Marley one, the great(est) boxer and the talismanic "founder" of reggae music are defined as "organically," if not prototypically, vernacular intellectuals. Through their various articulations, interventions into the national and global public sphere, from tiny Jamaica to postcolonial Africa, from resisting the Vietnam draft to paying (problematic) obeisance to Haile Selassie, Ali and Marley are read as figures who illuminate both the unusual possibilities for and the potential limitations inherent in being a vernacular intellectual.

The Language of Vernacularity

Vernacularity, though it emerges from below, from the periphery or the underclasses, is considerably more than a language of subalternicity. It is not only a language in itself, but a form public discourse sure of itself—sometimes inexplicably so. It is articulate and confident in its cadences, speech patterns, and intonations. Vernacularity is the language of the Other that, while conscious of its difference and Otherness, stands as a form of singular intervention. In some instances—such as Muhammad Ali's 1960s and 1970s press conferences, several Marley concerts, or contemporary hip-hop music—vernacularity conducts itself as the only modality of intervention into the dominant public sphere (which all too frequently signifies the white public sphere). Frequently, vernacularity is the mode of expression that has to bear the burden of overrepresentation: it is, in a disproportionately high number of instances, presumed to be the form of minority public expression that speaks for disenfranchised constituencies. Too many vernacular pronouncements are made to bear an undue weight, too many gestures are read as loaded, overdetermined with value (or the absence of value and "civilization") and valences possibly discordant with it.

The vernacular is, for this reason, susceptible to dilution, elision, misrepresentation, and, not least of all, cooptation by a dominant discourse. Marley found himself, despite his best efforts at ideological neutrality, at the center of the political debate in Jamaica, so much so that there was an attempt on his life just hours before he was due to play a peace concert in Kingston in 1976. Ali, icon of black self-determination and opposition to racism and colonialism, seriously considered fighting in apartheid South Africa. Hall, chief ideological critic of Thatcherism, despite his critiques of Tony Blair's government, has been linked—however fairly or unfairly—to New Labour's "Third Way" policy. (Impatient with the British Labour Party's repeated electoral losses, Blair and his allies fashioned the ideology of the Third Way. It is a program designed to modernize Labour, make it electable, loosen the grip—and the undemocratic structures—the trade unions had on the party and, most importantly, to find a middle ground, the third way, between democratic socialism—to which the party had historically been committed—and free-market capitalism.)[6] The vernacular, because it coexists so dialectically and symbiotically with the dominant culture, is ideologically vulnerable because the various state apparatuses understand how to appropriate, deploy (as a counterradical strategy), and transform radical oppositionality into a marketable commodity. From Ali's attempt, at the behest of the U.S. government, to convince African countries not to boycott the 1976 Olympic Games in Montreal (in protest against the New Zealand rugby tour to South Africa) to U2 front man Bono's efforts on his 2002 tour of the continent with former U.S. Secretary of the Treasury Paul O'Neill to rethink the debt policy that impoverishes African nations, vernacular figures have always found themselves both attracted to the trappings of state power and unexpectedly impotent in the face of it. The cooptation by the state confers, in a problematic if alluring way, a kind of social capital, authority, and location that vernacularity—a mode of intellectuality girded by oppositionality—cannot.

However, if the vernacular is vulnerable to the lures of the right, it is no less so in the face of left enticements and allegiances. Marley (through his refusal to critique Haile Selassie's peculiar brand of religious despotism), Ali (through his inability to recognize the failures of the Nation of Islam), and James (through his inability to recognize the postcolonial crises that Toussaint L'Ouverture's ascension in Haiti enunciates) demonstrate how the vernacular can be blind to corruption, violences, and exploitative workings of the anticolonial or the antihegemonic.[7]

Vernacularity is the discourse that encodes larger economic and political disenfranchisements. Overburdened by structural lack (historic absence of material resources and access to capital), vernacular speech is politicized as much by its content, though much of that may be superimposed, as by the absence of formal political channels of redress or representation. It is the minority discourse that stands in both for and as something else, for the other modes of resistances or oppositionalities that either cannot be voiced or have been drowned out; or, it takes the place of those protest votes that either cannot be cast or simply have no consequence or purchase in the dominant political sphere.

As delivered at a press conference by Ali, in Marley's reggae music, or in James's recounting of the peculiar vocabulary that attends cricket in colonial Trinidad, *vernacularism* is a "word, idiom, or mode of expression" that refuses to be modulated, intimidated, or silenced by the machinations of the public sphere.[8] At the very worst, it simultaneously accommodates itself to and undermines hegemony. Within this context the vernacular cannot be reduced to etymology, a series or history of speech patterns indigenous to a "country or district." It functions in this instance as a mode of linguistic expression, a repertoire of representation, a politics of being, particular to a racialized, ideologically marginalized constituency. The vernacular, as in the black or postcolonial vernacular, is not a marker of national or regional identity. It is simultaneously a sign of difference and disenfranchisement. In colonial and postcolonial societies, vernacular speech belongs to the colonized or the ghettoized communities of the metropolis. The vernacular is counterposed to (and is less valued than) the formal—or "proper"—speech of the colonizers or the metropolitanized discourse of the dominant society.

In the same way that the African-American blues was once unrecognized by America's Anglophone establishment, or the poetry of the Negritude movement was dismissed by the Francophone establishment, the vernacular, characterized by its informality, its nontraditional grammatical structures, its discursive hybridity, and its proclivity for drawing on and incorporating other cultural formations, even other languages, is also dismissed. The work of blues artists such as Robert Johnson or *Presence Africaine* authors such as Aimé Césaire or the poet-philosopher-statesman Léopold Sédar Senghor was at once the articulation of linguistic impurity and cultural innovation. That hybridity is so closely related to the overdetermined response the vernacular provokes signals a major conjuncture. The vernacular marks that intersection where the Other is both denigrated and turned into the object of xenotropic desire, the black body or history that is ridiculed or violenced against and the culture that is mimicked by the dominant society. Although xenotropia frequently produces immediate mimicry, it is also a temporally uneven process, divided between what we might superficially conceive of as "culture" and "politics." While the desire to adopt black modes of representation such as street couture or musical styles may be instant, there was and is generally a greater reluctance to identify with the ideological girdings of the culture. A post-1970s Ali (when he stumped for Ronald Reagan, then the California governor who had little more than a decade earlier sworn that "no draft dodger will fight in my state") has increasingly been adopted as a sanitized American icon, stripped of his radical past and the oppositionality it signaled. Hip-hop may enjoy widespread currency among white youth, but the black anger against structural disenfranchisement that sustains the music is all too frequently ignored.

The vernacular is, for this reason, the complex object that inspires hegemonic imitation and yet is despised—feared, even—because it is the incarnation and the articulation of that which is deemed culturally and economically lesser, the speech of the working class or the ethnic minority, the discourse of the racial subject. However, even when it is dismissed, the vernacular can still, in some if not all instances, stand as the enunciation of a threatening, angry resistance, a determination to speak within and against the dominant group with the hint of Fanonian violence. And, in the case of anticolonial revolutions—as in Cuba or Haiti or Kenya or Mozambique—the circumscription of the vernacular contains its own momentous capacity for violent action. When the subaltern subject is not allowed to speak in its own terms, its own discourse, its history, culture, or traditions, when it is alienated from its vernacularity, it is eminently capable of transcribing suppression into a violence aimed at the destruction of its oppressors. While it functions mainly at the level of the linguistic, the vernacular is—to invoke V. N. Volosinov's term—multiaccentual: it can, under extreme conditions or when particular alliances are made or certain modes dominate, articulate itself in more than one (oppositional) register, in more than one way.

Vernacularity is always, however, more than the language and mode of self-representation for the disenfranchised or dispossessed, the discourse that is almost invariably, despite or because of itself, imprinted with the mark of the politically subjugated: the immigrant, the working class, the black or ethnic community. Vernacularity has a contradictory function in that it is at once the marker of disjuncture, the form of speech that separates rich from poor, dominant from dominated, the speech that distinguishes black self-representation from its white counterpart, and an ironic conjoining.

Command of and the inhabiting of the vernacular, living it as a raced or classed subject, rather than mere mimicry or performance, identify it as a paradoxical sign of authenticity. The vernacular reassures the hegemonic group of their difference, their discursive, locational separation (that place where they stand, almost literally), and their linguistic superiority to—the command of, historic attachment and association with "proper" discourse, the formal expression of a particular language—that of the variously raced, gendered, and ethnicized underclass. Because of this, however, authenticity reveals itself as a dependent gesture, announcing a dialectical relationship between the vernacular and the formal. The authentic signifies difference rather than singularity (its authority derives from what it is not, the vernacular); it also indicates a reliance upon externality—that which is outside of and different from it—rather than essentiality—the pure, nonderivative epistemological being. The authentic can only enunciate itself as a formal discourse dialectically: in contradistinction to the informality and impurity of the vernacular, that to which it implicitly counterposes itself.

The Crisis of Vernacularity

For black intellectuals such as James and Hall, the engagement with vernacularity not only marks the coming to and deployment of popular consciousness, but also signals a (or sometimes *the*) major transformation in their work. It constitutes the moving away from one mode of intellectual production in the direction of another. Vernacularization entails the relinquishing of certain privileges, guarantees of access, academic status, and credibility in order to assume a decidedly different set of historical responsibilities. Vernacularization is never a historical inevitability; it is, rather, the direct consequence of a moment of intellectual crisis. It is that conjuncture when black figures, recognized by the dominant culture as conventionally trained and active intellectuals, confront in their work an incommensurability between their occupation in the academy (or the arts world) and their experience as minority spokespersons, a tension between the kind of work they are producing and the consequence it is having (or, failing to have) in the world. The crisis is fueled not by a fear of being silenced, but the prospect of a dual insignificance: excessive or extraordinarily successful interpellation, on the one hand, and a complete severing of the links between the black intellectual and his or her originary community, on the other hand.

The crisis of (re-)affiliation is the consequence of a recognition of limits: the knowledge that, after decades of immersion in Marxist and

Trotskyist activism, James realized that he had to adopt another mode in order for him to make substantive links with the Caribbean working classes to whom he had committed himself ideologically. Cricket, and the richly allusive way in which the sport is deployed in *Beyond a Boundary*, becomes the cultural practice that enables James to resolve his intellectual crisis through vernacularity. For Hall that moment has a much longer history, originating with his very arrival in England as a Rhodes scholar who was soon involved in the New Left movement. Hall's crisis turns on that instance when the question of racial identity and identification (both who he was and whom he primarily aligned himself with) becomes too urgent, too pressing to allow him to function simply as a New Left thinker or a cultural studies critic.

If Ali's and Marley's vernacularity emerges from within, marking an organic or essentialist vernacularity, James's and Hall's is the product of history—a response to the pressures, the changing conditions, the movement of social forces from without that compels a new kind of interpellation. Both experiences are salient as processes, however, marking the distinct—but connected— ways in which vernacularity manifests itself in the hegemonic sphere. The issue, then, is not whether vernacularity articulates itself, but from which locale and in response to what situation the vernacular(-ized) intellectual speaks. In some ways it matters less which minority public figure is considered a vernacular intellectual. What is more important is how and why they come to constitute themselves as vernacular spokespersons. However, Ali's experience of "internal exile" and Marley's of exile produced their own modalities of crisis for these vernacular intellectuals. Both crises were precipitated by their (different) encounters with the neoimperialist and newly postcolonial state. Ali, banned from boxing because of his refusal to be drafted into the Vietnam War, and Marley, driven from Jamaica because of internecine political violence in Trenchtown and other such ghettoes, each responded very differently to the confrontation with crisis. Ali remained, in part because his skills as political prognosticator verbally anticipated (and scripted) the repressive workings of the state, largely unchanged: his politics remained consistent (and idiosyncratically uneven)

in its oppositionality. But for Marley, the Jamaican crisis and its con-
comitant violence as well as his encounter with African postcoloniality
were ideologically productive. It led to a critical reevaluation of his
conception of Babylon, Zion, and the functioning of the postcolonial
state.

The Vernacular Intellectual

The vernacular intellectual, unlike the traditional and organic intellectual, is in no way connected to organized political structures. Not the
state, not the revolutionary party, not the elite of café society. These
figures emerge, quite literally, out of the vernacular experience, well
versed in the discourse of popular oppositionality but outside of its
formal articulations. Vernacular intellectuals craft a unique public space
from which to speak as they address the issues of the day that directly
affect their community. In his attempt to redefine the dominant conception of intellectuals and engender a rethinking of the role performed by
institutionally nonaccredited public figures, Jorge Castañeda argues for
a reconsideration of these figures: "Through their writings, speeches,
and other activities systematically substituted for innumerable institutions and social actors." Valid as Castañeda's notion of supplementarity
may be, to read vernacular intellectuals as "substitutes" is to detract from
the extent to which they act of their own volition. Figures such as Ali and
Marley are public figures because of their connection to the vernacular,
because their "speeches," lyrics, and social intervention echo, reinscribe,
and innovate within the hegemonic discourse. Vernacular intellectuals
speak differently, self-consciously so, but this does not mean that they
fail to grasp the importance of the political concern voiced by mainstream intellectuals; they know how to translate the interests of the populace into, and as, metaphors of the popular. Vernacular intellectuals
understand that the dominant discourse is not tone deaf, that it can hear
protests—and the resistances encoded therein—in many timbres. The
popular is not the evacuation or the dilution of the political; it is simply
its vernacular reinscription: it is speaking, cognizant of its various sus-
ceptibilities, in a different way, for and from different constituencies.

Figures such as Ali and Marley are grounded in the vernacular, are of the vernacular community, speak for the vernacular, in the vernacular, and yet they stand slightly removed from the experience: in it, of it, but not consumed or restricted by it, aware of how to make the transcription from subaltern to dominant sphere, always ready to oppose or transgress, even as they are vulnerable to the various cooptations at work. Michael Hanchard's description of black public figures is apropos for the kind of function vernacular intellectuals perform. These spokespersons stand, in Hanchard's terms, for a community "whose commentary and insights exceed the boundary of their celebrity. With neither political offices nor constituencies to hold them responsible, they use their highly visible public positions within the academy, arts, and letters to engage in public debate."[9] Vernacular intellectuals are oppositional public figures who use the cultural platforms and spaces available to them, but not ordinarily accessible to their disenfranchised communities, to represent and speak in the name of their communities. Celebrity status, acquired in the "nonpolitical" realm, empowers minority athletes to pronounce on an unexpected range of subjects in the civic domain; they are able to produce articulations for a public that far exceeds their narrow professional base—the arts or the academy or the sports arena. Ideologically mobile, these figures move back and forth between the popular and the political realms. These icons can be, simultaneously, cultural producers or political activists, speaking metonymically for themselves or their constituency—that body of subjects deliberately excluded from the formal public debate.

The difficulty in acquiring political office, for this very reason, never means that disenfranchised communities do not participate in public discourses; it simply means that their articulations are far more likely to emerge from informal, and frequently unacknowledged, public locales—and personages. As Hanchard reminds us, "The most significant figures within U.S. African-American communities—Fannie Lou Hamer, Malcolm X, Martin Luther King, Muhammad Ali, even Booker T. Washington—have never held elected public office."[10] These unelected office bearers were nominated through popular acclaim, determined largely by the commensurability between the elevated status of these figures and the access that status gives them to public platforms.

These figures participate in public debates not only as barely recognized spokespersons, but in a vocabulary unaccredited and often disparaged by ruling blocs—of both hegemonic and subjugated constituencies. The vernacular intellectual is constituted, as it were, by vernacular articulation. By introducing and strategically deploying vernacular speech patterns, idioms, and metaphors, iconic figures such as Ali and Marley alter, quite literally, the very language of the dominant discourse. Vernacular intellectuals intervene in the public debate about issues relevant for them and their community in a language inscribed with the history of their disenfranchisement and subjugation.

However, much as vernacular intellectuals speak for or in the name of their constituencies, so their very lack of "public office" represents a particular kind of alienation from and unaccountability to the minority constituency. More than any other American figure, Ali is symptomatic of the vernacular intellectual. Paraded now only as a figure of quiescence, a desire for American society to suture post–ipso facto the intense divisions of the 1960s and 1970s—to write out the atrocities, the defeat and internal violence produced by Vietnam, the multiple assassinations that rocked the nation's moral core; to sanitize or sentimentalize the counterculture; to forget the corruption of Nixon—Ali redefined the scope and possibilities for black figures transgressing and even invalidating the boundaries of the nation's public sphere.

Much like Marley's reggae would transform many forms of popular music (punk, rock, nascent rap) and black identity and historical imagination from Kingston to Kansas, from London to Lilongwe, Malawi, in the late 1970s, so Ali's vernacularity reconceptualized the 1960s understanding of politics and the actors who make, shape, disrupt, and impact it. Through their ability to pronounce, with an inimitable fluency and innovativeness, on boxing, culture, politics, and ideology, Ali and Marley were able to intervene in matters of public policy, give rare voice to black self-representation in the United States, the Caribbean, and diasporic communities in Europe, and align themselves ideologically with the newly postcolonial world in sub-Saharan Africa and Asia. Ali may be the first representative of the vernacular cosmopolitan—the African-American icon who translated the United States into and for newly independent peoples in Africa and Asia, the American who understood how to connect Kentucky to Kinshasa, Chicago to Kuala Lumpur. Marley was, arguably, the heir to that throne. What Ali and Marley demonstrate is the paradox of the vernacular: derived from and produced by the (American and Caribbean) local, the ideological content, style, and self-representation of the vernacular shows itself to be eminently translatable, globally applicable, politically usable in contexts well beyond its originary base.

The vernacular is ideologically mobile, responsive to crises, adaptable to its situation, able to translate and situate itself in nonnative locales; because of the workings of history and the reduction of geographical distance through cultural proximity, the vernacular has global purchase. The vernacular is situated but not physically—which is to say, geographically—restricted. The vernacular can be exported; or, it can make common cause with other vernaculars. The postcolonial condition constitutes its own global vernacular. It is no accident that Ali, more than Marley, was (at first) more readily accepted by the Third World and the black diaspora than he was by mainstream America. Similarly, Marley produced his most cogent, searing, but intensely lyrical critiques of the Jamaican and postcolonial state not from within Kingston, but only after his de facto exile after the 1976 attempt on his life at the (in)famous "peace" concert. Both Marley and Ali grasped the violence, linguistic and physical, that girds the vernacular although that recognition never inhibited their capacity to produce themselves as singular intellectual figures. The postcolonial, the work of James, Ali, Marley, and Hall suggests, can be understood in its full complexity only through the vernacular.

CHAPTER 1

Muhammad Ali, Third World Contender

> It was not with Jack Johnson, Joe Louis, and Joe Frazier that Ali
> stood, but with Garvey, DuBois, and Jomo Kenyatta.
>
> —Budd Schulberg, *Loser and Still Champion*

> America
> doesn't like a man who's good
> at what he does and wants
> to talk about it.
>
> —Lawrence Raab, "Why the Truth Is Hidden"

What's My Name? A Beating in the Dome

In a career filled with truly epic pugilistic battles, the 1967 boxing match between Muhammad Ali, holder of the world heavyweight crown, and his challenger, Ernie "the Octopus" Terrell, in the Houston Astrodome ranks unexpectedly as one of the most telling contests the champion ever fought inside the ring. As an opponent, the twenty-seven-year-old Terrell was not in the class of Ali's legendary adversaries—champions Smokin' Joe Frazier, George Foreman, or even the aging Charles "Sonny" Liston, the first title holder whom the then Cassius Clay had dethroned in February 1964. A lanky six-five, the Chicago native Terrell boasted a two-inch reach advantage and a solid jab but he lacked the awesome punching power and ferocity so innate to the boxing arsenal of Ali's fiercer foes.

The fight possessed no element of surprise such as had transformed Ken Norton and Leon Spinks overnight from ordinary heavyweights into celebrated conquerors of Ali. The Ali-Terrell match was completely devoid of the great drama that elevated the trio of Ali-Frazier contests to the level of fistic myth. But within the larger drama that was Ali's personal and professional life, this bout assumes an especial salience.

Houston 1967 represents one of the rare moments in Ali's career when his boxing skills, embellished by braggadocio, were used primarily, and brutally, to register political dissent.

At the peak of his illustrious career, as yet undefeated as a professional, Ali deployed his punches and his ringcraft over fifteen rounds with a very specific purpose: the Terrell fight was Ali's considered response to the rancorous sociopolitical forces lined up against him. A heavyweight champion then acknowledged by the mainstream American public and its media machine only as Cassius Clay, Ali made that Terrell victory ideologically significant by converting the Astrodome's ring into a battleground for the most basic form of identity politics: the right to name oneself. The process of renaming, to say nothing of the reconstituting, reconstructing, and resituating of self that is involved, is primary to any politics of identity. For Ali that right was particularly important because his new identity had for an inordinately long time been publicly symbolized by, and glibly reduced to, his Muslim name. By the time of the Terrell fight, Muhammad Ali was three years into his conversion to the Nation of Islam, a process that had culminated in his renunciation of what he dismissed as his "slave name," Cassius Marcellus Clay.

Renaming is, as Derrida reflects upon his own name in an interview, a crucial process "because the name, in a way, had to be coined and invented for myself, at the same time unique and iterable. That's what I can do to honour the name."[1] Cassius Clay's transformation into Ali both "honoured" the Nation of Islam (and its leader, Elijah Muhammad) and historicized the African-American and postcolonial experience. Through renaming himself "Ali," after having briefly adopted "Cassius X" as his name, the boxer rejects his enslaved past and brings into public view the effects of slavery—the ways in which it continues to haunt, inform, and shape black consciousness in America. By renouncing "Cassius Clay" for "Muhammad Ali," the name itself comes to constitute— or, constitutes itself as—a political event. The name "Muhammad Ali," simply by virtue of itself, attains meaning: it signifies simultaneously the act of negation (of the old) and self-construction (of the new), and both events iterate the acquisition of an unprecedented ideological agency.

The act and event of naming—and the name itself—produces affect; it demands recognition as a response; the act of renaming possessed an ideological scaffolding unseen, or sensed, by Terrell. He had to be made to see why the name Ali mattered. By shucking off "Clay" in favor of "Ali," he also narrativizes himself as a postcolonial figure. Through his "unique invention" of himself as Muhammad Ali, he "coined" a new personage that enabled him to situate himself within an anti- and postcolonial tradition of resistance to white (American and European) hegemony. Ali metaphorically charted through his own renaming the history of black opposition from slavery through resistance to liberation, enfranchisement, and postcolonialism. "Ali" iterates, in this way, postcolonial history: he at once speaks for and signifies beyond himself: he is simultaneously transgressive, oppositional African-American and anti- and postcolonial Every Man—and Woman, to a far lesser extent.

Because he renames himself and forges a new identity that resonates singularly (both as individual black man and within America) and collectively (as Third World spokesperson), Ali is able to build symbolic links with Third World subjects. His name locates him in relation to Africa and Asia (especially) in such a way that he draws attention to the histories embedded in names— a crucial issue for new postcolonial nations, as later discussions in the chapter will show—and how "honour" is claimed through the act of naming the self: of speaking in and with a new identity that is grounded in a history of resistance, of crafting the self as critically aware postcolonial subject, of restoring dignity, pride, and a tradition of accomplishment and self-respect to the denigrated black psyche. All of which would allow the oppressed or colonized subject to occupy either the hegemonic or the new postcolonial nation differently: as a being fully capable of self- (or nation-)hood.

Moreover, what Ali demands is not only the right to name himself, but the right to be recognized by that name. He wants his new name, and the reconstructed identity it signals, to be the name used: by insisting on the public use of his new name, Ali is explicitly demanding (by force, from Terrell, and forcefully from the rest of hegemonic America) that his new self be respected. The political and historical function of the name would have no public effect if the various others—from the dominant and the subjugated communities—did not use or invoke his new name. The name can only have public salience if it is routinely brought into public usage.

Through the athletic body, the vernacular, historically conscious iterations, and the deliberate situation of the black American self within the black postcolonial experience, Ali demonstrates how—within the moment of the decolonization, the Civil Rights, and black nationalist struggles within the United States and in several parts of the colonized world, all issues that obtain a certain pertinence in the construction of Ali as vernacular intellectual and that situate him, in an idiosyncratic way, as representative of postcoloniality in the 1960s and 1970s—the movement to claiming an identity through renaming was once the most important politics of all. The name, of the African-American boxer or the new postcolonial state, had to be more than "honoured." Its speaking marked only a single moment within that process. The more urgent aspects of that project required an acute understanding of why previous incarnations—of the self or the colonized community—were insufficient, demeaning, and "dishonourable."

Within this politics of naming, Terrell's main ideological failing was that he did not comprehend how deeply he was "dishonouring" Ali.

Despite repeated requests by Ali, Ernie Terrell and much of mainstream white (and black) America refused to address him by his adopted name or to acknowledge his new identity. His name remained, in Terrell's opinion, Cassius Clay. In the prefight interviews, *New York Times* journalist Robert Lipsyte reports that the champion "kept warning Terrell to call him Muhammad Ali, his name in the black racist sect."[2] Although Terrell's response was steeped in the usual boxing hype, his uncharacteristic defiance owes much more to the vituperative anti-Ali sentiments of the day: "'I met you as Cassius Clay, I'll leave you as Cassius Clay.'"[3] By fixing Ali in his earlier historical incarnation (and rendering him ideologically anachronistic to himself) as Cassius Clay, Terrell negated and dishonored Ali's conversion to the Nation of Islam. Girding Terrell's antipathy and his denial of Ali's right to announce himself a Muslim was the demonization of the Nation of Islam, in particular its leader Elijah Muhammad and public spokespersons such as Malcolm X—and followers such as Ali. So pervasive was the hostility in this moment that even longtime Ali sympathizer Lipsyte's turn of phrase is inflected by it. The *Times* journalist describes Ali's faith not as a bona fide religious movement but as a "sect," and a "black racist" one, at that.

Lipsyte's flip depiction of Ali is uncharacteristic of his writing on the champ, but the scribe nevertheless provides an accurate barometer of and vocabulary for white, Christian America's perception of Ali and his faith. Mainstream America took offense at a U.S. world champion who deviated so markedly from the personas of his predecessors and contemporaries by virtue of his remarkable public confidence and his highly controversial self-representation. Boxing historian Jeffrey Sammons, himself immersed here in a hubristic Ali ethos, provides a vivid sense of just how unprecedented a fighter the champ was: "His 'wolfing' or 'trash talking', his self-promotional poetry, and the 'Ali Shuffle' seemed to run contrary to the pattern set by the humble, unassuming, no-frills demeanor and style of Joe Louis. If Louis stood for quiet dignity then Ali represented loud arrogance. If Louis was blue-collar then Ali was somewhere between zoot suit and dinner jacket."[4] Evocative as Sammons's dichotomous dinner jacket–zoot suit image is, the historian relies on a sartorial bifurcation that the champion renders artificial. The Ali Shuffle was not simply a nifty boxing maneuver but a metaphor for a greater artistic adroitness: the ability to simultaneously inhabit and offset the formality and constrictions of the dinner jacket with the irascibility and verbal and (visual) spectacularity—a concerted aesthetic "wolfing," if you will. All of which, of course, made him unpalatable to large segments of white America. Lawrence Raab's pithy terms are, in this instance, apropos to Ali: "America / doesn't like a man who's good / at what he does and wants / to talk about it." Especially not if he's black, Muslim, and all too willing to talk about how good he is at what he does.

The major difference between Ali and Louis (and Ali and Terrell, and Frazier, and Foreman) was not class but ideology. It is paradoxical that Ali, flamboyant, colorful, and extroverted in the extreme, chose the sober black collar, and the severely starched white shirt, of the Nation of Islam as his political uniform in place of the mythic blue shirt, that venerated symbol of the (black) working-class hero made good, favored by Louis and Foreman. Ali's attire, much like his boxing style, was distinct because he viewed the world, as he makes patently obvious in his autobiography, *The Greatest* (what else could this work have been called?), through the lens of Elijah Muhammad's teaching. In the Nation of Islam the heavyweight champion saw the "liberation of black people from subjugation and slavery to freedom and equality and justice."[5] Motivated by a defense of his faith and his political principles, in addition to his customary confidence in his rhetorical and boxing skills, Ali was his usual boisterous self in the prefight theatrics for the Terrell encounter. But there was something ominous in his "warning" to Terrell to use his adopted, nonslave name. "What's my name?" he snarled to Terrell at the weigh-in, threatening the "same kind of slow punishment he had administered to Patterson" a year previously if the challenger did not respond appropriately.[6] Animated by the same anti-Ali forces as Terrell, ex–world champion Floyd Patterson had been sorely punished in the ring for his transgressions. In Ali's anger there was a caution Terrell ignored, at his own peril. His contempt for Ali came back to haunt him during the course of what would be, for him, a very long fight.

In constructing Ali as a vernacular intellectual, this chapter will map him as an oppositional cultural icon. In this regard the Houston bout lends itself as a central motif for Ali's singular vernacularity: it was a fight in which the champion demonstrated his athletic excellence, his ideological oppositionality, and his verbal dexterity. He articulated his position with a poetic brashness that was simultaneously publicly alluring, identifiably black, determinedly radical, and frequently echoed in locales beyond the ring and his native America.

As an international, black, postcolonial figure, Ali was a boxer whose name enabled him to situate himself as the popular cultural figure who makes interventions into antagonistic hegemonic spaces. While his capacity to champion the cause of African Americans is indisputable, I offer here a critique of his ability to speak for subjugated black populaces in the postcolonial world and an interrogation of the possibilities available to figures such as Ali and his efficacy as a vernacular intellectual.

White Man's Nigger

In the build-up to the Houston fight, the moderately talented Terrell was bolstered by an animosity to Ali that acquired a new dimension in the wake of his opposition to the Vietnam War. At a press conference about his draft status almost a year earlier Ali declared that he, unlike the U.S. government, had "no quarrel with them Vietcong." It was a position he held firmly and later transcribed into poetry ("Keep asking me, no matter how long. / On this war in Viet Nam, / I sing this song / I ain't got no quarrel with the Viet Cong"), making clear the racial motivations of his actions. He had no differences with a people whom, as he said, "never called me nigger." In an interview with Jack Olsen of *Sports Illustrated*, Ali expounded this position:

> Twenty-two million Negroes in America, suffering, fought in the wars, got worse treatment than any human being can ever imagine, walking the streets of America in 1966, hungry with no food to eat, walk the streets with no shoes on, existing on relief, living on charity and in the poor house, 22 million people who faithfully served America and who still loves his enemy, are still dogged and kicked around.[7]

With his usual hyperbolic flair underscored by no small measure of affect and social commitment, the champ mapped the degraded political experience of Negroes in America. Always historically cognizant and critical, Ali cleverly invoked the specter of black destitution—"walk the streets with no shoes on," "living on charity and in the poor house"—in a moment when President Lyndon Johnson had declared his "war on poverty."

Unlike Ali, the U.S. establishment and the media were reluctant to make the link between the nation's neoimperial aggression and its internal racism, the local effects of which he elucidated for Olsen with a colloquial intensity. Instead, the press immediately launched into a widespread denunciation of his position, labeling Ali variously a "trai-tor," "unpatriotic," and a "coward." Joe Louis, a nominal World War II veteran (he fought exhibition matches to bolster troop morale) and the only reigning heavyweight champ to be inducted into the armed forces, was most cutting in his censure. Playing to the dominant perceptions of the "Louisville Lip" as a loudmouth and a braggart, the ex-champ accused his successor of being a "guy with a million dollars worth of confidence and a dime's worth of courage."[8] By the time the Houston bout rolled around almost a year after his initial pronouncement, Ali's anti-Vietnam stance had transfigured Terrell beyond recognition. The Chicagoan was transformed into a more insidious cultural figure. Terrell became the "white man's nigger," a figure at once embellished and emboldened by the mainstream media hype and encumbered and under-mined by a racist discourse uncomfortable with his blackness.[9] The white man's nigger was a sociopolitical phenomenon that Ali encoun-tered before and would encounter after the Octopus.

In the absence of a credible white opponent (the proverbial, though all too fictitious "White Hope") Terrell was made to take up white America's burden.[10] It is ironic that Terrell should have been assigned this racial responsibility, even if only by proxy, because just a couple of fights earlier the only reputable white challenger, Croatian Canadian George Chuvalo, had tried to elide race and foreground indi-vidual dislike for the champion. "'I don't think the term white hope has any meaning today,'" Chuvalo claimed. "'People don't care if a fighter is white or black. They just want to see Clay knocked off. They resent Clay as a person, as an individual, not because of his color.'"[11] Chuvalo's line of argument is accurate (if not without the overtones of personal expedience) insofar as there was a public desire to see Ali beaten, but he conveniently mistook the desperate dearth of white contenders for race blindness.

Eldridge Cleaver's essay "Lazarus, Come Forth" is a firm rejoinder to Chuvalo's fallacious reasoning. "There is no doubt," Cleaver writes, "that white America will accept a black champion, applaud and reward him, as long as there is no 'white hope' in sight."[12] Terrell was the black boxer implored and sanctioned by white U.S. society to defeat Ali, the unrepentant "uppity nigger." That the uppity nigger's opponent was himself black was somewhat inconvenient. But ideologies are contradictory structures of political belief. They can be made to accommodate even blatant inconsistencies, such as the black body being adorned with the veneer of white racist supremacy. What mattered above all was that Ali be taught a lesson for his un-American values, among which his religious beliefs and his lack of patriotism were foremost. That he was made to learn that lesson was, at that moment, of greater consequence than the race of the man who performed the task. And necessity is, in any case, the father of ideological invention: the white physical threat to Ali's crown was a pale one, so a black-white hybrid would have to do. George Chuvalo fared no better in March 1966 than the white Englishmen Henry Cooper and Brian London did after him in May and August, respectively, of that same year. (Cooper, in fact, was a two-time Ali victim, having been stopped by the champ in 1963.)

Terrell was, however, not the first but the second (and certainly not the last) incarnation of the white man's nigger. Shortly after winning the heavyweight championship from Sonny Liston in 1964, Ali had encountered an earlier manifestation of Terrell in the person of Floyd Patterson, an ex-champ himself. Patterson, a black convert to Roman Catholicism, labeled his campaign against Ali as a battle to regain the championship for America and Christianity. "'I say it, and I say it flatly, that the image of a Black Muslim as the world heavyweight champion disgraces the sport and the nation. Cassius Clay must be beaten and the Black Muslims' scourge removed from boxing."[13] In addition to his public mission, Patterson also scripted the fight against Ali as a struggle for personal salvation. A notoriously sensitive man, so much so that he snuck out of his hotel room in disguise after his opening round knockout by Sonny Liston in their first fight, Patterson held himself vicariously accountable for Ali's status as champion: "'I do feel partially responsible for the title having fallen into the wrong hands because of my own mistakes. I want to redeem myself in my own eyes and in the mind of the public.'"[14] The patriotic Patterson may have considered Ali's the "wrong hands" because Liston was once in the employ of the Mafia and the Greatest was a Muslim. But Ali would have no truck with Patterson's psychic traumas and his endemic political conservatism. Instead Ali spoke out strongly against the religious antagonisms that animated his opponent. "'The only reason Patterson's decided to come out of his shell,'" Ali said in *Playboy Magazine*, "'is to try and make himself a big hero to the white man by saving the heavyweight title from being held by a Muslim.'"[15]

Patterson's effort was a hugely unsuccessful one. In this latter-day Crusade the Cross was soundly defeated by the (Nation's) Crescent Moon and Star: "Like a little boy pulling off the wings of a butterfly piecemeal, Cassius Clay mocked and humiliated and punished Floyd Patterson for almost 12 rounds tonight until the referee halted their heavyweight championship bout because the challenger was 'outclassed.'"[16] Ali put on a boxing clinic that night as he repeatedly beat his opponent to the punch and mercilessly extended the bout. At one point in the fight Ali so dominated the match that he shouted both at and past Patterson, with the intention of echoing way beyond the Las Vegas Convention Center, "'No contest, get me a contender.'"[17]

A Change in the Climate

By encapsulating the clash between religions, ideologies, and athletic abilities, the Ali-Patterson bout transformed and exceeded itself. Freighted with these tensions, the fight became a battleground: between two antagonistic manifestations of black American-ness. Although Patterson was mainly a reflection of his moment and Ali an iconoclastic shaper of his, the 1965 fight stands as a confrontation between two boxers whose conceptions of themselves as black men owed much to their historical context. Coming to athletic prominence in the early years of the Civil Rights movement, Patterson adopted those mid-1950s principles (radical enough in their moment, and beyond it) and that political paradigm as his own.

A life member of the NAACP and a model of mainstream integration with his white wife and suburban home, Patterson had realized his version of the American Dream. He had escaped from the poverty of his Bedford-Stuyvesant background (later home to another, more notorious, heavyweight champ, Mike Tyson) and graduated to a house in wealthy Scarsdale, New York. His investment in the Dream narrative was genuine, as was his opposition to Jim Crowism, and it was on this ground that the racial separation advocated by the Nation of Islam appalled him. Patterson opposed Ali and the Black Muslims because they did nothing but "preach hate and separation instead of love and integration."[18] In his views on this matter the NAACP man found considerable support in the black community. In its July 1965 issue, which preceded the fight against Ali by some four months, the always upwardly mobile *Ebony* echoed Patterson: "There are a number of Negroes who can't stand Cassius because they say that his beliefs are a deterrent to the civil rights fight that is seeking full and equal citizenship for all Americans, regardless of race, creed, or color. They do not believe in segregation, voluntary or involuntary."[19] Whatever Ali's disagreement with Patterson, the ex-champ represented a black constituency considerable in its dislike for the Nation of Islam's segregationist policies.

Ali, however, was not untouched by the Civil Rights campaigns of the 1950s. Emmett Till's death in Mississippi, especially, affected him deeply as a youth growing up in segregated Louisville, Kentucky; his religion, however, located him disjunctively from any other black cultural figure. Moreover, Ali's professional ascendancy coincided with the transition from the Martin Luther King–inspired Civil Rights movement to more militant forms of political activism, of the black and white variety. By the time Ali became champion in the mid-1960s, the political mood of the black community had shifted—in almost all sectors—from King's pacifist, Gandhi-inspired (*satyagraha*) appeal to white conscience to the militancy of Black Power.[20] The change in the climate of black politics and his intervention into international politics altered Ali's national status, transforming him into a lodestar for the decade's black radical movement (both culturally and ideologically, because of his affiliation to the Black Muslims) and a figurehead for the white New Left's various campaigns, if not for Students for a Democratic Society

(SDS) and the Weathermen. Ali's was the decade's ultimate "'crossover'" anti-Establishment symbol: a highly visible "personification of the discontent and the unrest" of the 1960s.[21]

It was with a black and white American audience in mind that Ali angrily explained and metaphorized his victory over Patterson. The champion invoked these terms that he would echo after his victory over Terrell (marked in this pronouncement is how much more sympathetic, despite his vituperative tone, Ali was to Patterson than he would later be to the Octopus):

> But it was not you [Patterson] that I was trying to beat and knock out. It was those backing you. I was talking back to them. I was saying, "I am America. Only, I'm the part you won't recognize. But get used to me. Black, confident, cocky; my name, not yours; my religion, not yours; my goals, my own—get used to me! I can make it without your approval! I won't let you beat me and I won't let your Negro beat me!"[22]

In Ali's view (unfair or not), Patterson was a black American in the hegemonically acceptable sense of the term: he was no race-proud, "confident, cocky" man. In terms of religion, generation, and ideology, Patterson was Ali's very antithesis, and he milked the binary for all that it was worth.[23] Justified though his displeasure was, Ali situated it in terms that were at least slightly disingenuous. Refracting his verbal attack on Patterson through the white U.S. establishment ("those backing you"), Ali positioned the ex-champ as a flag bearer for the larger social forces opposed to him. And he dealt with him accordingly in the ring. Patterson was the messenger, and he would be—if not shot on sight—then peppered with blows too numerous and telling not to be heard. He pummeled Patterson not only because he was younger (if only by seven years), stronger, quicker, and better than him: Ali administered a beating because he was politically opposed to Patterson. Ali made his bout with Patterson a "fight"—a deliberately punitive battle—rather than a "match"—a strategic, pugilistic encounter—between two boxers. In accentuating the personal and ideological animosity that underscored this "fight," Ali at once stripped boxing of its "scientific" veneer (the "Sweet Science," leading scribe A. J. Liebling called it) and demonstrated how his black body could, if so ideologically motivated, be employed toward atavistic ends. Ali used his superior skills against Patterson to enforce the professional rules of engagement that govern the sport. Patterson was not defeated by Ali; he was soundly, and intentionally, beaten. In the showdown between two generations of black men, the 1960s radical emphatically won out over the man he positioned as the 1950s "conservative."[24] In the process, Ali reserved the sting of his pugilistic and rhetorical virulence for the way in which Patterson accepted his role as "their Negro," for his inability to recognize the Dylanesque changing of the black and white times. Politically, athletically, and aesthetically, the "times they were a changing," and Patterson was out of step.

For all the resemblances between Terrell and Patterson, the historical pressures against Ali had increased so much as to render the two encounters only superficially and rhetorically similar. The Patterson fight preceded Ali's Vietnam pronouncement by more than fifteen months. After the bout with Terrell on February 6, 1967, Ali would fight only once more (six weeks later against Zora Folley in New York) before he was ousted from boxing for more than three years for following the dictates of his faith.

By the time the Terrell bout came around, Ali was less than three months away from taking that famous nonstep into the United States Army. Ali was never clearer about his religious convictions and his political principles than in that crucial moment: "I have searched my conscience and I find that I cannot be true in my religion by accepting such a call."[25] The Terrell fight was a precursor, an indication of the religious antagonism and political hostility that would soon be directed against Ali. Soon after he would be openly attacked by the international boxing authorities, the United States Army, and the Justice Department (one that eventually, though with no small measure of reluctance and finagling, recognized his status as a conscientious objector). Within hours of refusing to be inducted into the army, the WBA and the New

York Athletic Commission stripped him of his crown and his right to ply his trade in that state, for what has been called the "most widely observed non-induction in history."[26] California, where then-governor Ronald Reagan declared that "no draft dodger will fight in my state," and Illinois soon followed New York, as did several other states. There was there a veritable rush to declare Ali's title vacant, a move largely unopposed in the boxing establishment. The notable exception was Nat Fleischer, the feisty and curmudgeonly editor of *The Ring Magazine*, a man rarely given to adopting the (ex-)champ as cause célèbre. A "boxing championship," Fleischer solemnly intoned, "may change hands in the ring. This law is inviolate."[27] After the "non-induction," another event took place in Houston: Ali was handed the maximum sentence of five years, imprisonment and fined $10,000.

The two Houston moments represent different, though equally crucial, conjunctures of crisis in Ali's trajectory. The Terrell fight symbolizes a (temporary) triumph over American hegemony, while the sentencing inaugurates the instance of "greatest profit and greatest privation."[28] While the Houston verdict marked a "great privation" insofar as it prevented him from plying his craft, earning his living, and addressing his customary audience as a boxer, the outcome of the trial compelled Ali to reflect more deliberately on his standing as a vernacular figure. It represented a "great profit" in that it gave him direct access to new audiences (the American college circuit, where he could address students from the likes of MIT and Princeton), but it also forced him to understand firsthand the workings of a repressive society. The costs he incurred, both economic and psychic, were not articulated in his post-exile pronouncements (he had been prescient, after all; the state had simply acted as he had predicted, making him not only a visionary boxer but an astute political pundit), but they did enable him to substantiate his vernacular oppositionality with the experience of internal exile.

During and after his return to the ring, although it had no impact on his deployment of racist stereotypes against the likes of Frazier, he was able to situate himself as a cultural and ideological dissident. Ali could never again construct himself as "only" a boxer because he had been sentenced for his presumed ideological transgressions—the athlete who had rejected the duties thrust upon him by a state he recognized as neoimperialist and racist. Houston doubly inscribed him as the resistance of the vernacular impulse: the boxer who insisted on the proper speaking of his name, and the boxer who was punished because of what he had iterated by the speaking and adoption of his name. In Houston, the name "Muhammad Ali" came fully into its ideological own: it enunciated its uniquely political resonance and it inscribed the oppressed athlete as vernacular intellectual. While his moment of crisis did not visibly transform Ali, like Marley's did, it nevertheless signaled a major disruption—and irruption—of his self-conception: he had suffered privation at the hands of the state.

Champion of the Third World

Prevented not only from boxing locally but from traveling abroad and practicing his craft anywhere in the world was certainly one of the cruelest punishments inflicted on Ali. He had, after all, always played on the world stage. During a two-hour tour of the United Nations in March 1964, a few weeks after he had won the championship from Liston and just before he took off for a four-nation African tour, Ali told reporters, "'I'm champion of the whole world and I want to meet the people I am champion of.'"[29] In addition to visiting Senegal and Nigeria, he met the Egyptian and Ghanaian presidents—Gamel Abdel Nasser and Kwame Nkrumah (whom the champ dubbed his "personal hero") as he charmed the crowds in all four countries. "Ali kept firing cheering crowds with the question: 'Who's the greatest?' the replies were unanimous: 'Ali! Ali!'"[30] The road from the airport to his hotel in downtown Accra was lined with signs that read "Welcome to Ghana, Mohammed [sic] Ali." The impact of his victories and his (rare) defeats resonated well beyond the United States, particularly (and surprisingly, in those pre-TV and -satellite days) in those places where previously— or still-colonized—peoples saw Ali as championing the same struggles in which they were engaged.

Ali was, like no other fighter before him, a world boxer. He fought matches in venues that had previously staged no contests of international stature, such as Kuala Lumpur, Malaysia, and Kinshasa, Zaire (now the Democratic Republic of the Congo); he introduced the American boxing public to small-town Lewiston, Maine (because no big U.S. cities wanted to host a champion who was a Black Muslim), and he dazzled London, England, even as he dashed the title hopes of its native sons, "Our 'Enry" Cooper and Brian London. However, the defining characteristic of his internationalism became, undoubtedly, its Third World bent. Ali's most sensational, memorable, and dramatic bouts took place in Africa and Asia, not in Europe or even America, the first Frazier (Madison Square Garden, New York) and Norton (San Diego) fights aside. Ali's fights against Foreman in Kinshasa and Frazier in Manila overshadow his contests against the likes of Jurgen Blin in Zurich and Richard Dunn in Munich. In view of the dominance of black U.S. fighters in the heavyweight division, however, it is historically apropos that Ali's most spectacular bouts should have been against his compatriots. These fights are even more striking because Ali was able to "export"—for his own benefit—the U.S.-derived ideological tensions from America to the Third World. In this carefully staged political drama, Ali self-consciously scripted himself as a liberated ex-colonial subject doing battle against a (fellow) black American who had no racial identification or ideological affiliation with the newly postcolonial locals. He was the veritable, authentic black skin doing proxy battle against the foreign white mask, a troubling appendage he made Joe Frazier wear in Manila and, most (im)memorably, George Foreman in Kinshasa.

Ali's predilection for globe-trotting, for staging fights in exotic-sounding sites unfamiliar to the Western media and its public, was facilitated by a crucial, if not historic, conjuncture: the confluence of decolonization in Africa and Asia with the Third Worldist anticolonial tendencies that found articulation in black American political life in the period between the mid-1960s and the early 1970s. Anticolonialism was by this time a trope integral to black Americans' strategies of opposition: King's Civil Rights campaigns took as their inspiration Mahatma Gandhi's passive resistance campaigns against British imperialism in the

Indian subcontinent, the Panthers borrowed from the Mau Mau fighters in Kenya. But the "Sixties" represented a distinctly different postcolonial moment. Whereas the 1950s (an epoch inaugurated by Indian independence in 1947) marked the infancy of the postcolonial movement, the following decade can be characterized as its robust, frequently violent youth and optimistic early adulthood. In this era the postcolonial world expanded its scope to include not only Asia but also the Caribbean and sub-Saharan Africa (the touchstone for the black American struggle); the achievements of the anticolonial movement in this period owed more to the increasing militancy of the Mau Mau independence campaigns than to Gandhi's *satyagraha* philosophy.

The struggle against colonial rule intensified as armed resistance registered successes against, inter alia, the French in Vietnam (and Algeria) and the British in Kenya. For black Americans, who identified so closely with the African continent, Nkrumah's stature was undiminished (as Ali's visit to Accra demonstrated), but the allure of his anticolonial strategy was considerably less than that of Jomo Kenyatta, his East African counterpart. Kenyatta's accomplishment as leader of an insurrectionary force offered itself as a model of opposition in the 1960s.[31]

The liberation army was both a symbol and a modus operandi that resonated in the black American community. In an astute rhetorical maneuver, Stokely Carmichael at once stridently denied and invoked the linguistic importance of the black African–black American analogy. "It is more than a figure of speech," he claimed, "to say that the Negro community in America is the victim of white imperialism and colonial exploitation."[32] The Black Panthers went one step further, envisaging a global pan-Africanist struggle in which the battle against the United States would be pivotal: "To Newton and Scale the identification with world revolution is a serious business. They see the United States as the center of an imperialist system that suppresses the worldwide revolution of colored people. And, says Newton, 'We can stop the imperialists from singing it against black people all over the world.'"[33] As an indigenous anti-imperialist force, the Panthers sought to emulate the methods and borrow the revolutionary handbooks of their Third World comrades—

Frantz Fanon, Marcus Garvey, and Mao's Little Red Book was standard fare for the Panthers, as were the texts of native thinkers W. E. B. DuBois (by then already self-exiled to Nkrumah's Ghana) and Malcolm X. The symbolic significance of these explosive imported images was not lost on political commentators in the United States. With the radicalization of Student Non-Violent Coordinating Committee, its post-1966 activists were transfigured into the "American answer to the Mau Mau" and the Black Panthers were described as "full of revolutionary violence, seemingly out of place in affluent America."[34] As far as the Panthers were concerned their "revolutionary violence" was the only adequate response to a white American "affluence" dependent on the systematic oppression, exploitation, and cultural degradation of blacks. The anticolonial style struggle was "out of place" only if one did not read the United States as an imperialist state, which the Panthers clearly did. Within this context of a localized postcolonial militancy, Ali was able to construct himself as a self-consciously radical, oppositional black American, a 1960s Negro who aligned himself with the process of decolonization in the Third World.

The conjuncture of race and internationalism in Ali obtain (significantly) from his conversion to Islam, albeit a particularly black vernacular American articulation of that faith.[35] The champion's commitment to situating himself as an anti–American Establishment black man foregrounded his race and enabled him to make an essentialist connection with the decolonized world. While his oppositionality to the U.S. government cemented the radical aspects of those ties, it was his faith in Islam that enabled him to speak empathetically to Muslim constituencies in newly independent Arab and Asian societies. From the very moment he announced himself a Muslim, Ali was conscious of how his conversion allowed him to affiliate with a vast international community beyond the scope of even the black American postcolonial imagination. "Islam is a religion," he said at the February 1964 press conference where he made public his new faith. "And there are 750 million people all over the world who believe in it, and I am one of them."[36] Many of these Muslims lived outside the boundaries of the Arab world, providing Ali with a rare connection to postcolonial Islamic societies in sub-Saharan Africa and Asia. This link made Ali a singular postcolonial figure: an American boxer who had a privileged cultural affinity with a global religious movement, the African-American cultural icon who used a vernacular faith, oppositional, marginal, and nondominant even with the minority public sphere, to forge symbolic links with the international, religious Other: the convert to the Nation of Islam who identified strategically with orthodox Muslims the globe over. A citizen of a West that had over the course of centuries routinely denigrated, ridiculed, and caricatured non-Christian faiths, Ali now took on splendidly some of the religious and cultural garb of the Orientalized Other.

His religious beliefs positioned him equally uniquely in relation to both his black and white U.S. audience. His faith in Islam served the symbolic function of marking Ali as distinct from the dominant cultural ethic of white, Protestant America. Like the majority of his fellow African Americans he had been raised a Christian; unlike most of them he had publicly renounced the faith. At no point in his conversion, however, did Ali disavow the central cultural traditions of the black community. Ali represents the nonvernacular of the vernacular, the process of transforming a minority marginal subject identity into a publicly resonant one without renouncing vital elements of the (majority) marginal culture.

The Postcolonial Pugilist, Rooted Black Intellectual

Within the local and global community, across the racial and ideological spectrum, Ali has been represented in myriad ways. He has been construed as a loudmouth braggart, as a black nationalist and therefore a racist, sometimes as one and not the other, as the greatest boxer ever, as a confrontational athlete, as a misguided but genuinely religious man. He has been cast as a hero, as an antihero, as a man so radical that he was far ahead of the country's ideological curve (his moral stand foretold the futility if not the unnecessary brutality and violence of Vietnam). Like many prescient figures, he stands as a cultural icon fully recognized and applauded only after his moment has passed. Since his debilitating illness and his stirring though infrequent public appearances, Ali has assumed another, more problematic, status. The Greatest is now widely revered, not least by those who once instinctively vilified him, as a dignified victim of Parkinson's syndrome, a symbol of America's capacity to put the bitter cultural and ideological divisions of the 1960s behind it. The now-silenced boxer, the loudmouth upstart who can no longer speak where he once did nothing but hold forth outrageously, has been reclaimed by a (very different) American public that disdained him when he was at his athletic and political peak. From that most orchestrated of reclamations, his moving lighting of the Olympic flame at the 1996 Atlanta Games, to the most exploitative, the docu-drama *When We Were Kings* (a problematic, award-winning movie about his 1974 fight against Foreman in Zaire), Ali has been resituated in both American cultural history and its public imaginary. The 1960s radical has been strategically usurped by the ideologically sanitized 1990s rendering of him.

However, for all his ideological connection to and investment in the Third World, Ali has never been understood as a postcolonial figure. It is a conceptual lack that is easy to account for because the postcolonial paradigm has never been written through the experience of an icon of popular culture. However much Che Guevara's or Patrice Lumumba's faces adorn T-shirts from New York to Nairobi, however much Gandhi is invoked as a symbol of change from Johannesburg to Jakarta, however much Ravi Shankar's and Carlos Santana's music transcends cultural and geographical boundaries from Los Angeles to Lahore, their impact has been contained to either the political or the cultural realm: in Ali these social forces converged into a global, African-American vernacularity. Ali was, unlike other cultural figures, a universal phenomenon, the world boxing champ who became the icon of global, black resistance; the highly politicized cultural figure, the culturally inventive political spokesperson. Unlike the "historically fractious relationship between intellectuals and popular culture," the relationship between popular cultural figures and postcolonialism has traditionally been much smoother, if more hierarchical. As griots, as soothsayers, as poets, artists, dancers, and musicians, popular cultural figures have always been regarded as supplementary, if occasionally crucial, to the real political struggle—the encoders of a political vision, the decoders of contemporary events, and the quotidian voice of the masses. At a conjuncture where the paradigm of postcolonialism is the subject of intense scrutiny (its accomplishments, its failures, its viability, even, are all now being reconsidered) and cultural studies enjoins us to take the production of cultural practices and figures seriously, it may be opportune—and potentially instructive—to refract the figure of Muhammad Ali through the lens of postcolonialism. Phrased more interrogatively, How does postcolonialism function, what does it look like, when Muhammad Ali becomes its focus?

Ali's ability to speak in, to, for, and with the postcolonial world was shaped by his popularity as a charming, irascible boxer with a strong sociopolitical conscience. To identify and claim Ali as a spokesperson is to rethink our understanding of what constitutes a postcolonial figure, and a postcolonial intellectual. While C. L. R. James can be described as a Marxist theorist in whom the traditional, the organic, and the vernacular meld to produce an extraordinarily rich and complex postcolonial figure, and Hall can be identified as the prototypical Gramscian intellectual who grasps the significance and efficaciousness of the vernacular, Ali and Marley present us with a very different formation of a public figure who makes political interventions. Ali is a vernacular intellectual because he constructed himself as the spokesperson from a marginalized or oppressed community who gives public expression to the experiences of that constituency through the utilization and popularization of that grouping's linguistic patterns, its cultural rituals, rites, and mores, and its unique traditions.

Culturally, politically, and ideologically, Ali was firmly rooted within the black American community. Even if he was disjunctively linked to African Americans because of his religion, Ali consciously fashioned himself as a spokesperson for the struggles of black Americans in the 1960s. Ali's was, however, as his exchange with Bertrand Russell demonstrates, more than a recognizable vernacular situatedness within the African-American popular. Ali's intellectuality represents a complex interplay between the local, the black American vernacular, and the black (postcolonial) cosmopolitan. After returning from boxing exile, Ali had grown in political stature because support for his position grew steadily in the United States. Similarly, internationally his stance was endorsed by many, though none so prominently as that of the British philosopher Russell. Ali recalls the impact his conversation with Russell had on him:

> In a trans-Atlantic call, Russell asked if I had been quoted correctly. I replied that I had been, but wondered out loud, "Why does everyone want to know what I think about Viet Nam? I'm no politician, no leader. I'm just an athlete."
>
> "Well," he said, "this war is more barbaric than others, and because a mystique is built up around a champion fighter, I suppose the world has a more than incidental curiosity about what the World Champion thinks. Usually he goes with the tide. You surprised them."[37]

Evident here is Ali's disingenuousness (a false modesty, unusual for Ali), attempting to pass himself off as "just an athlete"—a boxer who has no ability to influence the way people think about significant events in the world. Salient about this exchange, however, is Russell's understanding of the champion boxer's "mystique" and his recognition that Ali is breaking the mold that boxers conform to by standing strongly against the political tide. In the process of bucking athletic and political convention he "surprised" those who so publicly doubted and ridiculed his belief in the principles of Islam and those who failed to comprehend his commitment to the Third World.

As a vernacular figure Ali, in Derrida's terms, conceived of an alternative set of duties for himself. Ali "eschew[ed] the rule of ritualized decorum" that "demand[ed] that one go beyond the very language of *duty*" (original emphasis).[38] Derrida's discussion of "duty," which turns on the proscribed, demonstrates how Ali reframed the limits of what was permissible for and he implicitly interrogated what was expected of the athlete—especially the African-American athlete. Through rejecting his duty as quiescent boxer, Ali offered a new conception of the athlete. In his paradigm, the African-American boxer or football player (where the example of Jim Brown is pertinent) had a responsibility not to the dominant culture but vernacular oppositionality. Ali is not so much preoccupied with exceeding the "very language of duty" as he is with crafting a new language of duty to and in the vernacular. In this way Ali simultaneously rejects, accepts, and draws into question the ideological implications of "duty" since—and perhaps especially—even when the athlete is silent, he or she is performing in the service of a set of values, traditions, preconceptions –about the role of the athlete, about race, about gender or sexual orientation. As Russell understands, Ali's critical sense of duty represents an intellectual intervention: the exceptional athlete as radical public figure, the sport's icon as cultural revolutionary. Ali is positioned here as the intellectual who assumes the role of radical community spokesperson, articulating the cause of his—and more globalized—disenfranchised community/ies to a frequently hostile American public, exceeding a narrow vernacularity by fashioning himself as a cultural icon at once intensely localized and spectacularly international.

Clearly, however, Ali's intellectual acumen, his sense of morality, his conception and experience of political (in)justice, grew out of, was shaped and nurtured by, his black American-ness. His modes of self-representation drew extensively on the experiences and resources of his primary community. Ali's stylistic repertoire (his celebration of the black body, his public articulations) was grounded in the black American vernacular experience. Nowhere is that reliance on black culture more evident than in his penchant for poetry—often glib, frequently incisive, though never without rhythmical verve. Here Ali not only accessed old oral traditions within the black American community (the "dozens"; borrowing from the style of Southern black preachers), but also, as a proto-rap artist, borrowed from, renovated, and adapted those speech patterns for a wider American and international audience. Ali's clever wordplay, employed to unsettle opponents and gain an advantage in the ring (though he mostly did not need that) signified more than showmanship and weigh-in theatrics.

Ali's was always a verbal dexterity with a sharp political edge. Frequently he used his linguistic skills to portray himself as the authentic black fighter in battle, reducing his (black) opponent to the status of a boxer only spuriously connected to the race. Invoking this binary, an artificial, ideologically troubling one, he promised in his first championship bout that he would beat Liston because of the "Bear's" superficial blackness:

> He's not doing as he should,
> Because he lives in a white neighborhood.
> And because he doesn't like black,
> I'm going to put him on his back!

Ali's use of language as a cultural resource is in and of itself unique; no other boxer used it to indict his opponents morally and ideologically. More problematic, however, is how he used it to accuse not only Liston, but Patterson, Foreman, and even Frazier of that ultimate crime against black America: he implicitly and explicitly labeled them race traitors.

Ali's reliance on uncomplicated but discursively effective binaries in his fights against his fellow African Americans is disturbing. It depends upon his portrayal of himself as the organic (authentic) black Third World champion in contradistinction to his ability to cast his black opponents as insistently prointegrationist and therefore ideologically subservient boxers. William Nack argues that in the process of situating himself as radical, Ali "played to the most insidious racial stereotype": "the dumb and ugly black man"; Joe Frazier or George Foreman was featured in the ongoing Ali drama as that ultimate black subservient: "Uncle Tom."[39] In order to establish his own political credentials, Ali invoked the racist imagery and stereotypes regularly deployed by white America against their black counterparts. It is an Ali tactic in which political irony, public relations savvy, and strategic adroitness commingle with a certain ideological unease. Ali's media consciousness and tactical astuteness establish him as the lodestar for radical democracy, yet he is shown capable of employing the tropes of white racism because, showman that he is, he recognizes that his stature is founded upon singularity and polarization. "Any black who thinks

Frazier can whup me is an Uncle Tom," he would say, taunting his opponent, the black and white American Establishment, and anyone who would support Frazier or Foreman over him.[40] Ali's desire for athletic and political salience, for an elevated standing in the American and postcolonial left, and the need to see himself as Third World champion motivates this need to posit his boxing opponents as ideological enemies.

Because of the way in which opposing fighters were sociopolitically sanctioned by the white Establishment and often accepting of that positioning, especially in the period between his conversion to Islam (1964) and his banishment from the ring (1967), Ali developed a natural pugilistic antagonism into an unrelenting ideological animus. Historically understandable as Ali's position was, girded as it was by his penchant for verbosity and banter, it becomes most ideologically slippery when he denounces his black opponents as "ugly" and "dumb." Joe Frazier, the youngest of nine children, son of a South Carolina sharecropper, found the deployment of these racist (or racially based, at the least) stereotypes offensive; the sullen, introspective Sonny Liston was unmoved by these appellations. While clearly making these aesthetic judgments based on his own good looks (though, by whose standards was Liston "ugly"?), Ali's ability to appropriate these racist, white-identified pejoratives and reinvent them becomes a questionable project—one tainted and overdetermined by the very constituency to whom he is so vehemently opposed. The final irony is that in aligning his pugilistic opponent with the white Establishment, Ali adopts not only their tropes but their very racist vocabulary—and its considerable metaphoric baggage—in order to undermine and overpower hegemony inside and outside the ring. The vernacular intellectual, linguistically expedient and not as conscious of history, tradition, and the effects of linguistic jabs as he should have been, drew upon the wrong idiom in order to maintain his status in his primary communities—black America and the Third World.

Always the master of self-promotion, Ali utilized his status as anti-Establishment cultural icon to inject political tensions where they frequently did not exist. Patterson and Terrell set themselves up for the treatment they got in the ring and George Foreman's flag-waving at the 1968 Mexico City Olympics (after Tommy Smith and John Carlos's defiant Black Power salute) made him an easy target for Ali and his fans in Kinshasa. But it is questionable whether or not Joe Frazier should have been subjected to the most derogatory of black radical put-downs. There was little motivation for Ali to indict Frazier since there was nothing of the compliant black man in the South Carolina native's past. Frazier was, however, made to bear the brunt of Ali's post-1971 linguistic vituperation: "From their first fight in New York City, on March 8, 1971, until their third and last in Manila on Oct. 1, 1975, Ali humiliated and enraged and ultimately isolated Frazier, casting him as a shuffling and mumbling Uncle Tom, an ugly and ignorant errand boy for white America."[41] Locked into a polarized mindset, Ali's own history, his appetite for selling his own fights, and his successful deployment of an overdetermined racist discourse prevented him from producing another idiom—one rich in metaphor, images, and symbolism—in which adversarial relations with other black boxers could be conveyed without easy recourse to dominant stereotypes. Ali was able to use this language expediently (never unreflectively since he grasped the ideological value of his representations) and with rhetorical success, because he had been granted ideological carte blanche. These neat and historically rich binaries played well, for both Ali's supporters and his opponents, in the United States and abroad.

Ali escaped censure on this issue because he was not critiqued by either the black or the white Left for his racist depictions of his African-American opponents and because he commanded language like no athlete before or since. Few other boxers dared to predict the round of their opponent's demise, and no other boxer did so in rhyme. Rejecting "ritualized decorum," in effect the Derridean silencing of black athletes, Ali spectacularized boxing as a cultural event both through the magnificence of his athletic skills and his introduction of an identifiably black speech into forums dominated by a white aesthetic of reserve, an arena where blacks were objects of rather than producers of commentary. Ali converted boxing's traditional venues from spaces that privileged the black body as mute spectacle into a platform for black physical and intellectual articulation. Versed in the linguistic cadences of his marginalized community, Ali the vernacular intellectual appropriated previously "neutral" public spaces—everything from the notoriously dour and monosyllabic boxing weigh-in to the rote, predictable press conference and the sacredly nonverbal gym (where grunts and inaudible instructions constitute the verbal norm)—and transformed those forums through theatricalized, culturally black occupancy. He spoke from those venues and to the same audiences, though vicariously so, in the same ways that Martin Luther King Jr. used the pulpit and Stokely Carmichael and Malcolm X the political meeting.

Like these recognized political leaders, Ali reached beyond the immediate audience he was addressing. Except, of course, that as the most popular athlete of his century (after Michael Jordan or Pelé, some would argue), his reception area far exceeded even King's, Malcolm X's, and Carmichael's. Ali's pronouncements, whether a prediction about the fate of an unfortunate opponent or a contemplation about American foreign or domestic policy, had global echo. Ali internationalized his persona not only via his media-worthiness, but through his ability to align himself symbolically with communities who shared—in uneven, discrete, and even unrecognizable ways—his experiences of subjugation, racism, and persecution for religious or ideological purposes. Ali's skills as political observer were astutely delivered in resonant, if occasionally stereotypical, metaphors. However, they were always rendered in linguistic tropes that appealed to and were identified with by people in distinctly varied geographical locales. Ali's crisp witticisms, his forthright, hyperbolic sociopolitical evaluations, his physical attractiveness, and his sense of moment enabled him to transcend his public and make ideological connections across the world.

As a member of the Nation of Islam, he received a sympathetic reception in the resident Muslim community in the United States, in the Middle East, and North Africa; his critique of U.S. imperialism was applauded in Asia, Africa, the Caribbean, and in various sectors of the

Western left. Out of these disparate constituencies, Ali forged a contingent, dispersed vernacularity: transcending the boxing ring, through his political and cultural interventions he became a spokesperson for and a symbol of (often unaccredited and reluctantly so) a dispersed range of struggles; in large part, of course, because he was himself appropriated by movements—such as the Nation of Islam and the anti-Vietnam campaigners—he supported. In the process, the boxer Ali was positioned as the public articulator, the lone, idiosyncratic member of the vernacular intellectual vanguard. Ali integrated himself, if only transiently and symbolically, into an array of oppressed communities, enabling him to act as the unofficial oral historian who lent poetic voice to the battles of that grouping—sketching with a rhetorical magnetism its political, economic, and cultural vision. Ali was, in his heyday, the poet laureate of black global oppression. His media visibility provided him with ideal opportunities to make forays into debates about public policy and culture.

The Vernacular Intellectual

As much as Ali invoked and made common cause with postcolonial communities, he always did so in his own vernacular. He rarely invoked other cultural paradigms (as he did in Kinshasa when he learned and turned the Lingala chant of "Ali, bomaye!" against George Foreman), relying instead on his own range of experiences and traditions. In the process he inadvertently situated himself as the inveterately (black) American, the international icon who contributed to the African-Americanization, to borrow Cornel West's concept, of global culture in a way that predated (and differed from the more unreflectively corporate modes) how figures such as Michael Jordan and Michael Jackson would Americanize the late-capitalist twentieth century. The antihegemonic black American whose stature in the postcolonial world increased to a degree commensurate with the extent of his internal dissent, Ali became, because of that construction, an inadvertent purveyor of the international exportation of U.S. hegemony. Internationally constructed as opposed to American hegemony (also reduced, in certain moments, to an indictment of white hegemony, white-identified Christianity, the American military apparatus), Ali's status, his visibility, the very platforms afforded him, derived from American capital and technology.

Because all of his radicalism was inconceivable without his antagonism to the U.S. state, Ali's iconographic status in the Third World was a double-edged sword: the anti-American American, a complex subject position, girded as it was by principle, strategy, and even expedience. Ali the anti-American enabled the exportation of American popular culture: Ali's (African-)American vernacular allowed for the globalization of that vernacularity. Through Ali (aided by American capital and its media apparatus), in a phenomenon later utilized and exploited by American athletes, actors, and musicians from Michael Jordan to Michael Jackson, American popular culture became, in contradictory, dynamic ways, the global vernacular. Ali might have been anti-American Establishment, but he remained—despite his protestations and the momentary adjustments to his personality—an American. What he stood for, how he said it, and where he—in the main—said it from, affirmed his standing as American. Through Ali the American vernacular assumed a hegemony it did not have before: he transported, and exported, the American vernacular.

Within the context of the postcolonial world and U.S. society, the Terrell fight and the question that shaped it so indelibly—What's my name?—were of huge consequence. At more or less the same moment of the Houston bout, the issue of identity started to assume considerable importance within the United States and within the new postcolonial nations—and a great many places besides. It is now a question being investigated with increased urgency as black, gay, and ethnic communities living in the metropolis and the periphery struggle to define their place in the world. Stuart Hall writes on the question of cultural identity in the Caribbean:

> The issue of cultural identity as a political quest now constitutes one of the most serious global problems as we go into the twenty-first century. The re-emergence of questions of ethnicity, of nationalism—the obduracy,

the dangers and the pleasures of the rediscovery of identity in the modern world, inside and outside of Europe—places the question of cultural identity at the very centre of the contemporary political agenda.[42]

In its 1960s manifestation, identity was a question that turned, from internal groups such as African Americans to newly (or nascent) post-colonial nations, mainly on the issue of naming. Key to this process was the renouncing or rejection of old names (pejoratives such as *nigger* or *spic*); the insistence upon new ones (Afro- or African-American); appellations to which an individual or nation responds (not Bechuanaland but Botswana); the name that such an entity independently assumes after having renounced an earlier, imposed one; the status afforded an individual or a nation by the local or world community (the usage of a proper noun, Miss or Mister, or the Republic of . . ., where it takes its seat at the United Nations). Whether or not that new name is respected, and the different place the subject assumes in the world before and after its new political character is adopted, were vitally important.

For the world heavyweight champion, the process was no different as he undertook the transformation of Cassius Marcellus Clay, known in the early part of his career as the "Louisville Lip," into Muhammad Ali, which means "one who is worthy of praise." This new name, given to Ali by Elijah Muhammad, is symptomatic of the struggle for a distinctive, antihegemonic and nonpejorative black identity in U.S. society. The name Muhammad Ali can stand, metaphorically, for those same anti-colonial struggles in Africa and Asia. Muhammad Ali registers not only the alteration of a name, the iteration of deliberately reconstructed self, but a fundamental change in political philosophy. Within the United States, activists in the Civil Rights movement and the black nationalists —in all their various manifestations—struggled for the recognition of the traditions, culture, and material depravity of an oppressed community. It was a struggle that, as Stokely Carmichael put it, turned on the "necessity to reclaim our history and our identity from the cultural terrorism and depredation of self-justifying white guilt."[43]

During the late 1950s through the 1960s, in the midst of which

Clay became Ali (1964), the transmutation of identities was a recurrent feature of the postcolonial world. In this period many newly independent nation-states in the postcolonial world rejected their colonial names in favor of ones that gave expression to their black history and culture, as well as their vision as autonomous political and ideological entities. The Gold Coast became Ghana, the Belgian Congo became Zaire, Bechuanaland Botswana, and Northern Rhodesia Tanzania—to mention but a few. Previously, in the late 1940s, Ceylon had become Sri Lanka and long thereafter, in the early and late 1980s, Rhodesia would become Zimbabwe and South-West Africa Namibia.

In many instances, colonial names merely reflected exploitative colonial aspirations, geography, or else they represented derogatory ethnic terms. Rhodesia, for example, was named in honor of the imperial vision of Cecil John Rhodes, a colonialist who dreamed of raising the Union Jack over all of the continent—from Cape to Cairo, as he so grandly proclaimed. Conversely, the new names signaled political—but not necessarily economic, as would be quickly recognized—independence, the freshly manufactured flags symbolized entry into the world of free nations, and the new national anthems expressed the voice of a liberated people, the new currencies sometimes denoted the adoption of a divergent ideology—capitalism for socialism. Often, of course, the new, unified political structures that served to suppress dissent failed to articulate more than a single viewpoint or ideology, and represented a shift to neoimperialism rather than a break with capitalism. But, whatever the new postcolonial nation's shortcomings, and there have been far too many, Ghana and Botswana announced a major rupture with the colonial past.

In *Loser and Still Champion* Budd Schulberg recognizes, in a work noteworthy for its treatment of Ali as a serious political figure, the Greatest's role within the United States as a postcolonial voice. Drawing on the oft-made analogy between Ali and Jack Johnson,[44] the first black heavyweight champion (1908–1915) who was a dissident figure in his own right, Schulberg provides a framework for Ali's internationalism, a conception of the globe that was distinctly Third Worldist in its outlook. "Johnson had fought with his mocking smile and his wicked tongue," Schulberg writes. "Cassius would fight with weapons never before carried into an American ring, his faith in a non-Western religion, as well as his growing awareness that while he might be part of the minority 10 percent in the United States, he was also part of a global family of nonwhites among whom Caucasians were in turn a minority."[45] Recalcitrant as Schulberg is in his refusal to acknowledge the champ's new name, his comparison of the two most self-confident and confrontational black boxers is nevertheless still valid and valuable and, to be sure, an analogy of which Ali was all too aware. Experiencing tremendous difficulty in staging a bout after his Vietnam statement, Ali remarked on the similarities to the Johnson situation some forty years prior: "The fight game is getting like it was in Jack 'Papa Jack' Johnson's day. You have to go outside of the country to hold fights."[46] Exiled to Europe (where he worked for a while as a strongman in a circus in order to earn his keep) by the federal government on a trumped-up charge, Johnson was the original "bad nigger" boxer. He defied the society's governing sexual mores, marrying and conducting affairs with white women at a time when it was against the laws of several of the Union's states.

However, it is in these Johnsonian predilections that the Schulberg comparison is most instructive because it allows us to identify what distinguishes—beyond the religious differences—the two pugilists from each other. While both black men were radical figures in their (decidedly different) day, the Greatest was much more self-consciously a race man. So much so that during his enforced exile from boxing Ali refused an opportunity to play the boxer in a movie about Papa Jack's life because he was ideologically opposed to Johnson's relations with white women. More than simply a global fighter, Ali situated himself squarely within the history of the entire black world. Developing this notion of the Greatest as an international (and transhistorical) persona, partly through invoking the comparison with Johnson, Gerald Early writes, "Ali had become, merging the tragedies of Jack Johnson and Paul Robeson by combining both a black physical presence and racial political utterance into a spellbinding saga, the most self-conscious black man in history."[47]

Ali clearly saw himself as a historically conscious black man, a figure of DuBoisian perception, almost, as someone who had a keen sense of his place in his people's past and an eloquent vision of his role in their future. Ali recognized, as Schulberg and Early do, his own exceptionalism, and the complications of that position. He was the most visible spokesperson for a U.S. minority who opposed the denigrations of that status by situating himself as a fully enfranchised member of the black world beyond his country's borders. Unlike Johnson, vilified without ever providing a cogent political response, Ali offered incisive, scathing critiques of American society. But while, like Papa Jack, Ali never renounced America, neither would he be driven from his home into European exile. Ali's race may have circumscribed his claims upon American citizenship, but the persistence of Jim Crowism or U.S. warmongering in Southeast Asia would not prevent him from challenging the (im)morality of those restrictions.

For all their dissimilarities, Johnson was, as Thomas Conklin argues, Ali's athletic and ideological progenitor: "There hadn't been a fighter as interesting, as provocative, as Clay in quite some time, perhaps not since the widely reviled Jack Johnson, the first black heavyweight champion. Johnson, too, was boisterous, with lightning reflexes and a rich sense of humor. As champion ... he became famous for his love of the high life, his gold teeth, and his taunting of opponents."[48] Johnson and Ali were both boxers given to verbal banter in and out of the ring, both drew the ire of white America, and they were the only two heavyweights—no surprises here—not invited to the White House during their reign.[49] The two champions drew aesthetic attention to themselves as black men, and they both won—Johnson against Tommy Burns in Sydney, Australia, and Ali against Foreman in Kinshasa, Zaire—and defended their titles outside the United States. As champion, Johnson was forced to fight Jess Willard in Havana because the federal authorities threatened to arrest him if he returned to America because of his relations with white women.

Johnson and Ali were the rare U.S. champions who fought not only in the old world but the Third World as well. Johnson, however, did so only once, in his controversial 1915 loss to Jess Willard in Cuba.[50] Ali did so several times, most notably in the "Thrilla in Manila" or the "Rumble in the (Zairian) Jungle." Ali's different historical conjuncture enabled him to extend, redefine, and reinvigorate the first black champion's radical model. He was aided by technological developments, such as international TV and media coverage, and political changes, such as postcolonialism. Ali could reach new audiences, critique dominant ones, and make transnational links with newly independent societies in Africa, Asia, and the Middle East. The singular aspect of both men's careers is that no other boxer—or athlete, for that matter—before or since has opposed so vigorously and so publicly the norms, the socioeconomic inequities, and the racist practices of his day.

Budd Schulberg's pronouncement at the opening of this chapter ("It was not with Jack Johnson, Joe Louis, and Joe Frazier that Ali stood, but with Garvey, DuBois, and Jomo Kenyatta") is a provocative but insightful explanation of Ali's status as a boxer whose importance exceeded the ring. However, while Schulberg's formulation is allusive, it is conceptually lacking because it cannot fully account for the unique sociopolitical role Ali created for himself. Schulberg's pantheon of heroes is imaginatively constructed, but he emphasizes division where Ali produces the unprecedented melding of sport and politics. For Ali it was Johnson *and* Garvey, DuBois *and* Louis, rather than Kenyatta as *opposed* to Frazier. Ali symbolically "stood" as much with the black American pugilists as he did with the anticolonialists from the Caribbean, the United States, and east Africa. As a symbol of political dissidence and a fugitive from U.S. "justice," Jack Johnson was as radical, if not as critically engaged, as Marcus Garvey, the back-to-Africa black nationalist; DuBois the philosopher on race; and Kenyatta, the African revolutionary. These political impulses and outlooks merge in Ali, vernacular postcolonial intellectual. Ali is the black American cultural figure who writes himself onto and into the African experience, the American who makes common cause with Africa, giving spectacular visage to the Panthers' iconographic borrowings from the Mau Mau. Schulberg's dichotomy, which artificially privileges those publicly recognized as

"intellectuals" over those deemed mere athletes, and between intellectuals and sportspersons, is rendered invalid by this postcolonial athlete.

Ali is a boxer who incorporates in his persona the most charismatic
elements of the fight game and black political activism. He was the consummate showman—"Float like a butterfly, sting like a bee. Ready to
ruuumble!" was a ringing and highly quotable fight chant he developed
before the Liston bout with the help of his Falstaffian sidekick "Bundini" Brown and it became his trademark ritualized fight entrance at
important bouts. Ali used the public platform boxing afforded its practitioners to attack not only his pugilistic rivals, but his political antagonists as well. At the February press conference on the morning after he
defeated Liston in Miami, he proclaimed (after much speculation in the
media about his association with Malcolm X) defiantly his conversion to
Islam. And then he went on, in words now famous and more memorable
than the announcement of his new faith: "I don't have to be what you
want me to be, I'm free to be what I want," he said, confounding a media
and an international public that had definite ideas about how (as Russell
told him) the new heavyweight champion should act, what he should say,
and what faith he should practice. It was an act for which he would pay
dearly—boxing journalist scribe Al Buck claimed incorrectly, but with a
large measure of public support, that Ali's "troubles began when he was
converted to Islam"—but his opposition to the Establishment position
rarely wavered.[51]

More capable of serious commentary than he is generally given
credit for, Ali could be remarkably deliberate in the public presentations
that demanded it. After refusing the induction in Houston, he criticized
the U.S. media's reporting of his decision: "I strongly object to the fact
that so many newspapers have given the American public and the world
the impression that I have only two alternatives in taking this stand:
either I go to jail or I go the Army. There is another alternative and that
alternative is justice."[52] Ali not only refuted the political binaries of popular media perception ("either I go ..."), but he implicitly invalidated
the United States' imperialist incursions in Asia. Invoking instead a
highly moral discourse, one he would refine through his immersion in

Islam, he shifted the focus from his alleged transgressions to "justice." And justice, as Ali saw it, involved the withdrawal from Vietnam and redeploying those war resources to fight domestic poverty, racism, and a concerted distribution of wealth to poor black communities in the rural South and the northern inner cities. Lipsyte puts into perspective Ali's appropriation of these public spaces: "He refused to play the mild and politically uninvolved sports-hero and began to use the news conference as a platform for socio-political theory."[53] Small wonder then that his pronouncements were eagerly anticipated and widely received, and that this was as much for the theatricality of his prefight predictions as for his political commentary—in its several guises, some more unusual than others.

Ali's capacity for politically inflected repartee, his ability to make his interventions around issues such as Vietnam ring with poetic cadences, undermined the distinction between politics and sport; Ali made his form of political meditation count as much, certainly with a great deal more flamboyance and with a more direct public reception, as DuBois's. With his unforgettable phrases such as "I'm the greatest," uttered in a rhythmical tone that sounded as if he was about to break out into song, Ali reached and influenced audiences exceeding those of Garvey, Kenyatta, and DuBois. He did so by expressing his politics as integral to his boxing—the ring as battleground interchangeable with any forum in the political arena. For Ali, one was inextricably bound up in the other; no disjoining was possible. He was the popular cultural and intellectual figure who, as Schulberg says in an earlier moment, "not merely reflected his times ... but, as a superb athlete-activist, was beginning to shape his times."[54] Ali's vernacularity was founded on his understanding of his own unique agency: how he used, as no one before him had, public space and the possibilities for intervention afforded him by virtue of his standing, as Russell recognized, as world heavyweight champion.

What's My Name?

Relishing his unique historical formation as boxer and cultural revolutionary, there was no way Terrell could have matched the Greatest. But he did provide a platform for Ali to transform and focus his acute anger at white America's virulent political and ideological onslaught against him. Terrell's disrespect for Ali's name, his religion, and his sympathy for the Vietcong, as well as his apparent indifference to the history of black people around the world, their struggles, and their subjugated place in many parts of the globe, lent the bout a disproportionate significance. Ali converted his vituperation into a pointed taunting and a punishing, even sadistic, performance in the ring: "The champion of the world outjabbed, outboxed, outmaneuvered, outpunched and outtalked his challenger while giving him the merciless 'whuppin', spankin' and humiliatin'" he had promised. No matador ever stabbed a helpless bull more cold-bloodedly or efficiently."[55] Soundly beaten, Terrell, his face looking like it had been put through a "hamburger grinder," was "cold-bloodedly" shown to be out of his league.

Ali punctuated his uppercuts, left hooks, and stinging jabs to his opponent's head and body with the constant refrain: "What's my name! Uncle Tom! What's my name!"[56] After fifteen rounds of absorbing this physical pounding and psychological punishment—Ali the vengeful "matador" deliberately did not knock his hapless and barely conscious opponent out—Terrell submitted. The Octopus conceded in the ideological and, for all intents and purposes, in the physical sense. In between the final blows Terrell replied, in a barely audible whisper, to the champion's query: "Muhammad Ali." It would take white Christian America somewhat longer than Terrell to acknowledge Ali's name and his religion and to engage the ideological import of his new identity. Ali had already accounted for mainstream America's ideological recalcitrance, but he wanted his message heard just the same—loudly, particularly by those outside the ring who supported Terrell's position. "I wasn't just talking to Terrell," Ali said as he echoed his stance in the Patterson postfight interviews. "I was talking to all those people who keep calling me Cassius Clay. They wouldn't call Sugar Ray Robinson, Jack Benny, Howard Cosell, or Edward G. Robinson by the old names they junked. Why do it to me?"[57]

Indeed, why? Because Ali fashioned himself as an oppositional athlete he was singled out for continued vituperation among those who had "junked" their previous names. Unlike the others Ali listed, athletes and artists alike, he alone took a determined stand against the prevailing mores in U.S. society. (Howard Cosell is an exception of sorts here. As the host of ABC's *Wide World of Sports*, he was renowned for his verbal sparring with the champ and in the wake of Ali's exile from the ring Cosell continued to support his favorite guest. Cosell's loyalty, which included public campaigning for his reinstatement, earned him the wrath of some sectors of the public—he was once dubbed a "White Muslim.") In rejecting the role of the politically quiescent boxer, Ali redefined the existing model of the black American athlete. "Whereas [Joe] Louis and [Jesse] Owens fit neatly into the social space allotted to African Americans," Othello Harris argues, "Ali went beyond the white limits of acceptability in his beliefs and his behavior. Pride in his black-ness was taken as a sign of arrogance, and his embrace of Islam and his name change were interpreted as indications of contempt for whites, both serious indictments for an African American in the 1960s."[58]

Ali made it clear that he shared none of Joe Louis's patriotism— "There ain't nothing wrong with this country that Hitler can fix," Louis had replied to questions about American racism. (Ignored in Louis's dis-claimer is his implicit critique, typically muted, of the American system and its racism. Hitler may not be able to "fix" America's problems, but that is in itself a recognition of the inequities, segregation, and difficul-ties prevailing in the United States.) His morality came from a deep and distinctly non-American place, and indicted though he was, compro-mised he would not be. He went on to make it clear, in a belligerent response to detractors (who included ex-champ Gene Tunney, in addi-tion to the "Brown Bomber") of his antidraft position, that the domi-nant athletic Louis-Owens mold and mode would not be applied to him:

> I felt an urge to declare even more strongly why I felt the war was unjust
> and why I would not myself be used to help it in any way. Those who were
> denouncing me so bitterly had never said a single word against the injus-
> tices and oppression inflicted upon my people in America. I felt they were
> saying they would accept me as the World Heavyweight Champion on

their terms. Only if I played the role of the dumb, brute athlete who chimed in with whatever the Establishment thought at the moment even if it was against the best interest of my people or my country.[59]

Evident here is Ali's sense of outrage. More important is his sense of political history, manifest in his ability to explain his opposition to the war in terms that read like a universal indictment of oppression. The war in Vietnam against a people fighting for their liberation is (generalized and) translated easily by Ali into an analogy for the "injustices inflicted upon" African Americans within the United States itself. No Vietcong soldier or supporter, we remember, had ever called him "nigger." On that basis alone he shared substantial common ground with Ho Chi Minh and his people. Here was a community that was derogatively labeled, by U.S. forces and the media, as "gooks" and "chinks," to say nothing of the requisite "commie" label. In a rhetorically adroit maneuver, and with a conviction that strikes one as more personal than Bobby Seale's, Ali symbolically strengthens the African-American/Vietcong bond by collapsing two historically distinct constituencies: those Americans who criticize his respect for the Vietcong cause are rendered indistinguishable from those who have been historically silent about the oppression suffered by blacks in the United States.

Ali's own profession, the racist lineage of which he was intimately familiar, enabled him to make his case aggressively. He publicly indicted two of the previous white heavyweight champions, among his most vociferous critics, to illustrate his point about amnesia about domestic racism. (Ali concentrated his ire at his fellow boxers because it was within his own ranks that the criticism was more vituperative; Joe Louis was in agreement with his white predecessors about Ali's antiwar stance. It was for this reason that Ali did not attack stars from any other sports, though he easily could have since no white star from football or basketball had exhibited behavior any different from that of Ali's "own kind.") During their reigns Gene Tunney and Jack Dempsey had refused to face black challengers. "They had never," Ali impugned his predecessors, "dared speak out against the lynching terror against blacks in the

South which was raging while they held the title. They had been 'White Champions.'"[60]

Ali represents Dempsey and Tunney—and we could easily include Jess Willard in this dubious pantheon—as metonymic and emblematic of a propensity for unreflective, unhistoricized, white American racism and selective political memory. Motivated by a keen sense of injustice (the fact that his democratic right to oppose a war and not participate in it is being disrespected by his peers), Ali counters the (almost inevitably expedient) tendency to separate the cultural from the ideological— sports from politics—by fully inhabiting his role: the vernacular intellectual as sports activist. Ali positions himself strategically as the boxer who recognizes the cultural authority vested in him, especially as heavyweight champion of the world, and the ways in which it empowers him to make interventions into his political moment, particularly when such a figure is able to give public articulation to the cause of a disenfranchised constituency—such as Southern blacks who lived in fear of their lives. Ali understands, and deploys, his own cultural enfranchisement and he is reminding, through his own example, his boxing predessors and peers of their (continuing) political abdication. By not using the power of their "cultural office," Ali positions Dempsey and Tunney as complicit in the racist practices of their, and his, day.

The white champions' silence, deriving in large measure from their subscription to rather than a critical engagement with the political order, represents a mode of being a boxing champion that Ali rejects. While black champions such as Louis and Patterson were by no means in agreement with the U.S. race policies of their day (Louis's "nothing-Hitler-can-fix" remark indicates a consciousness of the problem, even an implicit, muted critique; Patterson's affiliation with the NAACP suggests a more formal, even activist, engagement with American race politics), they never set themselves directly in opposition to the dominant order. Ali's conception of himself as vernacular intellectual separates him clearly from other boxing title holders—and all other sportspersons, for that matter—because he deliberately, and consistently, takes upon himself as heavyweight champion the political responsibility of critiquing racial inequity, discrimination, and injustice in whatever quarter of society he finds it. As a vernacular intellectual Ali's greatest skill was indeed, as *Ebony* editorialized here in its chastisement of the champion, his ability to use the boxing ring for purposes it was never intended: "If Cassius Clay wishes to win public favor ... [he must] stop using the ring as a pulpit."[61]

Whereas *Ebony* intended the pulpit analogy as a criticism, it refracts as a singularly apt one. Metaphorically the pulpit highlights the (sometimes overtly religious) fervor of Ali's speech, his capacity to draw people toward him, and his natural aptitude to situate himself at the center of a public gathering. More than that was his refusal—one that girds his attack on Dempsey and Tunney—to isolate the boxing ring from the various contestations, antagonisms, and debates that shaped life outside it. (John Carlos's and Tommy Smith's Black Power salute on rostrum in the Mexico City games is, after Ali's anti-Vietnam statement, the most spectacular—and defiant—gesture by sportspersons to thrust politics squarely into the cultural arena and draw attention to the battles being waged by black people in the world beyond the boxing ring or the track. The winner's podium in Mexico City became briefly, instead of a celebration of U.S. athletic prowess, a pulpit for the struggles and the ideas of the Panthers and like-minded groupings in the black community.) Like the legendary African-American preacher, Ali is easily given to parable—he is, after all, the boxer who spoke in verse, even if it wasn't iambic pentameter. However, always a man of his moment, Ali was adept at parlaying his cultural capital into effective political commentary—in, needless to say, richly metaphoric speech. Ali took seriously the stature that prizefighters occupied in the popular psyche—"[The] world has a more than incidental curiosity about what the World Champion thinks," Russell pointed out to him. He used the pulpit, the unique public space he had carved out for himself, and transformed it into a platform from which he could show how the conflicts in the ring were rendered insignificant in relation to the struggles African Americans faced on a daily basis.

It is because the "Negro's been lynched, killed, raped, burned, dragged around all the through the city" that Ali saw no choice but to intervene in the public sphere. In his angrier, less poetically embellished moments, Ali the activist overshadows the champion boxer, reducing sport to a backdrop; boxing becomes a mere vehicle for Ali's vernacular forays into the dominant public sphere. However, these instances are the exception. Most often he is able to conjoin the two arenas, making one stand for the other, and locate himself squarely in both struggles. "I'm fighting for my freedom and carrying the hopes of my 30 million black people here and that's what my mission is," he remarked on the Supreme Court decision that overturned his draft conviction and at a time when he was preparing to fight Joe Frazier.[62]

The Greatest

Unlike his black and white predecessors in terms of his politicization of boxing, Ali was even less like them in his aestheticization of the sport. Ali reveled publicly in his beauty, taking a pleasure in it such as no boxer ever had. Sonny Liston, dubbed by boxing commentators as the Bear, was in Ali's estimation "too ugly" to be heavyweight champion—he cast similar aspersions upon Frazier and George Foreman. As Budd Schulberg points out, Ali was the "first black champion to proclaim his blackness ... the ideal practitioner to tap out on the heads and bodies of his opponents the message: Black Is Beautiful."[63] For many constituencies, among them black nationalists (cultural and otherwise), reconstructed Civil Rights activists, the anti-Establishment white left, the counterculture movement, and 1960s youth of all races, "Black Is Beautiful" was the anthem for the second half of the decade. The counterculture and the radical left, which included some sectors of the student movement, took as its poster boys of black militancy and aesthetics the battle-fatigued Latin and local revolutionaries Che Guevara and Huey Newton.

For other sectors of the student left, fans of the decade's soul culture, and the population in general, an icon such as James Brown ("I'm Black and I'm Proud," he proclaimed) was more identifiable as a symbol of black beauty. Ali's conception of black aesthetics, and his celebration of it, combined the cultural joie de vivre of the "hardest working man in show business" (Brown) with the brooding intensity of Che and Huey—though the Greatest seldom publicly shared their intensity and aptitude for dourness. With his natural, neatly coiffed afro, he represented, as opposed to James Brown's heavily processed locks, a more "authentic," chemically unaffected, Nation of Islam blackness. He added humor and cheek to Elijah Muhammad's spirituality and leavened Malcolm X's seriousness. With his nifty turn of phrase his radicalism was more accessible and quotable than either the Panthers' Minister of Defense or Castro's one-time lieutenant. In the 1960s "Black Is Beautiful" functioned simultaneously as a critique of the ruling white aesthetic and the adoption of a black culture that had been routinely derogated by the mainstream American public.

Black bodies and repertoires of representation, hairstyles, dress codes, speech patterns, body postures, music, and so on, were embraced by a range of groups opposed to the society's dominant values. Ali reveled in the blackness of his body, took pride in his trimmed, manicured afro, and with his unscarred face and his lyrical tongue neither looked nor acted like a "pug"—an age-old abbreviation for *pugilist*, which had long descended into boxing's equivalent of the unthinking basketball "enforcer" or the ice hockey "goon." He was, as he continually reminded everyone, not only "the Greatest," but also "the Prettiest."[64] As a boxer he was perforce required to display his body, but as a sports figure conscious of the history of the black body's negative inscriptions, he drew attention to his physicality as a sociopolitical commodity to be enjoyed and consumed by all Americans. By focusing on his looks, he distanced himself from and elevated himself aesthetically above the ways in which the sullen Liston and retiring Louis presented themselves. He proclaimed himself "the Prettiest" in opposition to Liston's "Ugly Bear"; he played the "Bronzed Adonis" to Louis's "Brown Bomber."

Unprecedented as an outspoken sportsperson, Ali had a rhetorical confidence that grew as much out of his political convictions as it did out of his pugilistic innovativeness. Ali did not remake the sport, but his ring-craft and style became de rigueur for every heavyweight with athletic pretensions who came after him. Some heavyweights, such as the late champion Big John Tate, borrowed from Ali, but they did not have the arsenal of fistic tools—the foot- and hand-speed, the swift jab, the ringcraft, and confidence—necessary to emulate him. Ali revolutionized boxing insofar as he introduced its audience and practitioners, boxers and coaches alike, to talents never seen before. *Sports Illustrated*'s Gilbert Rogin dubbed him a fighter of "undeniable virtuosity" and barely five years into his professional career ex-heavyweight champ Jersey Joe Walcott, who refereed his second contest with Sonny Liston in Lewiston, Maine, proclaimed him the "greatest heavyweight champ of them all." But it was appropriately his trainer, the Italian-American Angelo Dundee, who intuitively grasped the uniqueness of his charge and the inexplicable way in which historical moment and pugilistic genius came together: "Before him there was no one like him. After him there'll be no one like him. This ain't every one of my fighters. This is a new kind of person, a new kind of human being. This is a special case where you can't give orders."[65] Ali was not only a unique cultural icon, he was a boxer sui generis.

C. L. R. James wrote in 1969 about Gary Sobers, the greatest all-around cricketer the game has known, in a way that instructively echoes and illuminates Angelo Dundee's comments: "All geniuses are merely men who carry to an extreme definitive the characteristics of the unit of civilization to which they belong and the special act or function which they express or practice."[66] In the world of boxing, Ali was certainly a "genius," the most creative "practitioner" of his sport. However, his real genius was his firm grasp of the "defining characteristics" of his historical conjuncture: his comprehension of, capacity to give expression to, and ability to situate himself within the intense ideological conflicts of his moment. Intuitively brilliant as a boxer, he had a confident new style that reflected the impact black Americans were making in U.S. culture and political life. However, what was most "special" about Ali was the way in which he seized the possibilities of his moment: it enabled him to merge his boxing talents, his verbal dexterity, and his ideological commitments into a vernacular persona that presented itself as ambiguous "extremity" in the 1960s. "Extreme" in that it was read in antagonistic quarters as a wanton, self-aggrandizing radicalism (the "poet laureate of the busted beak variety," he was dismissively called). More important, it represented a rare political engagement by an athlete who challenged his particular "unit of civilization" on a variety of fronts—social, political, cultural. In the process Ali came to personify definitively the potential for and cost of resistance, self-reconstruction, and stylistic innovation in a turbulent, deeply divided society.

As an evaluator of talent and as a trainer, Angelo Dundee ranks among the best of his profession. (Ali was undoubtedly Dundee's crowning jewel, but the Greatest barely outshone the brilliance of the Italian-American trainer's later prodigy, "Sugar Ray" Leonard, the late-1970s to late-1980s welterweight. Leonard, who took his moniker from the 1950s middleweight Sugar Ray Robinson, is the boxer who most approximated Ali in terms of style and pure athletic gift.) In the hyped world of boxing, that the usually restrained Dundee recognized Ali's singularity carries an especial resonance, one that was important because it had significant consequences for their professional interaction. Because Dundee saw what Ali represented, it enabled trainer and boxer to forge an unconventional relationship, a "special case" where the coach did not "give orders" but allowed for a negotiated approach to training, to the prefight regimen and the tactics for the bout itself. The usual trainer-boxer hierarchy where the coach (usually white) instructed and planned for the fighter was invalidated—Joe Louis used to swear by Chappie Blackburn, the exceptional case where a black champion was coached by a black trainer, and Patterson (as well as Mike Tyson early in his career before the coach's death) took orders from another Italian American, Cus D'Amato. Ali and Dundee established a new kind of pugilistic partnership, one that privileged the boxer over the trainer. It was also a unique boxer-trainer relationship because the latter did not verbally represent the former in the media. "Angelo does not speak for me," Ali used to say. As Dundee reflected in a candid moment, "Muhammad changed the way things work. In promoting boxing, he made the fighter the main guy."[67] Before him, fighters had been vehicles for white promoters and trainers; Ali inverted this racial hierarchy and redefined the economics of boxing. Because of Ali, fighters earned more, gained greater personal exposure, and established themselves as personalities distinct from the people who trained and promoted them. Ali achieved a rare athletic and ideological agency for black boxers: he installed them as central to the event, as the very raison d'être for the sport.

An unprecedented figure outside the ring, Ali was an equally great anomaly in the "square circle." He defied the rules of boxing as easily, and arguably more successfully, than he did the political and cultural conventions of the day. Accused of bad boxing technique ("I can't punch, I hold my guard too low, I lean back. But I'm still here," he taunted his critics), Ali used weapons unconventional for fighters, especially those in the heavyweight division: speed of hand and foot.[68] Ali's power as a puncher was often underestimated, even though he knocked out twenty-three of his first twenty-nine opponents (including all six fighters he faced in 1962), because his lightning reflexes overshadowed his more conventional skills. He could knock opponents out with a single blow, but his trademark was more singular: he was a cerebral boxer, a fighter who outthought an opponent long before he outboxed him. "Boxing is psychology," Budd Schulberg muses in an epilogue to Jose Torres's biography of Ali. "Boxing is outguessing which means outthinking your opponent."[69] Ali was the consummate master of "outthinking" and out-psyching opponents. He flustered and disconcerted opponents because he was quicker to the punch, fleeter of foot, and hence more difficult to hit. Ali moved like a much lighter man, say, the middleweight Robinson or the welterweight Leonard, than a leaden-footed heavyweight such as Primo Carnera or Mike Weaver. To recall his own memorable expression, Ali could "float like a butterfly and sting like a bee." And like Terrell and Patterson, his opponents always felt the punch of Muhammad Ali.

Always athletically creative, Ali fashioned unprecedented tactics such as his famed "Rope-a-Dope" and the "Ali Shuffle." Both these tactics relied on a certain measure of taunting, elusiveness, and a sure defense (the very staple of a good boxer). However, most of all, these Ali qualities were based on confidence—"I am confident in my abilities," Ali was wont to say early in his career. Here was a confidence announcing itself, in full view of the world, the antistereotypical, aesthetically self-aware, and unconquerable presence of the militant black body. During the course of making this statement, the black body may absorb some blows, but that serves only to demonstrate its resilience. Ali's confidence, Michael Oriard writes, was always a pronouncement not without professional hazards: "When Cassius Clay first declared, 'I am the greatest!', this was an original and radical act . . . It was also full of risk: proclaiming himself the greatest, Clay/Ali challenged opponents to beat him into a liar."[70]

Other boxers rarely beat him—he lost only five times in his entire career—because he was considerably more ingenious than them. "Rope-a-Dope," to describe one of his most innovative tactics, was a phrase Ali coined to celebrate his ability to use the ropes spanning the ring; it was a strategy that confused and exhausted opponents. During this maneuver the normally nimble Ali leaned against the ropes, deliberately making a target of himself, giving his opponent the dangerously false sense of being—in boxing terminology—"on the ropes," vulnerable, perilously close to defeat. Because of his extraordinary long forearms, Ali invited his opponent (none more famously than George Foreman in Kinshasa in 1974) to flail away. Invariably, his opponent punched himself out without really doing any serious damage to Ali, making himself a "dope" because, instead of moving in for the kill (as he expected), a fighter such as the remarkably strong George Foreman was only really tiring himself out. In the later rounds, a still fresh and strong Ali would confront—and inevitably beat—his now exhausted opponent. In Rope-a-Dope Ali functions as a pugilistic Brer Rabbit, the boxer as trickster; moreover, in this unique maneuver Ali's rhetorical acumen and his boxing innovativeness come together—the language of Ali the cerebral, verbal boxer and his boxing strategies conjoin.

Reflecting on Ali's boxing style, Pacheco provides us with a profile of his amazing talents as a boxer:

... he had the leg speed of a welterweight. And hand speed. And radar for incoming punches. And a granite chin. And one of the greatest brains ever seen in a boxing ring. What else can one ask of a fighter? One thing: a mouth. Nonstop talking, bell to bell, to frustrate you, to wear you out, to confuse, befuddle, distract.[71]

Ali's physical skills were matched by his mental prowess, assets he combined astutely in the ring. While his opponent flailed away, all the while the victim of a barbed running commentary on his futile efforts, Ali counterpunched to great effect—jabbing, uppercutting, and hooking inside his rival's futile efforts. Derision and mockery followed every time the opponent's blows missed. In the 1974 Kinshasa bout, the younger, stronger, heavier-punching George Foreman fell victim to all these tactics in the early morning Zaire (as the Democratic Republic of the Congo was then known) air. (The bout was scheduled for four in the morning in order to reach the American audience.) Already thirty-two, Ali realized that he could not outpunch Foreman. Instead, he adopted the Rope-a-Dope strategy (accompanied by an especially sharp verbal attack, even as he was taking some serious blows to the body, fewer to the head). Ali set himself up against the ropes, Foreman punched himself out in a flurry of misses (though he dominated the fight in the opening rounds), and the rest is, as they say, postcolonial history: against a frenzied postcolonial backdrop, a famous Ali victory, a triumph unexpected by the pundits.

Problematics of the Postcolonial Intellectual

"The Rumble in the Jungle," as the Foreman fight has become universally known, is a phrase that is both catchy (in no small measure because that bout is so etched into "1960s" cultural memories, a moment made available to later generations with *When We Were Kings*) and politically disturbing. It is an event, linguistically and politically, that certainly bears renewed scrutiny in our consideration of Ali as a vernacular postcolonial figure, an American cultural icon who exported U.S. discourse to—and imposed an unfamiliar set of tropes upon—the Third World.

Both the linguistic terms of that famous fight are grounded in a 1960s American inner-city idiom. *Rumble* is a colloquial term for a fight (often a description of battle between two gangs) and *jungle* was a disparaging reference to underresourced black and Hispanic areas. By uncritically applying a U.S. metaphor to the Kinshasa bout and describing the Zairian capital city as a "jungle," Ali demonstrates the dangers—because of derogatory rhetorical confluences—of his appetite for language that rhymed. To equate Kinshasa with a jungle, in a moment when newly independent African states were trying to establish themselves as modern, industrialized nations, is to recall and underwrite a long and very recent history of racist and imperialist discourse. The appellation *jungle* reinforced the (still barely residual) colonialist notion of black Africans as crude, premodern subjects; as nonrational beings who inhabit lush tropical environs. Undermined by Ali's verbal pyrotechnics is the de facto condition of the decolonized African state—the stadium in which the fight was held also hosted international football (soccer) matches, Kinshasa's architecture was modern and its infrastructure and facilities technologically advanced. But in the American (and to a significant extent the world's) imagination the location is a dark (post)colonial outpost, replete with sweating black bodies jostling inside and outside the ring.

While the U.S. media coined "Rumble in the Jungle," its idiomatic roots could be traced directly back to the Ali camp itself. In a ritual that originated with the 1964 Miami fight against Liston,[72] Ali and his sidekick Bundini Brown used to yell on the walk from the dressing room to the ring: "Rumble, young man, Ruuumble . . . !" And what rhymes better with "rumble" than "jungle," a chant animated in this instance by the fact that Africa, the proverbial Dark Continent, was hosting the bout? A decade after the original *rumble* in Miami, the term found its fullest rhythmic articulation. Coined in the hype that surrounded Ali's bouts, the phrase assumed colonialist overtones unintended and unforeseen by the Greatest's camp. Ali, who at no point intervened and rejected the phrase, demonstrated a lack of consciousness about the phrase's pejorative implications. Instead, he immersed himself in the "colonialist" spirit of things, as it were, and on several occasions—both in the United States and in Kinshasa—he invited George Foreman to rumble.

Ali's lack of a critical historical perspective on Africa's reception in the West is in and of itself disturbing, but it becomes even more problematic because it is not without precedent in Ali's history. As a political faux pas, Ali's inability to recognize the Orientalist tendencies of the phrase recalls an ideological blunder he made about the continent during the 1960 Rome Olympics. Asked by a journalist from the Soviet Union about racial segregation in the United States, Ali (then still Cassius Clay) provided a knee-jerk American response. The most telling aspect of Ali's reply, which puts one in mind of Joe Louis's World War II Hitler remark, was that his patriotism not only disabled him from engaging the matter of U.S. racism but that in so doing he resorted to a primitivist description of Africa: "'Look here Commie. America is the best country in the world, including yours. I'd rather live here in Louisville than in Africa 'cause at least I ain't fightin' off no snakes and alligators and livin' in mud huts.'"[73]

A remarkably unreflexive statement from a man who had grown up in a deeply segregated Louisville, Kentucky, and whose father had frequently reminded his two sons of the condition of black people in the U.S. South. But perhaps it is not so surprising if one considers that, for all his difficulties with the U.S. state, he was still decidedly shaped by it and subject to its representations of other peoples and parts of the globe. "Like other Americans, black and white," Thomas Hietala points out, "Ali had formed images of Africa that had originated with movies about 'the dark continent.'"[74] Ali quickly regretted his derogation of Africa after he encountered a "young Nigerian" Olympian who clearly felt that he had overestimated Ali's understanding of and empathy for his homeland. "'I thought we were brothers,' the Nigerian said, 'You don't understand.'"[75] Ali did not and he acknowledged, in his autobiography written almost fifteen years later, that his 1960 position was born out of ignorance and the prevailing racist and neocolonialist perceptions of the continent—"I knew nothing of Russia and little of Africa, except what I'd seen in Tarzan movies," he admitted.[76] By 1974, his conversion to Islam, his respect for African leaders he had met, his anti-Vietnam stance, the impact of civil rights and the black nationalist struggles, and extensive travel to the Third World had certainly disabused Ali of these notions. As he says, "I saw modern cities, met talented, artistic people and got to know something of the culture and contributions Africa had made in the ancient and modern worlds."[77]

Despite these insights, however, in key cultural moments Ali was too involved in the promotion of the fight and his own causes—regaining and defending the heavyweight crown—to either critique the offensive ideological underpinnings of the fight (such as was required in Zaire) or reject offers from politically unsavory quarters. This is a trend, hauntingly reminiscent of his "Africanist" moments, that is most evident in Ali's flirtations with the continent's most racist and repressive regime—apartheid South Africa. In 1972 the white minority government of Prime Minister B. J. Vorster recognized the value of Ali as an iconic black figure, a boxer, and a vernacular intellectual: if he could not absolve the regime for its policies and invalidate its pariah status, he alone among black cultural and political figures could secure it a temporary respite from international sanction. At the very least, the apartheid state reasoned, his very presence could take the edge off the invective it was routinely subjected to by both its African neighbors and the world at large. Toward this end, the Vorster government made two efforts in 1972 to woo Ali to its shores. In July of that year the *New York Times* reported that "Muhammad Ali has been offered $300,000 for ten lectures in South Africa December 20 through January 2 and plans to accept if he can obtain a visa to that racially troubled country."[78] It is shocking that Ali would even have considered such an offer, profoundly disturbing that he "planned to accept"—pending a visa being granted. While it certainly matters that he did not go (though it has never been fully explained), what is more problematic is his ideological vicissitude: his inability to recognize that as a radical black figure he was charged with the responsibility of always representing disenfranchised and oppressed people. That Ali may have gone to South Africa for financial reasons, or because he believed that his ten lectures could have an impact, points to a serious limitation in Ali's ability to read the non-American political landscape and to comprehend how his international stature could be exploited—though what he would have said that the South African government would have approved of is quite unfathomable.

Later that year a fight between Ali and an unknown black American in South Africa was negotiated and again Ali was prepared to go ahead with the bout until some major African political bodies intervened. Dennis Brutus, longtime antiapartheid activist and the guiding influence behind SANROC (the South African Non-Racial Olympic Committee, a sports body that fought for decades to have the apartheid state barred from Olympic competition), and Ambassador Abdulrahim Farah of Somalia, chair of the United Nations Special Committee on Apartheid, conferred with Ali. Brutus, who had once been imprisoned by the apartheid regime, and Farah convinced Ali of the importance of isolating South Africa politically and culturally. The Greatest agreed but just six years later (this after the Soweto student-led uprising had exploded on the world's television screens), when black opposition (and state repression, commensurately) had intensified, Ali was again poised to visit apartheid's shores. Following his unexpected February 1978 loss to Leon Spinks, Bob Arum (a boxing promoter with strong links to apartheid society) made him yet another tempting South African offer: "Bob Arum reached a tentative agreement in 1978, with a South African hotel chain (Sun Hotels) to stage the Muhammad Ali–Leon Spinks return match in Boputhatswana."[79] The bout would have taken place in Sun City, capital of the nominally independent South African homeland, and a haven for the casinos and adult movie theaters outlawed by a puritanical Pretoria government—Sun City was the South African equivalent of Las Vegas.

Yet again the proposed bout did not take place, but once more Ali behaved inexplicably. A deeply principled and moral man, a cultural figure who understood the machinations of politics beyond gesture and rhetorical flourish (otherwise he could not have taken the anti-Vietnam stance and paid so high a professional price for it), in his post-1960s manifestation Ali revealed himself unable to adopt ideological positions on the Third World consistent with a critical vernacular postcolonial intellectual. If ignorance of the South African situation was clearly not a mitigating factor in 1978, Ali certainly showed himself no more adept a reader of the rest of the African continent just a couple of years later—a situation in which South Africa again played a significant symbolic role. Using the Soviet Union's invasion of Afghanistan as a pretext for the United States to boycott the 1980 Moscow Olympics, President Jimmy Carter appointed Ali special envoy to Africa to mobilize support among nations there for this position. Ali failed miserably in this role, both because the State Department briefed him inadequately and because he lacked the kind of insights necessary to be a convincing unofficial ambassador for American foreign policy—a status in itself replete with irony given that Ali's capital in the continent derived from his opposition to the U.S. government, not his subscription to its policies. A sense of recent Olympic history, on the part of the Ali-led U.S. delegation, was also absent here. Most African countries had boycotted the 1976 Montreal Games because the hosts would not withdraw their invitation to New Zealand, a country that was sending its rugby team to apartheid South Africa—at the same time as the Olympics were being held, no less. The New Zealanders were adamant, in spite of appeals by black African countries to isolate its racist neighbor culturally, and the rugby tour took place as scheduled even as the Soweto uprising of June 1976 wracked the country. The black African states had received no support from the United States in their bid to bar New Zealand, and many of them had more allegiance to Moscow, both literally and metaphorically, than they did to Washington. Claiming the right to keep sport separate from politics, the New Zealand rugby team (known, ironically enough, as the All Blacks) embarked on a tour through a turbulent South Africa.

More than any other Ali commentator, Jeffrey Sammons has tried to account for this tendency in the Greatest. The South African episodes, within the historian's argument, represent an ever-increasing trend in Ali toward conservatism: "The truth is that the radical who had abandoned Christianity to become a Black Muslim, who had refused military induction and in general defied the Establishment, was never really a radical—society merely perceived him as one because he did not follow the guidelines that had been set. In the post–Malcolm X era the Nation of Islam was no more threatening to the American order than Booker T. Washington's Tuskegee group."[80] Sammons clearly overstates his case here because Ali, even by his definition, was nothing if not a cultural radical—transgressing the "guidelines" required an alternate and oppositional conception of the world. Without a doubt, Ali possessed that. Even within the Nation of Islam he was a radical, a figure so influential that he convinced Elijah Muhammad to suspend the movement's ban on participation in professional sport. The Nation believed that sport corrupted and, more importantly, that it functioned as an opiate for the black American masses, hence the moral opprobrium directed at organized sport. Recognizing Ali's public allure, the champion as a source of funds for his organization, and his singular gift for popularizing the Nation, Elijah agreed to grant the champion special permission.

Despite all this, Sammons's critique (which, interestingly, positions Ali as a Booker T. as opposed to Schulberg's DuBois) provides a moment for historical reflection on Ali's Third World (and domestic) politics and the opportunity to explicate the Greatest's limitations as a postcolonial figure. It is not so much that Ali became a conservative in the "post-Malcolm" phase, because this is after all a period that pivoted on his refusal to be inducted into the U.S. military and demonstrates his capacity for political sacrifice. Rather, it is that in the wake of his favorable 1971 Supreme Court ruling (an unsigned opinion that overturned his fine and his prison sentence) we see the (re)emergence of reactionary political strains that first found articulation in his "primitivist" comments at the 1960 Rome Olympics. In Ali it is clear that while his radical tendencies dominate in the period of his vernacularity, there are always dormant (and not so dormant) conservative strains that coexist with his left leanings. The three South African incidents and, as disturbingly, his 1980 endorsement of Ronald Reagan represent some of the more troubling instances of Ali's conservatism. As part of his support for Reagan, Ali, flanked by Joe Frazier and Floyd Patterson, posed for a telling picture with the Republican candidate. The caption for the photograph, which shows Ali taking a punch from Reagan, reads: "You're the man." This endorsement for a man who refused him the right to fight in California in the late 1960s because he was a "draft dodger." For this reason the period between 1964, when he reengages Africa as heavyweight champion, and 1971, which peaks during his banishment from the ring, stands as Ali's most radical. The moments that precede and follow them are, at best, ideologically ambiguous—an admixture of inexplicable political conservatism and incisive articulation.

The reappearance of a predilection for poor political judgment can be attributed, unevenly, to three factors: a change in the domestic ideological climate, a recognition of opportunities in the postcolonial world, and Ali's status as transient postcolonial subject, an amalgamation of factors in which the last is the most important and requires the greatest engagement. With his readmission to boxing in October 1970 when he fought and defeated Irish-American Jerry Quarry, yet another forlorn White Hope, Ali began his slow but definite reintegration into the mainstream of American cultural life (a development that establishes itself more firmly from the mid-1970s on). After his victorious comeback in the Atlanta fight, Ali's stature grew as public support for the war in Vietnam declined and opposition increased. The bloody failures of American foreign policy had a tremendous domestic impact, among which was the (re)clamation of Ali. Addressed now by his adopted name, he had shown himself to be a man ahead of his time, and the radical 1960s martyr was publicly reinscribed as a man of conscience and principle. It was a protracted but sure process, and one that for possibly that very reason in no way detracted from his Third World cachet. Ali, of course, was also remarkably adept at devising his self-representation to suit the moment, the audience, and the geographical context. He easily abandoned his changed (or changing, to be more precise) status in the United States in order to avoid alienating his fans in the Third World. In cities such as Manila and Kinshasa, he foregrounded his history as the black anti-American in contradistinction to the U.S. Establishment–identified Frazier and Foreman.

Most important, in accounting for Ali's limitations as Third World spokesperson is his condition as transient postcolonial subject. Postcolonialism was an experience that Ali moved in and out of, a political concern to which he was generally committed but in which he was invested only at strategic moments. In some instances, Ali's dedication to the cause of decolonization was intense; in others it was restricted to a highly stylized gesture. Ali claimed his ties to the Third World selectively, always with a strategic boxing eye. The effects of Ali's status as part-time postcolonial reminds us, in instructive ways, of the conditions and challenges faced by contemporary decolonized intellectuals. Decolonization, diaspora, deracination, and mobility between metropolitan centers and the erstwhile periphery characterizes the lives of postcolonial subjects, requiring them to speak in, about, and for disparate sites, to a whole spectrum of audiences, and on a range of subjects. Often these spokespersons undertake these projects from positions of dislocation within the first and the new worlds, with uneven levels of competency or political investment. These are all tasks postcolonial and other intellectuals, of the organic, traditional, or vernacular variety, take on with different degrees of efficaciousness, although their commitment may be unwavering. In their own way some of these intellectuals are, like Ali, transients. They live the condition of what Bruce Robbins has called, in another context, "cosmopolitanism": to inhabit places that are at once strange and familiar, locations that their allegiances have simultaneously rendered as identifiable as home, yet they struggle to overcome their sense of being aliens in a foreign country. Variously interpellated by these contradictory experiences, they possess some measure of cultural and ideological literacy.

What marks these postcolonial subjects as transients, however, is their unreliable access to the status of local political memories. Often they do not know which ones are sensitive, which sacrosanct, or even which public recollections are of most consequence. Here Ali's charisma is both political asset and impediment. Nowhere did the Greatest use his Third World political cache, his verbal finesse and charm, so potently as when he integrated himself into the local situation at the expense of his opponent. Ali and Foreman arrived in Zaire as "extended family—but Ali was the better politician. By visiting the neighborhoods, kissing babies, and mugging for the camera, he seized the people's vote."[81] An underdog, Ali endeared himself to the locals, an immersion that culminated in the Lingala chant of "Bomaye, Ali, bomaye!" ("Kill him, Ali, kill him!") on the night of the fight. Ever the expert at manipulating situations, at home and abroad, Ali was at the top of his game in Kinshasa.

However, because Ali's postcolonialism was of the transitory variety, in specific encounters such as Zaire not even his background, a black American shaped by a history of racist injustice, could compensate for a longer memory of colonialism's indignities and rhetorical vituperativeness. In the decolonized world, more so than in the United States, *jungle* is an overdetermined term impacted with subjugation, ridicule, derogatory stereotype, and exploitation. It is not a term that a permanent postcolonial spokesperson could invoke solely with the intent of humor or rhythmic language. The fact that the phrase "Rumble in the Jungle" has been insufficiently critiqued can be attributed only partly to Ali's uninvestigated status as a postcolonial spokesperson. Ideologically, the Foreman-Ali encounter was a strangely complicated fight. Sponsored by the newly independent black African government of (CIA-sponsored) "president for life" Mobutu Sese Seko, promoted by a black American matchmaker (Don King) for a record purse ($10,000,000, equally divided between the two boxers), and featuring two black American fighters, this bout announced Zaire's political autonomy. In a fight underwritten by profound political antagonisms between the two black Americans exported to another continent, the Africans supported the boxer who had historically shown himself to be ideologically in sync with the postcolonial movement. Kinshasa was a clash between fighters who, after achieving similar Olympic and professional successes, represented divergent political tendencies within the black American community.

Ali's (or Clay's, to be more precise) moment of Olympic patriotism was long forgotten (perhaps never even known, let alone remembered), surpassed by his status as cultural revolutionary. On the other hand, Foreman's infamous patriotic gesture at the 1968 Mexico Games still reverberated six years later for the Greatest and his fans; or, it was recalled and amplified by Ali and his entourage. Foreman's "spontaneous" action, waving an American flag after he beat his opponent for the gold Olympic medal, was read in (significant sections of) the black American community as a direct counter to Smith and Carlos's defiance.[82] Kinshasa provided the stage for Ali to attack the champion he had designated, not without some validity, as an Establishment fighter.

Ali's defeat of Foreman, much like his triumphs over Terrell and Patterson, signaled the symbolic victory of black American militancy over black conservatism—Ali had "outrumbled" a fighter determined not to offend white America. The resounding chants of "Ali, bomaye" entreated the interpellated postcolonial to literally punish the misguided 1968 gold medal winner. Foreman, who became a metaphor for white America and the forces of colonial oppression, had to be rudely dispensed with, if not "killed." Ali's eighth-round knockout of Foreman to the chant "Ali, bomaye" marked the moment at which an endorsement of black American radicalism and a celebration of the symbolic end of colonialism conjoined in the Kinshasa dawn.

Among others, the Manila and Kinshasa bouts demonstrated this case amply. These fights showed that the Greatest could put previously unknown and little-known cities—even countries—on the world map. Ali's status in the postcolonial world was such, Ferdie Pacheco argues, that a visit by him could deflect attention from the indigenous forces lined up against his repressive hosts. Pacheco is rather blunt, but politically provocative, in his description of this particular Ali-inspired phenomenon. Ali, the fight doctor writes, "enjoyed the courtship of small countries that needed him to distract their unhappy populaces from political insurrection."[83] It is unclear whether Ali understood these invitations quite like this, but he could not have been completely unaware of the repression of internal dissent in states such as Zaire and the Philippines. Ali was, after all, a vernacular intellectual whose critiques depended on a familiarity (however imperfect) and (lyrical) engagement with popular events. He understood the significance of Third World independence so he has to have known, either explicitly or implicitly, that Mobutu Sese Seko of Zaire and the Philippines' Ferdinand and Imelda Marcos, to be sure, fell squarely within the category of leaders with "unhappy populaces." At no point did Ali reflect on his symbolic alliances with these Third World despots, or why fighting in Jakarta or Kinshasa was ideologically and morally unacceptable; he never refused to fight in any of these ethically questionable venues. Quite rightly, he had "no quarrel with them Vietcong," while here he had every reason to differ from—and take to task—those in central Africa and east Asia who paid his purse. Ali's reticence about critiquing postcolonial elites belongs to a disturbing, double-edged, antiradical tendency within his vernacularity. On the one hand, there was the propensity for silence in relation to issues of what may be conceived of as "race loyalty," to his faith and Third World leaders; on the other hand, as we have seen, there was the capacity for a rightward turn toward a conservatism that was expressed through but not restricted to race (such as his support for Reagan).

At the time that Ali fought in Zaire and Indonesia, both governments had poor enough records as democratic institutions and there was opposition enough to their regimes. Historian Sean Kelly dubbed Mobutu, handpicked by the CIA to replace the assassinated Patrice Lumumba (a victim of the Cold War intrigue because of his sympathies to the Soviet Union), "America's tyrant" in central Africa. It was rumored that Mobutu has thousands of dissidents imprisoned beneath the stadium in which Ali fought Foreman. By staging Ali's bouts in their capitals, these leaders secured the kind of cultural and ideological sanction—and a measure of quiescence—that could not be culled from any other international figure. Ali was then, just by virtue of his presence, implicated in the internal political wranglings of the Third World— he could speak in the international name of black people, but he could not always measure the impact of articulations in every site where he said it or where it reverberated.

However, highly regarded as Ali was in the postcolonial world, and the world in general for that matter, it is doubtful that a boxing match featuring him could have staved off a revolution. This is not to suggest that sports events cannot spark or inhibit a major political upheaval. Nations have gone to war over the result of a football game, and the outcome of boxing matches—such as black Jack Johnson's defeat of white Jim Jeffries on July 4, 1910—have wreaked havoc with the white American psyche, but not even Muhammad Ali could have stayed an "insurrection." Without completely dismissing the Pacheco hyperbole, we can say that the socioeconomic questions inadvertently raised by it about postcolonialism—and Ali's implication in that process—is infinitely more interesting than the theory itself. Ali's commitment to the Third World, as athletically unique as it was, is mediated not purely by ideology but also by the spread and workings of global capitalism.

Ali endorsed independence and freedom for black people in the many forums he occupied internationally—he spoke to it during press conferences, in interviews, and in other public engagements. In the process, however, he also earned bigger purses—ones occasionally underwritten by the local government itself, such as the Kinshasa bout—than he might have had the bouts been staged in the United States. Ali knew, of course, that he alone could attract mammoth crowds and a huge press corps to places in the world few people had ever heard of. By converting Ali's Third World cultural capital into hard cash, he and his manager Herbert Muhammad—Elijah's son—grasped the economic opportunities presented in athletically uncharted waters. In the five years following his 1970 return to the ring, marked by his victory over the white Irish-American fighter Jerry Quarry in Atlanta, the Third World was a site Ali frequently visited with exactly these fiscal ends in mind.

The most striking aspect of Ali's fights in the postcolonial world is the transition from exhibition matches to bouts of boxing consequence. All the exhibition fights—such as those against Jimmy Ellis, his sparring partner and fellow Louisvillian, in San Juan, Gothenburg, and London—took place before 1967, the year he is effectively banned from boxing. After his return from athletic exile, Ali never again fought an exhibition match and all his fights in the Third World are either for the championship belt—against Foreman—or a title defense. During his exile Ali's financial resources had been seriously drained and he needed big paydays to replenish his funds. The Third World provided excellent opportunities in this regard. The Third World became, as it were, Ali's personal goldmine. In the process, Ali becomes a postcolonial "colonialist"—a figure for whom the Third World represents both an ideological commitment and an economic opportunity. Although figures for the purses Ali received are not available, we know that while exhibitions can be profitable, "real" fights usually guarantee greater returns. (Exhibition matches carry their own risks. Fighters can sustain serious injuries in bouts where there is really nothing at stake, thereby endangering their livelihood.)

Already a hero in the postcolonial universe, his victory in Zaire made him an even more fetishized commodity. Ali was now able to secure, by exhibiting his skills in previously little-known sites, purses that he could not have if the fights had been staged in the United States or Europe. In return, cities such as Jakarta, Kinshasa, and Kuala Lumpur positioned themselves prominently—if only momentarily—on the world stage. Nowhere are the ideological complexities and tensions attendant to an Ali Third World event as evident than in his Jakarta fight with Ruud Lubbers. Jakarta, the capital of Indonesia, was home to a Mohammed Sukarto government that has had a longstanding policy of state-sponsored extermination of the East Timorese. By fighting there without speaking out against the Indonesian genocide, Ali compromised himself ideologically. At the very least, we are confronted here with the shortcomings of Ali's postcolonial knowledge; or, to put it more bluntly, we are reminded here of his ignorance about the internecine struggles that marked the local terrain. Ali becomes, in this instance, more than simply another Third World spokesperson or intellectual who overlooked the failings and brutalities of the new regimes just because they had only recently assumed power. Ali's was a problematic allegiance, one that spared Mobutu and Suharto the kind of criticism he routinely aimed at the administrations of LBJ and Nixon. Cognizant of his role as Third World champion, Ali understood how his critiques would resonate for mainstream America—it would confirm their Orientalist perceptions and implicitly make him a traitor to the Third World nation-state, the leaders who feted him and paid his large purses, and the populace who so readily embraced him. Unable to produce a vocabulary that could critique the leadership without simultaneously indicting the Third World itself, Ali opted for troubling silence—a reticence that could be, given his elevated status in this site, be read as a political abdication.[84]

Ali reveals himself here as a singular black American vernacular intellectual. Sympathetic to a symbolic Africa, he is a figure with a circumscribed and inadequate grasp of the postcolonial world that has inordinate cultural and ideological currency in the Third World. Here it is precisely his reliance on vernacular preconceptions—the circulation of annotated information and the dissemination of popular images or, worse, failing to acknowledge and act on the information and the images—rather than engaging in more scholarly, ideologically unencumbered research that prevents him from fully understanding the specificities of the several localized struggles with which he aligned himself. Since he was grounded in the U.S. experience, he could give incisive vernacular critiques of it, but his Third World interventions required a more studied approach—a strategy he did not, at some cost to both him and the peoples he symbolically represented, cultivate. Ali certainly knew how to work the Third World crowds and how to invoke the region as a political metaphor. He did not, however, always know enough about them nor did he estimate accurately the impact of his persona on and in these sites.

Ali did not comprehend how his presence alone could deflect international and national attention from the atrocities that marked everyday life for marginal communities in the sites in which he fought his (largely) symbolic postcolonial battles. Ali's limitations as postcolonial figure rest, finally, with his inability to critique—either through a lack of knowledge or familiarity with the conditions, or a lack of political will—those institutions in which he had, symbolically and ideologically, invested so much. He revealed himself to be a "metropolitan activist who was postcolonially reticent."[85] More importantly, we are confronted here with the paradox of the vernacular intellectual as a "popular culture intellectual." While the organic, traditional, or Gramscian (as Stuart Hall might sometimes be conceived of) intellectual is required to be articulate and interventionist, the athletic or artistic star runs the risk of losing popular appeal in proportion to his or her willingness to speak out—thereby reducing, ironically enough, his or her very popularity and thus capacity to make interventions. Celebrity status is a double-edged sword, empowering even as it retains the threat of popular disenfranchisement. As much as anything, celebrity frequently depends on (implicitly or directly) affirming the status quo or remaining obdurately silent about its failings.

To offend, especially ideologically, is to risk the loss of celebrity—which results in marginalization or, worse, cultural irrelevance. Having exceeded the boundaries and experienced the restrictions of celebrity first hand, Ali had created the possibility for reconciling public acclaim with oppositionality. Ali's celebrity, however, is always a complex phenomenon. There are moments in which Ali acts primarily as a celebrity—a public figure who seeks public endorsement; there are also occasions on which his oppositionality is incidental, or simply accidental to his celebrity mode; there are times when his celebrity is completely secondary to his larger ideological commitments. His public standing meant that sometimes his athletic pronouncements were read as political articulations. Ali's celebrity was so deeply ideological that it was always presumed to be indivisible from his politics. Ali is a celebrity who represents the entanglement of self-aggrandizement, political protest and ideological stamina—the one as much a derivative of the other. Throughout his career, Ali was the unusual celebrity in that he would not be silenced: the threat of public sanction, opprobrium, or even incarceration made him more, not less, outspoken.

It is because of his predilection for articulation that the rare instances of political silence resonate so loudly in his career. Ali's reticence is no more telling than in the furor surrounding the assassination of his friend and early mentor in the Nation, Malcolm X. "Outspoken about everything except the assassination of Malcolm," Ali did not comment on this momentous event because of—we can safely presume—

speculation that members of the Fruit of Islam, the Nation's security forces, were responsible for Malcolm's death.[86] Although Ali broke from the Nation in the period immediately following Elijah Muhammad's death in order to join the more orthodox Islamic movement of Wallace D. Muhammad, it is still a subject he will not breach. Loyalty to the Nation, and Elijah in particular, is probably the main reason for his continued silence in this matter—though he has long since distanced himself from the theological and ideological girdings of the man many journalists called his "surrogate father." This is an act of reticence salient in the Ali narrative, and arguably the one moment where we can question his political forthrightness. In a critical moment, a heavily compromised Ali would not take his own to task, much like he would not bite the postcolonial hand that (repeatedly) fed him—both because he was not always "intellectually" able to and because he was reluctant to. The fight in Jakarta echoes some of these concerns, if only mutely and idiosyncratically.

The Lubbers bout provides a clear demonstration of the intersection of capitalism and postcolonialism, the tensions between the colonial legacy and the new era of independence, and racial conflict as a barely disguised subtext. Indonesia was chosen as the venue, there could be little doubt, because Ruud Lubbers was a white heavyweight from the Netherlands. Since Indonesia had been a Dutch colony, and Lubbers was simply an unknown white European opponent in the United States, Jakarta would ensure a much more lucrative return for all concerned. Jakarta could stage the bout as the symbolic victory parade of the battle against colonialism. Ali's triumph, which was never in danger, would culturally usher in the new era of Asian postcolonialism. Like most Indonesians, Ali was a Muslim and by extension a member of the reimagined and expanded (inter)national community. Needless to say, his opponent Lubbers was a Christian. For Indonesians Ali was the postcolonial representative par excellence, the Jakarta ring transformed into his (and their) domain. The several binaries in place and an Ali victory guaranteed, the Indonesians settled down for a boxing conquest whose effects emanated from and echoed far beyond the Jakarta ring. There was, however, a hollowness in that victory over a less than worthy opponent. Contextually surrounded as the post-Kinshasa moment (until his retirement in 1981) was by Ali's South African shenanigans, the pugilistic (the fight an unequal battle) and ideological vacuity (his inability to bring his domestic radicalism to bear on a Third World site where he was so feted) of the bout anticipated his turn toward an ideological conservatism, away from the vernacular radicalism innate to his boxing career.

Expediently denigrating his black opponents in the hegemonic discourse, stumping for Reagan, reticent in his postcolonial critiques (and often, willfully? blind to the consequences of Third World dictatorships), Ali reveals how the vernacular intellectual—the minority intellectual as figure of cultural and ideological resistance—is (as capable as any other) of a turn to the right, of a conservatism that endorses the very status quo the vernacular figure has spent a career opposing. Vernacularity, Ali shows, is not in and of itself a guarantee of career-long (or, postpugilistic career, in Ali's case) radicalism; vernacularity is not necessarily a permanent condition. The vernacular figure can easily be, as Ali was and has increasingly been since the late 1970s and early 1980s and especially since his status was so dramatically transformed when he contracted Parkinson's syndrome, appropriated by the dominant American discourse. The loss, or abdication, of vernacularity—a movement away from the subaltern culture and its ideological girdings—produces a sanitized transformation, or transcendence, into "American iconography." The postvernacular Ali, though he is entirely capable of transitory, strategic, and witty recourse to the vernacular, is the third incarnation of the Greatest. After Cassius Clay, "Muhammad Ali, Black Muslim, anti–U.S. imperialism, Third World champion," he became the orthodox, conservative Muslim, stricken by a condition that eviscerated—but did not eradicate completely—his verbal and physical skills, but a figure who could now be claimed and celebrated by all of America; a cultural icon of legendary verbosity and poetic intelligence who now charms, despite his physical disabilities. The radical African-American anti-American neutered into a recognizable, nonthreatening U.S. identity, a symbol of America's capacity to embrace—even if only post–ipso facto—racial, religious, and ideological difference. It is ironic that Ali, the "essentialist" vernacular intellectual, retreats from radicalism into hegemonic interpellation while the self-constructed vernacular intellectuals James and Hall, who achieve their status through crisis, sustain their oppositionality. The older they become, the more, not less radical they become; the older they become, the more ensconced they become in their (historically obtained) vernacularity. Some vernacularities have greater longevity than others. (It is, of course, difficult to speculate about Marley since he died young. However, he was about the same age as Ali when the Greatest aligned himself with Reagan. Whatever the more conservative aspects of Rastafarianism, Marley maintained a radical sociopolitical critique in his music.)

Metaphorically phrased, James, Hall, and Marley (though the reggae artist did, like Ali, adopt a different faith—or, "denomination" of Christianity) did not change their names but they retained (or transformed) their radicalism. In truth, after the Foreman fight, Ali undermined his own significance as a vernacular figure. It is not that he had forgotten the lesson he had so brutally taught Ernie Terrell, but that he no longer realized, post-Kinshasa, that his (new) name was never simply a proper noun. "Muhammad Ali" was an identity, a moniker self-consciously chosen (even though it was a name given by Elijah Muhammad), an act of self-making that resonated in historically radical timbres. When he assumed that identity, Ali spoke not only differently from when he had been Cassius Clay, but from the lowest frequencies with the greatest vernacular articulation. In his second incarnation, he spoke as the 1960s hybrid of Ellison's Invisible Man and the all-too-visible African American.

Ali spoke on the same (not always low, or lowest) frequency, for a range of racially and economically discrete but always culturally and ideologically (however loosely) aligned constituencies. Ali spoke, well before the Houston bout and for almost a decade thereafter, in his own name and for those who grasped what his name meant, when Ernie Terrell and those who supported him could not and would not understand the imperative that sustained his interrogation. It is doubtful that those who would not hear the question "What's my name?" could ever fully understand the import of the answer for African Americans, anti- and postcolonial subjects from Africa to Asia, and, least of all, to Ali himself.

CHAPTER 2

C. L. R. James, Marginal Intellectual

This closeness to the lives of ordinary men and women was something
James consciously developed; but he never shook off his sense of being
an outsider, of looking on rather than being a participant in the
vibrancy of the barrackyard communities.

—Anna Grimshaw, *The C. L. R. James Reader*

The Maple Man: The Crisis of Shannon

It is not unusual for a single ideological crisis to constitute the most
formative political event in an intellectual's life. It is rare, however, that
such a moment should arrange itself around the choice of a sporting
institution. This was exactly the case for Cyril Lionel Robert James
when he was a young man trying to make a decision about which cricket
club in Trinidad he would join: "This, apparently simple [decision],
plunged me into a social and moral crisis which had a profound effect
on my whole future life."[1] James was in a crisis because, in choosing
between Maple and Shannon cricket clubs, he was negotiating directly
between his middle-class background and his as yet barely conceptualized attempts to situate himself as a spokesperson for the experience
of working-class Trinidadians.

The Caribbean island's cricketing structure emblematized the
entire society, James wrote in *Beyond a Boundary*, as the "various first-
class clubs represented the different social strata in the island within
clearly defined boundaries"; by joining a club James was deciding about
far more than for whom he would bat, bowl, and field on a Saturday
afternoon (55). By affiliating himself with either Maple or Shannon,
who represented very "different social strata," James was making a political gesture that favored one West Indian constituency over another.
Maple was the "club of the brown-skinned middle class. Class did not
matter to them as much as colour. They had founded themselves on the

principle that they didn't want any dark people in their club" (56). Shannon, on the other hand, was the "club of the black lower middle class: the teacher, the law clerk, the worker in the printing office and here and there a clerk in a department store. This was the club of Ben Sealey, the teacher, of Learie Constantine, the law clerk, and W. St. Hill, the clerk in a department store" (56).

In counseling James, Mr. Roach, a Maple member "openly contemptuous of these colour lines," explained to the future Maple player that ultimately their natural affinity lay with the middle class: "'I understand exactly how you feel about all this God-damned nonsense. But many of the Maple boys are your friends and mine. These are the people whom you are going to meet in life. Join them; it will be better in the end'" (59). This exchange is telling because it reveals the slender—even precarious—nature of James's link to the Shannon constituency. Faced with a crisis, James turned to those who, in class and cultural terms, most resembled him. He did not approach Shannon's Sealey, Constantine, or Wilton St. Hill for advice.

Roach's counsel and his choice of Maple belong within the broader framework of the social forces that shaped James's life as a middle-class Trinidadian: "The social milieu in which I had been brought up was working for me. I was teaching, I was known as a man cultivated in literature, I was giving lectures to literary societies on Wordsworth and Longfellow. Already I was writing" (59). James's was an unprecedented position in his society since the "coming" cricketer was also a "coming" young intellectual, "already writing" and "giving lectures," as eager to contribute to the literary debates on Longfellow as to the cricketing fortunes of a club in the island (59). Mr. Roach sought simply to avoid a rupture between the young man's sports and social lives.

Although Shannon played "brilliant cricket," it lacked the cricket-arts continuum that James required at that moment in his life (58). Despite all the subtle arguments for athletic-scholarly integration and the tacit social pressures to which he was subjected, James's final decision to don his cricket whites for Maple rather than Shannon was tinged with ambivalence. Although the pressure of his "social milieu" effectively restricted James's choice to Maple, the club where he believed he could most easily reconcile his intellectual and cricketing pursuits, he was, as he says, "not altogether convinced, but reassured" by Mr. Roach (59).

It was the wrong decision, and James realized this soon enough. A longer process was involved, however, before he could articulate the ways that Trinidadian social history, racial discrimination, and the political underpinnings of cricket embroidered themselves into the fabric of the sport. The ideological tensions generated by joining Maple thrust James into direct conflict with Shannon, compelling him to read cricket as not only the central, but the most ideologically loaded Caribbean cultural practice. By linking up with Maple, James had not only made a poor cricketing choice; he had also aligned himself with a profoundly conservative political constituency:

> My decision cost me a great deal. For one thing it prevented me from ever becoming really intimate with W. St. Hill, and kept Learie Constantine and myself apart for a long time. Faced with the fundamental divisions of the island, I had gone to the right and, by cutting myself off from the popular side, delayed my political development for years. But no one could see that then, least of all me. (59)

When confronted with the "fundamental divisions of the island," James did not, contrary to what he argues, "go to the right." Instead, he remained in the place where he had always been: to the right of Shannon and the Trinidadian working classes, deeply embedded in the middle-class experience.

In choosing Maple, James demonstrated how he was, as Anna Grimshaw reminds us, forever plagued with a "sense of being an outsider," how his formation as an anti- and postcolonial intellectual was consistently marked by ambivalence. The Trinidadian's career is characterized by the struggle between his radical ideological commitments and his psychic remove from those constituencies whose political causes he championed. Even as he made common cause with the working class,

James observed rather than involved himself in the "vibrancy of the barrackyard communities." His dominant political persona was that of what is being characterized here—borrowing a typology from Mr. Roach—as the Maple Man: James is the incarnation of the Maple Man, the intellectual who opposed colonial Trinidad's color prejudices and who admired and ideologically identified with Shannon but could never completely overcome his middle-class sensibility. James respected Shannon, as he could never respect Maple, but he could not bring himself to join the lower-middle-class cricket club; Shannon and its working-class supporters occupied a psychic locale beyond the boundary of James's middle-class consciousness. Shannon was the club with whom he was ideologically identified, but Maple was where he—however reluctantly—belonged.

Deploying the figure of James as the Maple Man, as the organizing trope of alienation, the striving after integration (into the radical working class) and (eventual) vernacularity, this chapter engages the process by which James constructed himself as an anti- and postcolonial intellectual. By exploring the relationship between the diasporic Maple Man and his native community, how that relationship changes with time and distance, the complicated ways in which he negotiates his relationship to the peripheral home he left behind from the dislocation of (which is, of course, also a relocation to) the metropolis, how he utilizes the distance from his originary community, and the ways in which the peripatetic James's constant movement between metropolis and periphery was intellectually enabling, this chapter posits the Trinidadian as an anti- and postcolonial intellectual who thrived on—and, arguably, because of—his particularly impacted marginality.

Reading *Beyond a Boundary* as the foundational—but not prototypically—Jamesian text, this chapter demonstrates how this book animates one of the most resonant tensions in the Trinidadian's corpus. More than any of his other writing, this work foregrounds James's negotiation between his conception of real and cultural politics. It is through *Beyond a Boundary*, a work that might be construed as his ideological bildungsroman, that James gives most eloquent voice to the knotted, entangled conflict between his divergent, but not dialectical, commitments. In this text the Trinidadian produces a commensurability, and occasionally even a poetic harmony, between his investment in traditional political institutions—leftist parties, radical philosophical groupings—and his growing understanding of and appreciation for the kind political function cultural practices such as cricket had historically performed in Caribbean society. It is in and through *Beyond a Boundary* that James was able to resolve the tensions and the ideological problematic attendant to being a marginal intellectual inherent in *The Black Jacobins*.

Preceding, without counterposing, the enunciation of politics as inscribed in cultural practices is an explication of *The Black Jacobins* (and *Modern Politics*, to a lesser extent) as James's most important intervention into postcolonial history and theory. These works, however, illustrate more than the range of the Jamesian corpus. Read metonymically (because they are discussed in relation to the texts that preceded—and produced—them), *Beyond a Boundary* and *The Black Jacobins* mark different chronological moments and distinct political modes (though they clearly impact each other), and they represent the Trinidadian's engagement with the questions of politics, culture, and the formation of the anti- and postcolonial intellectual—and the complicated ways in which these issues intersect—from an array of ideological vantage points.

C. L. R. James: Intellectual on the Margins

Because of the significant body of critical work that has been published on him since his death in 1989, James can no longer be said to be an underengaged postcolonial intellectual. However, despite his prodigious output, James's work has, as Stuart Hall explained in a 1992 essay,

> never been critically and theoretically engaged as it should be. Consequently, much writing on James is necessarily explanatory, descriptive, and celebratory. However, major intellectual and political figures are not honored simply by celebration. Honor is accorded by taking his or her ideas seriously and debating them, extending them, quarreling with them, and making them live again.[2]

The critical neglect Hall alludes to has been significantly redressed, but the earlier condition of James studies had a great deal to do with the Trinidadian intellectual's tendency to situate himself, on three continents, within groupings on the fringes of the political mainstream. James's proclivities for the margins of the political left were borne out of his radical ideological commitments, and they were manifested in every context in which he was politically active, ranging from his decision to affiliate to the Trotskyist Independent Labour Party (ILP) when the dominant left organization in Britain was the Labour Party, to his work with the Trotskyist Johnson-Forest tendency rather than the Communist Party in the United States, and to his pivotal role in the 1965 founding of the Workers' and Farmers' Party in Trinidad in opposition to the People's National Movement (PNM).[3] All these radical leftist affiliations demonstrate what Hall calls the "hard edge in James's political position."[4]

Ideologically peripheral and psychically alienated though he was, James occupies an intellectual position that is not always outside of the community he is engaged with in his work. He represents a location that is, in Foucault's terms, "'somewhat ahead and to the side.'"[5] As committed to the end of European domination as any anticolonialist of his or any other generation, James located himself disjunctively as a postcolonial thinker. In a career that spanned more than six decades, from his early forays into creative writing in his native Trinidad to his final days as a supporter of Poland's Solidarity movement from his final home in Brixton, London, James's work made him a unique figure among twentieth-century intellectuals. He was frequently in the forefront of imagining of a socialist, postcolonial future, from outside the left of the ideological mainstream. James's critiques were sharpest when he worked at a remove and an odd angle from dominant left political thinking. Because he wrote from the margins, from an intellectual boundary that allowed him to survey the field of ideological play, inspired by an eclectic collection of political interests and aesthetic passions, he was often prescient and deft in his reading of anticolonial resistance. James's construction as an intellectual enabled him to become the first scholar of his era to take seriously the role of cultural politics, to develop himself into the most astute interpreter of the popular of his (and several subsequent) generations of leftists, and to become (like Fanon and Césaire) an expansive, incorporative thinker about both a Pan-African and a Pan-Caribbean consciousness.

In *The Black Jacobins* James draws on the nineteenth-century anticolonial resistance experience of the Francophone colony of San Domingo to rethink the possibilities for postcoloniality in twentieth-century Anglophone colonies in the Caribbean and Africa. He uses the example of historic black opposition to European colonization to demonstrate how the anticolonial paradigm marks, across the vast expanse of time and geographical distance, a shared history and a desire for postcolonial sovereignty. James's notion of a Pan-Caribbean consciousness obtains with greater specificity, and with a troubling salience for contemporary Trinidad where Afro-Indian Caribbean tensions abound, in his only novel, *Minty Alley*. (Shortly after *Minty Alley* James abandoned fiction and committed himself completely to philosophy, an intellectual transition that initiated his work as a left political theorist.) While it stands as James's only full-length work of fiction (he also published several short stories), it is a singular text in the field of Anglophone Caribbean fiction. It is the first work within this genre to engage the situation of blacks and Indians, their shared class location, their different cultural backgrounds, and their everyday interactions in the barrackyards of Trinidad. Moreover, *Minty Alley* gives muted but critical voice to the experience of the *dougla*, the offspring of the Afro-Indo Caribbean racial exchange. The product of those ideologically distinct diasporas, the slavery of the Middle Passage, and the indenturement of the *kala pani* (voyage over "dark waters"), *douglas* speak at once of the attraction between these constituencies as well as the potential for racial, ethnic, cultural, and historical conflict between the two main groups in the Caribbean. *Douglas* constitute a growing constituency within Caribbean societies such as Trinidad, but their subject position remains precarious in a region where Afro-Indian ethnic tensions run dangerously high.[6]

In *Minty Alley*, in a mode that would later become characteristic but is here still in its infancy, James registers the presence of the different disenfranchised ethnic groups in Trinidad through the recurring motif of his own marginality. The novel's depiction of Haynes, a lower-middle-class, culturally bourgeois protagonist who bears a striking resemblance to the author, is the first instance within the Jamesian oeuvre of the alienated intellectual.[7] Faced with a mortgage he cannot meet after his mother has died (and with it her ambitions for her son's Oxbridge education), the bookstore clerk Haynes is forced to rent his own house and take up lodgings in the barrackyard of 2 Minty Alley. Haynes's servant Ella advises him against taking the room because, as she warns him, "They are ordinary people, sir. Not your class of people."[8]

Nowhere is the difference in class between the new lodger and the other residents clearer than in Haynes's relationship with the young woman Maisie, by far the most dynamic protagonist of *Minty Alley*. Maisie initiates Haynes sexually, and yet she continues to clean his shoes for him, serve him dinner, and call him "Mr. Haynes." This difference in the form of address most pronouncedly marks the class divide between the James-like figure and the other yard inhabitants. Haynes is unable to grasp the ironies of his position. Like the hero of the nineteenth-century novel (an era of the genre so beloved by James), Haynes never reflects on the fact that the woman who cleans his shoes is also his lover. He regards her lessons in love (and in the ways of the world outside the confines of his small, bourgeois circle) and sexual availability less as his right than he is inattentive to the effects of his own privilege; similarly, he is unaware of how the fecund young Maisie (and the other women of the alley) has replaced the aging Ella as his domestic help. Maisie and Ella share a class, if not a set of sexual mores, and Haynes is oblivious, like the hero of the bildungsroman, to how these women usher him into maturity, often at considerable emotional (Maisie is the woman who provides the young bourgeois man's sexual training, not the woman he— nor Ella, for that matter—can conceive of marrying), if not economic, expense to their own lives. Haynes's lack of class-consciousness is not a critical blindness repeated in James's philosophical work. The ideological shortcomings of the novel would, as it were, be redressed in *The Black Jacobins* and *Modern Politics*. Fictional alienation would be replaced by ideological commitment.

Throughout *Minty Alley*, Haynes retains his status as slightly inexperienced but benevolent bourgeois outsider within the barrackyard community. He offers advice to the Indian servant girl Philomen, brokers several uneasy peaces between Maisie and Philomen (whom Maisie calls and treats like a "coolie"), talks Mrs. Rouse through her emotional crises, and his rent (as well as his small loans) keeps the household financially solvent. It is not that Haynes's commitment to the female-dominated yard can be questioned; it is simply that he remains detached from their lives even while he is located in the very midst of them. If *Beyond a Boundary* is the work in which James's marginality—in its various guises, personal, ideological, and sociopolitical—is dramatically overcome, *Minty Alley* is the text in which his alienation expresses itself most poignantly. It is the first articulation of James's coming to political consciousness, his initial foray into exploring how the alienated middle-class intellectual might, however tentatively or naively, integrate himself into the history of the island—its cultures, its cultural struggles, its cultural differences, those deemed by Ella to not be (Mr.) Haynes's class of people, those barrackyard residents who lived beyond the purview of Mr. Roach and the other members of the Maple constituency.

Tradition and Betrayal

Constructing James as an intellectual who incorporates elements of colonial culture into his thinking is both facilitated and complicated by the etymology of the word *tradition*. Contained within the Latin root of *tradition*, *traditio*, are two possible meanings that appear to be in ideological conflict: (1) to "hand down" or "on"; and, (2) "betray."[9] As a traditional intellectual in the former sense of the word, James participated fully, though not unproblematically, in the customs, cultural practices, and values of colonial Britain. James was, as Edward Said explains, a "remarkable" thinker "whose early formation in British colonial schools brought forth a wonderful appreciation of English culture as well as serious disagreements with it."[10] James's reflection in *Beyond a Boundary* on his schoolboy days in Trinidad bears out Said's insight: "It was only long years after that I understood the limitation on spirit, vision, and self-respect which was imposed upon us by the fact that our masters, our curriculum, our code of morals, *everything* began from the basis that Britain was the source of all light and leading, and our business was to admire, wonder, imitate, learn" (38). Critical as James is of the extent to which Britain "limited" the scope of his intellectual life and his perception of himself, the Arnoldian metropolis also represents the cultural model according to which James shaped his life. Contained within the proper noun *Britain* is an encoding of the historical trajectory that produced, at its far end *(Beyond a Boundary)*, the dialectic between James's "wonderful appreciation" for colonial culture and his "serious disagreements" with the ideology of the metropolis.

However, when James traces his ideological lineage to the literature of nineteenth-century English realism and not the nineteenth-century radicalism of German philosophy ("Thackeray bears the heaviest responsibility for me, not Marx"), the Trinidadian identifies himself as a native intellectual participating fully in the traditions of a co-optive culture (25). In this articulation James maps the process by which he was interpellated into Anglophone hegemony, a culture in which he has secured an ambivalent place for himself. James was doubly implicated in the "traditional" culture. He was a recipient of the cultural practices handed down by the imperial power and he was, through his work as a teacher at Queens Royal College (where future Prime Minister Eric Williams was one of his students), interpellating future generations of black colonial subjects. Himself educated at Queens Royal College, James was actively involved in handing on colonial culture. Moreover, as the different modes and moments in his oeuvre attest, the colonial culture was able to perpetuate itself by moving through the corpus—the life and work—of C. L. R. James. Ideologically mediated by metropolitan thinking, James was located in a series of ambiguous relations to his primary community—black Trinidad—and to the colonial structures he was interacting with in his daily life. As a full participant (relative to his black Trinidadians) in the colonial traditions and as exceptional practitioner (in the perception of the colonial community), James cut a marginal intellectual figure. He belonged to an elite class of colonized subjects far advanced in traditional cultural literacy.

James's cultural ambivalence and his complicated fidelity to two different cultures (Trinidadian and British, colonizer and colonized), his bourgeois marginality, borders on "betrayal," the second possible meaning of *tradition*. Intellectually positioned as he was, James transforms his double-edged cultural (in)felicity into a highly charged, ideologically ambiguous term, because betrayal is founded here upon a recognition of the conflicted (and conflictual) relationship with an antagonistic set of traditions. Implication and participation in traditional culture does not, however, equate with the "treason of the intellectuals" critiqued by Julien Benda in *La trahison des clercs*. Benda's attack on the "betrayal" of early-twentieth-century intellectuals is founded upon a bitter disagreement with the historically unprecedented politicization (which he understands as ideological support) of intellectuals: "At the end of the nineteenth century a fundamental change occurred: *the 'clercs' began to play the game of political passions*. The men who had acted as a check on the realism of the people began to act as its stimulators (emphasis in original)."[11] In James's case there is no sympathy with the disinterestedness of the "clerical" class that, in Benda's view, has through the ages constituted a special social category motivated by the purer philosophical instincts and not "political passions."

James's career was profoundly shaped by political passions of his moment, a sure sign for the Trinidadian of his broader societal affiliations as an intellectual. There is, however, at the core of Benda's argument, still a dilemma that applies provocatively to James: commitment to a particular constituency. What is at stake for Benda is, as he imagines, fidelity to a history of clerical impartiality based on universal values such as truth, justice, and intellectual independence. James, however, did not regard political alignment as a binarized choice, negotiating as he was between metropolis and periphery, and grappling with the different demands of various, often competing, cultural practices. Marginal thinker that he was, betrayal was a concept that neither arose for James nor could be reduced to questions such as, Which set of traditions is being betrayed? The hegemonic culture of the colonizers or the publicly marginalized practices of the colonized masses?

Betrayal, in any ethically mundane sense of the word, offers little assistance in constructing James as an intellectual. But the term does act as catalyst for interrogating what is being given up and what is at stake in the process of partial or wholesale cultural renunciation, that moment when certain practices are embraced and others, as a result, fall into disuse. James's relationship to different traditions enunciates a conflict because he was ultimately partial to both as much as he was (in-) capable of betraying both. The Trinidadian not only inhabited the two traditions unevenly; he did so from a location at the very edges of these different cultures. From a locale "ahead and to the side," James created an intellectual vantage point that was neither distinctly British nor Caribbean, nor did it always mark the intersection of those traditions. James's was an anomalous position, not merely a hybridized product of (uneven) cultural exchange nor an ambivalent "third" space. He worked from the fringes, drawing selectively on antagonistic (and dependent) cultures, crafting a paradigm that acknowledged his primary cultural influences while always thinking beyond it, aware of left debates but almost invariably at variance with it, and always informed by his brand of radical politics, his love for high culture, his growing appreciation for the popular, and his conflicted, dialectical movement toward the vernacular.

James's Organicism

In articulating the concept of the organic intellectual Gramsci carefully delineates how the functions of the traditional intellectual were implicit in the former category: "Every social group, coming into existence on the original terrain of an essential function, creates together with itself, organically, one or more strata of intellectuals which give it homogeneity and an awareness of its own function not only in the economic but also the social and political fields."[12] The organic intellectual is distinguished from the traditional one, R. Radhakrishnan explains, by a "traditional intellectuality that seeks to be timeless and unitary and an organic intellectuality that posits historical contingency and conflict-uality."[13] The "timeless and unitary" structure that the traditional intellectual wants to maintain, which Radhakrishnan's outlines, is in direct conflict with the organic intellectual's commitment to social reorganization so that the majority can secure access to the resources of the hegemonic bloc from which they are effectively excluded; or, in Gramsci's terms, the organic intellectual is serious about redressing the "imbalances and inequalities within the same society."[14]

The organic intellectual has a specific function in this political process, taking on, as Radhakrishnan puts it, the role of "'persuader'": the "intellectual is inserted into historical participation whereby his or her eloquence is given terms of purpose. Someone is being persuaded by somebody toward some determinate purpose: the persuader is thus made accountable historically and politically."[15] The organic intellectual is characterized by two main attributes: first, an embeddedness within a specific community that drives the attempt to restructure the broader social order; and, second, his or her intellectual labor, motivated by a keen sense of historical and political responsibility to that constituency.

James's entire political career represented a commitment to the struggles of oppressed and exploited communities across the globe. His work is characterized by an enduring responsibility to the histories and political complexities of the communities he aligned himself to. James imaginatively affiliated himself with several different contexts of struggle where his "eloquence" was put to the task of "persuading," giving voice to the position (politically, ideologically, socioeconomically, culturally) of the community in which he situated himself; these articulations represented an engagement both with James's community and their antagonists. Organicism, however, was an especially difficult experience for James as an intellectual. Organicism comprises, at both an ideological and a political level, a network of social links that are established through shared experiences, common struggles, and a remove from resources, links that bind a community together, sustain it in the face of repression, and motivate it to restructure the organism that is society.

This formulation of organicism gestures implicitly toward a notion of the community that is critical of society as a "natural" or an organic phenomenon, in the etymological sense; such a formulation recognizes that the human interactions that facilitate group construction and maintenance assume a physical situatedness, a grounding within a geographical confine.[16] Despite the quotidian nature of the social interactions, it is only through understanding the significance of these exchanges that those seeking to integrate themselves into the community can form meaningful bonds with (and within) that grouping. An actual or imaginary situatedness within, in addition of course to ideological alignment with the particular constituency, is crucial for the intellectual attempting to achieve integration. For James there was a massive disjuncture between his unqualified ideological affiliation and his personal inability to situate himself, physically or imaginatively, in the community of the barrackyards and the cricket oval.

James's failure to find a more rooted place for himself within the working class did not affect his theoretical, philosophical, and political work for, and in the name of, that constituency. This incommensurability between his ideological (imaginative) interpellation and his physical remove finds expression in James's corpus from *Minty Alley* to (a lesser extent) *Beyond a Boundary*. James's qualified, contingent organicism, transformed into vernacularity in *Beyond a Boundary*, finds its most telling expression in his ongoing negotiation, with varied success, between the demands of the indigenous and the colonial traditions. This tension reveals itself in the poignant description of the Barbados novelist George Lamming: "James was growing up a middle-class boy, a schoolmaster's son, but he was looking out the window at working-class boys playing cricket. They were not five hundred miles away. This reciprocal influence across the class lines was permanent and continuing."[17]

Lamming correctly points out that the cricketing experience crossed class lines and that the "influence" was "reciprocal," but the windowpane magnified the distance between James and his (same-age) peers considerably. Although not "five hundred miles," the slight thickness of the window alienated the intellectual who sought a closer connection with the "working-class boys playing cricket." James's organicism was limited from the earliest moments of his childhood. His political commitment and his physical and psychic remove remained in conflict throughout his life, sometimes ameliorating but more often complicating his marginality.

James was nothing if not an enthusiastic cricketer, but his friend Lamming captures a portrait of his involvement in the cricketing activities plagued by a sense of the vicarious, too often without direct participation. The window of class difference, of social aspiration and expectation, separated James from those with whom culturally he had a great deal in common. However, if James is too much the boy at the window, "looking out" and insufficiently involved in the experience of playing the game itself, then the "pane" (and the psychic pain) of separation marks both the attenuation of alienation and the vernacular conjuncture. Through watching (and playing) cricket across class lines, James symbolically, viscerally, and culturally identified with the working-class boys on the other side of the windowpane. The distance, and the difference, for James are not simply between the high (traditional) aspirations of his (lower-) middle-class family and his desire for inscription into the organic. It is also an illustration of how deeply cultural an identification the organic is, how the organic functions as the gateway to the vernacular.

The young boy James wants to participate as an unadorned equal (stripping himself of the class privileges at the root of his cultural alienation: the organic) and to learn the discourse of the game (the vernacular). James wants to understand its function, how the sport connects to the lives of the players, what role it plays in community life. The complicated desire for interpellation into subaltern life, so repressed in *Minty Alley*, opens up the possibility for James to comprehend the full import that cricket carries for colonized Trinidadians. In James's case (much like Hall's), the vernacular can be achieved only by and through the organic. The vernacular represents the transcending of the organic: that moment, and modality, when the textured meanings of the popular (cricket) are grasped as a nettlesome—and therefore dynamic—conjuncture.

In order to explicate James's ideological identity (the vernacular-through-the-organic), it is necessary to "ground"—to invoke Bruce Robbins—the Trinidadian within the community (-ies) he operated in, those he wrote about, and those he saw himself as part of, either in practice or in his political imaginary. "Grounding," Robbins explains, "includes two logically antithetical but historically coexistent senses: (1) to strand, beach, confine to quarters, restrict the movement of, and (2) to base, establish, serve as foundation of."[18] Naming James the "Maple Man" reveals considerably more about him than the resilience (and residualness) of his middle-class roots, though that forms a dominant trope within his intellectual narrative. As a rhetorical device, the Maple Man metaphorizes James's class grounding by explaining how his background severely restricted and qualified, at numerous moments, his political—if not his ideological and imaginative—mobility. It was, however, James's cognizance of the dialectical complications of that grounding that compelled him simultaneously to investigate the problematic of his social location and the possibility of transcending the limits of his bourgeois ideology. These contending, antithetical historical forces coexist in an ongoing struggle, reshaping, informing, and even temporarily eliminating each other, in James's work.

Deeply troubled about but firmly anchored within his privileged quarters (as Haynes was often tethered to his "outside" room in *Minty Alley*), James was nevertheless resourceful in his efforts to construct, through and out of his political work, solidarity with those people who experienced subjugation or oppression in any form. James sought to overcome—not through denial of the skills that his background had afforded him—his middle-class status through a creative utilization of those attributes, without having to engage the process Gayatri Spivak has called the "unlearning of one's own privilege as a loss."[19] James at no point regarded himself as handicapped by middle-class privileges, his superior education, his involvement in the colonial high Anglophone culture; his status as teacher did not constitute a "loss." There is little indication that James was unduly burdened by his privileges, and he sought to overcome his alienation by engaging the phenomenon, continually, through his writing. James's thinking could be represented as post-"unlearning" because he committed himself directly to the process of protracted intellectual alchemy: the extended transmutation of his middle-class advantages, the base material of his privilege, into a political force that could assist in the project of radical social restructuring.[20] Participation in the struggle to reorganize society transforms the metaphor of alchemy into a lengthy process that pivots on the notion of investing in a social grouping with the intention of securing, through various forms of political activism, the prospect of a more luminous future. Protracted intellectual alchemy, therefore, enables members of the elite, irrespective of how they are positioned by their privilege(s), to convert the advantages of background into a commodity that has radical and lasting social value.

Reductively phrased, *learning* can be harnessed for tasks by dissenting members of the ruling elite beyond the ideological scope of that class. In this way, James's remaking of himself—through his writing, his public speaking, and his general political involvement without ever eschewing the bourgeois foundation of that self—demonstrates the potentialities of protracted intellectual alchemy. The position of Marxist oppositionality that James took up marks the endpoint in this process.

The Jamesian Margins

As a voracious reader of fiction, history, and political theory; a thinker with a particular fondness for an Arendtian "life of the mind"; a radical philosopher and a creative writer; and a Marxist committed to democratic social change, James represents the point at which the intersection of the traditional and the organic intellectual transforms itself into a different mode of being an intellectual. His career marks that difficult, conflicted conjuncture where these two modes of being an intellectual confront each other, where they overlap and diverge, and demonstrate how such an encounter complicates their position in relation to their communities—the ones they come from and the ones on whose behalf they are attempting to speak—and enunciates itself as a complicated, resonant, and philosophically productive marginality.

James's marginality articulates itself as a distinct remove from both the hegemonic (traditional) and a difficult, problematic alienation from the resistant (organic, or, later, vernacular) cultures. His marginality resists the several disenfranchisements of the peripheral locale delimited for her or him by both communities. Instead, James works to transform that interstitial location between the antagonistic communities—which is both an aporia (an opening up) and a border (a liminal point)—into a critical and creative space that is available in neither the traditional nor the organic constituency. Because the disjunctiveness so inherent to marginality is often difficult to identify ideologically, and is thus interpreted as a potential threat to both the hegemonic and the oppressed communities, the space occupied by intellectuals such as James is all-too-frequently actively suppressed in and by both communities.

However, the marginal intellectual's training and philosophical predisposition means that he is epistemologically integrated into and retains substantive links to both communities. In possession of an interstitial subjectivity, the marginal intellectual acquires a salient bidiscursivity. These figures have the facility to operate between, outside, as well as within and on the margins of two communities. The advantages of this bidiscursivity, the benefits of a critical disjunctiveness, are complicated by the historical burden of articulating the possibilities of marginality out of a language that is deeply marked by the ideological residues and sociopolitical context of the two communities to whom, in a very real sense, he (or she) continues to belong. The marginal postcolonial intellectual is ambivalently located, confronted with the difficult historical task of negotiating between the maintenance of the remove from both sociopolitical organizations and the recognition of the profound implication (and investment) in and involvement with them. Within the context of the diasporic effects of colonialism and postcolonialism, the marginal intellectual (who, like other members of the intelligentsia, often availed himself—it is far more rarely herself—of the opportunity to move to and/or between the erstwhile periphery and the metropolitan center) has to negotiate the demands of functioning in a mode where dislocation, relocation, and deracination all conjoin and complicate still further the intellectual's position within society; particularly difficult is the relationship to the communities he or she engages.

Marginalization is at the core of the diasporic experience. The dispersion of a previously settled social grouping involves the loss of place (signifying primarily home and community) and the often violent interruption, if not termination, of a people's history and the resituation at the outskirts of a foreign environ. As a specific social category (which is how Gramsci sometimes thinks of intellectuals), intellectuals are particularly well endowed with a cultural literacy—deeply familiar with the values, customs, and traditions of the colonial power—that enables them to adjust to the demands, and the potentialities, of the diaspora, so much so that they are very soon able to participate in the colonizers' sociopolitical forums. The intellectual's cultural literacy, however, is always tempered by the anxiety about an inexplicable cultural unfamiliarity with the metropolitan experience, as James reveals in *Beyond a Boundary*, as he recounts his trepidations on the eve of his first visit to England: "The British intellectual was going to Britain. About Britain I was a strange compound of knowledge and ignorance" (114). The initial moment in the diasporic experience is, for this reason, invariably a kind of marginalization: the first, and sometimes only, experience of the colonized in the center is marked by a specific form of alienation whereby he or she continues to constitute and occupy, to metaphorically and metaphysically live in, the periphery despite inhabiting the metropolis itself.[21] For many intellectuals (and other migrants) from the colonies the first experience of marginality is particularly disconcerting because here "ignorance" exceeds "knowledge," temporarily invalidating the intellectual's immersion in and familiarity with the colonizer's culture.

One of the more creative responses, and the most effective antidote to this attack of "metropolitan-induced anxiety," is the engendering of a critical consciousness of their relation to the dominant culture;

what they are struggling against is the "place" the dominant culture has assigned them as colonial subjects within the metropolis.[22] The trajectory of the British-identified intellectual James is representative of the community, but it is also marked by a continual diasporic resettlement/dislocation and an articulate opposition to colonialism and capitalism. James's marginality, however, is marked by a determined effort to overcome the debilitating effects of the phenomenon, especially the loss of community. He attempts to achieve this in two ways: by expanding the community within which he can locate himself, and by reinscribing himself into what he claims as his primary community in his native Trinidad, an endeavor that is at the very core of *Beyond a Boundary*.

The first of these methods, based on James's construction of a universal working class, is his preeminent mode of countering his marginality. The second method—what might be conceived of as his antidiasporic mode, an ongoing investment in and maintenance of links with the primary community despite the deracinating effects of continuous relocation—raises more intriguing questions about the relations between postcolonialism and the diaspora. We are confronted here with the task of articulating how the postcolonial intellectual and her or his community of origin construct, maintain, and reconstruct an understanding of community that counteracts the disruptive (and, sometimes, liberating) effects of diaspora. The process requires an investigation of antidiasporic strategies, the strength and resilience of community ties, the residues and renewal of that connection, and (most important in James's instance) the imaginary reconstruction of that relationship.

Toussaint and the *Sans Culottes*

By undertaking this process of transformation, James sought to situate himself in a different, vastly expanded political constituency: the working class. As the scope of his projects expanded, that class was conceptualized by James as the international proletariat. The international proletariat contained within its ranks the revolutionary vanguard through which James gave voice to the unique historical agency of the working class that constitutes (as *Beyond a Boundary* makes clear) one of the fundamental tenets of his writing. It is precisely the trajectory of James's political imaginary—the means by which he attempted to link himself to the class that his work was committed—that should, as Robbins says, serve as a "reminder that no portrait of intellectuals alone, flattering or unflattering, can usefully speak to this issue [of class]; what counts are relationships with other social actors and forces."[23]

The working class, James asserts, is capable of effecting a broad-based unity that grounds itself, primarily in the second sense that Robbins outlined, in a such a way that it exceeds its immediate context. This expansive grounding is a project that appears in various forms in James's work, but is most astutely and fully developed in *The Black Jacobins*, his 1938 rewriting of the San Domingo slave rebellion—a historical conjuncture at which the working class's actions are invested with an ideological significance that resonates far beyond its Caribbean setting. *The Black Jacobins* was conceived as an extended critique of the imperialist Italian invasion of Abyssinia, a project first undertaken by James two years earlier in his essay "Abyssinia and the Imperialists." The 1936 essay was written in the process of James's involvement with the International African Service Bureau (IASB), an organization founded in London in 1935 to oppose Mussolini's colonialist forays into the Horn of Africa. A founding member of the IASB, James worked alongside other anticolonialists such as Amy Garvey, his fellow Trinidadian (and childhood friend) George Padmore, and future postcolonial statesmen Kwame Nkrumah and Jomo Kenyatta.

In his account of the San Domingo revolution, James carefully reveals the means by which ideologies transcend geographical distance, from Paris to San Domingo and back, and translate themselves into distinct practices in apparently discrete contexts. James is, as ever, alert to the differences, but he engages with the process by which revolutionary impulse is taken to new heights in a location—the French colony of San Domingo, with its huge slave population—remote and ostensibly so unsuited for dramatic sociopolitical restructuring. James identifies in the ex-Haitian slave Toussaint (as he calls him) the apogee of the revolutionary doctrines that underpinned the French Revolution:

The blacks were taking their part in the destruction of European feudalism begun by the French Revolution, and liberty and equality, the slogans of the revolution, meant far more to them than to any Frenchman.
That was why, in the hour of danger, Toussaint, uninstructed as he was,
could find the language and accent of Diderot, Rousseau, and Raynal, of
Mirabeau, Robespierre and Danton.[24]

By locating the revolt of the San Domingo slaves within the historical
framework of the "destruction of feudalism begun by the French Revolution," James adroitly forges close ideological links between the metropolis and the colonial periphery. The revolutionary struggle that the
slaves in the faraway Caribbean are conducting is being waged in the
spirit with which the French peasants eradicated feudalism. Toussaint's
troops are extending that battle to a distant site, but the enemy is a common one, the French aristocracy and their functionaries:

The workers and peasants of France could not have been expected to take
any interest in the colonial question in normal times, any more than one
can expect similar interest from British or French workers today. But now
they were roused. They were striking at royalty, tyranny, reaction and
oppression of all types, and with these they included slavery.... Hence-
forth the Paris masses were for abolition, and their black brothers in San
Domingo, for the first time, had passionate allies in France.[25]

The newly "roused" revolutionary classes in France, now armed with the
insight that they were not the only victims of "royalty" and "tyranny,"
transformed their conception of the revolution into a critique of their
country's colonialism and the racism implicated in that policy. This revolutionary recognition, achieved in the midst of the struggle against the
feudal state and its repressive apparatus, motivated the "Paris masses" to
rally against the enslavement of "their black brothers in San Domingo."
Embattled in the alleys of Paris, the "workers and peasants of Paris," that
new social group Foucault calls "*la plébe*, the common people of Paris,"
claimed "their black brothers" as Caribbean comrades engaged in the

same struggle.[26] The Parisian revolutionaries extended their political horizons beyond the local battles and beyond their society's construction of race; in making this epistemological break, the Paris masses became "passionate allies" of the San Domingo slaves.

The Black Jacobins reconstructs the events of 1789 in France as an international phenomenon that redrew the revolutionary paradigm of the eighteenth century as racially diverse and that incorporated several oppressed classes—the San Domingo slaves and la plébe. As the text moves seamlessly between Port-au-Prince and Paris, James demonstrates that the French Revolution was not simply an insurrectionary experience restricted to Europe. The Black Jacobins introduced its twentieth-century public of radical metropolitans, anticolonial activists, and nascent postcolonial theorists to discrete moments and different sites, one historically familiar, even overdetermined, the other new, previously nominal, and apparently out of historical congruence. James, however, makes clear to his various publics that they are in the throes of the same revolution. Geographical distance, The Black Jacobins insists, is no real obstacle in a situation such as this signal historical conjuncture where the slave community and the French masses share an ideology. The San Domingo slaves are remarkable, however, in that they exceed even the French peasants and the fledgling Parisian proletariat in terms of their bravery and their commitment to the basic tenets of the Revolution. "Liberty and equality, the slogans of the revolution," James points out, "meant far more to them than to any Frenchman" because they stood to gain considerably more from a victory over slavery and colonialism.

The San Domingan slaves believed more fervently in "liberty and equality" than their French counterparts, but their leader demonstrated in his political correspondence with Paris how immersed in the historical unfolding of the metropolis the periphery really was. Toussaint, "uninstructed as he was," captured in his missives to the capitol the very "language and accent" of the philosophers who gave voice to the democratic thrusts of the disenfranchised French masses. This barely literate son of slaves, who dictated most of his letters to secretaries scores of times until he was satisfied with them, was able to emulate the philosophical impulses of Rousseau and Danton and give them (an incipiently) Third World articulation. In recognizing how located he was in their ideological orbit, the French philosophers became for Toussaint comrades who provided him with the theoretical underpinning to articulate the experiences and the liberatory visions of his people; Diderot and Robespierre and Toussaint belonged to the same intellectual fraternity, and while the Frenchmen provided the philosophical guidelines, it was the ex-slave who took the Revolution's democratic impulses to its most radical end. Toussaint saw himself and the Haitian slaves as fellow members of a movement, fully enfranchised and empowered by the Declaration of the Rights of Man and equally dedicated to the liberation of those subjected to centuries of aristocratic rule: "The San Domingo representatives realized at last what they had done; they had tied the fortunes of San Domingo to the assembly of a people in revolution and thenceforth the history of liberty in France and of slave emancipation in San Domingo is one and indivisible."[27]

The "indivisib[ility]" that is established between the political contestations in France and the drive toward emancipation in San Domingo emblematized, for James, the successful construction of a radical international working class. The French peasants and proletariat and the San Domingo slaves formed a unique late-eighteenth-century political community. The alliance spanned continents, rendered racial differences temporarily insignificant, and forged ideological unity so that metropolitan "revolution" and peripheral "emancipation"/"revolution" were incorporated within the same political project. As a phenomenon of its time, the French Revolution was obviously a historical aberration; there were no other contemporaneous instances of such efforts to construct an international, nonracial proletariat. However, James used the collaboration between an embryonic metropolitan proletariat and a non-European revolutionary class to signify beyond its historical confines, in some regards with a critical prescience and in others with a retrospective vision more incisive than his ability to understand—as the later discussion of the postcolonial nation-state will demonstrate—the philosophical value of the problematic that he raises in *The Black Jacobins*. In its more retrospective mode, James is projecting into and onto a sub-Saharan Africa displaying the first signs of its readiness to embark upon a revolutionary campaign against its European occupiers along the ideological lines that the San Domingan slaves had mapped out.

The Black Jacobins marks a phase when James was both a Trotskyist and a Pan-Africanist, negotiating the varying demands of each of these political tendencies within the context of his involvement with the ILP in Britain. At his friend Learie Constantine's urging, James joined the ILP, where he made his first serious acquaintance with the works of Marx, Lenin, and, most importantly for the conception of *The Black Jacobins*, Trotsky. As a philosophical blueprint, no text was more crucial than Trotsky's *A History of the Russian Revolution*. Oswald Spengler's *Decline of the West*, along with Trotsky's *History*, provided James's recovery, and reconstruction, of the San Domingan revolt with a historiographical model. Writing in the posthumously published *American Civilization*, James acknowledges his debt to Trotsky: "*A History of the Russian Revolution,*" he recalls, "gave me a sense of historical movement: the relation of historical periods to one another."[28] *The Black Jacobins*, a work preoccupied with the "relation of historical periods to one another," represents an intellectual juncture where James—in a difficult, dialectical conversation with Trotsky—reoriented and expanded his conceptualization of a radical political community. Written in the declining years of the Marxist Third International (which had started with the Russian Revolution), James's work on the San Domingo revolution reveals how steeped he was in the ideology of the Trotskyist movement and how close he was to breaking from it. Unlike the Second International, which favored a policy of gradual social change through parliamentary democracy, the Third International advocated the Leninist-Trotskyist line of the global revolution headed by the proletariat.

The radical ideological parameters of the Third International were politically synchronized with the conditions in which the alliance between *la plébe* and the San Domingan slaves had been constructed. Implicitly included within the imaginary of the Third International, though never explored as creatively by any Marxist historian of the period other than James, was the potential for alignment of political forces in the metropolis and on the periphery. Such an international solidarity of working-class forces was eminently possible in the technologically advanced mid-twentieth century; if the colonized Africans' struggle for liberation and independence matched or exceeded the achievements of the San Domingan slaves, then the relationship with the metropolitan classes would be even more dramatically altered than in Toussaint's conception of revolution. In a moment when the metropolitan masses and the colonized peoples were subjugated by the same class, bourgeois capitalists (that constituency which had replaced the European aristocracy as the hegemonic grouping), the two communities were fighting significantly different battles. In the late 1930s the European masses were fighting against fascism, a struggle that would ultimately draw the colonies into World War II; the participation of colonials in the war played no small role in reconstituting the metropolis-periphery relationship as the battles dispelled the myth of racial supremacy, a founding tenet of the colonial enterprise. The subjugated peoples, meanwhile, on the now vastly expanded periphery, were starting to resist, as the pre–World War II Abyssinians (contemporary Ethiopia) demonstrated, the shackles of European domination.

Through his analysis of events in San Domingo, James was able to identify—from a signal historical vantage point he had created—the underlying political forces and energies that spurred oppressed indigenous populations to achieve national independence. Toussaint and his people symbolized, in and through *The Black Jacobins*, the determination of oppressed peoples to throw off the yoke of colonialism, a historical event that James transformed into a metaphor for the resistance movement then unfolding vigorously in Abyssinia and more variegatedly on the rest of the African continent. The struggle for sub-Saharan African liberation would find, in the aftermath of World War II, full and often violent expression in anticolonial struggles from Kenya to Zimbabwe—a movement that lasted some five decades. It is through his work on Abyssinia and San Domingo that James came to recognize the limitations of the Third International, an insight that precipitated his break with this line of Marxist thinking; all the while, however, he remained unable to glean the precipitous lessons imparted to him by the fractious violence that emerged from the historical saga surrounding Toussaint and Dessalines' leadership.

James was fully committed to the world revolution, but in *The Black Jacobins* he registers his impending rupture with the Third International because he did not see it as capable of accounting fully for the anti-imperialist struggles the African peoples were about to engage. The ideological undergirdings of these battles for liberation and national sovereignty would be, for reasons Anna Grimshaw points out, unrecognizable to European Marxists. "First of all," Grimshaw argues, James "cast doubt on the assumption that the revolution would take place first in Europe, in the advanced capitalist countries, and that this would act as a model and a catalyst for later upheaval in the underdeveloped world. Secondly, there were clear indications that the lack of specially trained leaders, a vanguard, did not hold back the movement of the San Domingo revolution."[29]

By displacing Europe as the revolutionary hub, undermining the role of the vanguard, and thereby invalidating the leadership responsibilities of the "Party," *The Black Jacobins* establishes the slaves as fully developed political agents. The Third International's main limitation, for James, was its inability to accommodate the unique agency of the San Domingan slaves, a class that fought a successful revolutionary struggle without adhering to the fundamental principles of Trotsky's Marxism. Toussaint and the slaves demonstrated that revolutions on the periphery could be conducted in forms, and by exercising strategies, which in significant ways contradicted and ideologically superseded—the theories of European political thinkers and their constituencies. Among the major accomplishments of *The Black Jacobins* is that it established the periphery as a distinct political force capable of interacting dialectically with the metropolis, but equally capable of a singular agency.

James recovers the San Domingo revolt as a radical, sui generis anticolonial event. Read within the paradigm of this text, the great failure of the French Revolution was that it was bourgeois. The French

Revolution simply facilitated the transfer of hegemony from the aristocracy to the merchant class, diluting the authority of the monarchy and accommodating itself to new historical forces. Because of Toussaint's struggle, however, this transfer of power from the colonial regime and the white plantocracy was an experience only repeated, with disastrous historical consequences for the political heirs of the *sans culottes*, after an extended period in the newly sovereign Haiti. The crucial difference between San Domingo and France is that in the ex–French colony the interregnum—the moment between the transfer of power from the old ruling class, the French colonial functionaries, to the new one, the liberated slaves—was sufficiently (if, regrettably, too transiently) extended by the slaves themselves so that they were able to complete a more revolutionary transformation. Toussaint and the slaves accomplished a radical reorganization of the social order that was premised on the very terms of the bourgeois revolution—liberty, equality, and fraternity— which they thought they were merely emulating. From where the slaves stood in relation to the history they were making, liberty and equality resonated with the prospect of a very different social reality to the only one they had known. Although the slaves were soon subject to the same political expediency in Port-au-Prince as their comrades in Paris, the promise of liberty and equality sustained a revolution on the periphery where it had merely facilitated the transfer of power from one class to another in Europe.

As a Marxist and a Pan-Africanist, James grappled in *The Black Jacobins* with the discrete demands of the two ideologies (the class-based analysis of the former versus the race-based one of the latter) and the extent to which imperial oppression entangled the two categories. In his research on Toussaint and the slaves, James constantly had to weigh the significance of race against that of class in the designs of empire, setting up a dialectic between the two ideologies that he returned to again and again. Although *The Black Jacobins* identifies James as Marxist first, Pan-Africanist second, the text is marked by a skillful negotiation between the two historical forces. Although James's pronouncements are securely grounded in Marxism, they are also adroitly qualified, as he writes in

Beyond a Boundary: "The race question is subsidiary to the class question in politics, and to think of imperialism in terms of race is disastrous. But to neglect the racial factor as merely incidental is an error only less grave than to make it fundamental" (283).

The ideological hierarchy is in place for James, and the "race question is subsidiary to the class question," but the impact of the former is such that it can never be left out of any political consideration. The class question may be the fundamental one, but its importance is always predicated on its relationship to race. The *black* in the title of the San Domingan text is therefore particularly significant. *Black* establishes the San Domingan upheaval as parallel to, and implicated in, the white Jacobin revolution. James therefore transforms what was previously considered a historical oxymoron and sets it up as a revolutionary precedent. The black Jacobins, furthermore, represent a creative, not uneasy, union of James's dual ideological commitment. James's deep investment in the revolutionary potentialities of both Marxism and Pan-Africanism finds an ideological reconciliation in the title, and within the workings of the text itself. James's class-race hierarchy is thus shown to be a fluid intellectual arrangement that is maintained with considerable ideological effort.

The ideological tension (if we might call it that) between the title and the content demonstrates James's effort to locate himself with relation to the demands of Marxism and an emergent Pan-Africanism. It was an ideological tussle that James could never resolve, but his Marxism, if anything, became more sensitive to the notion of context, and the particularities of each site of struggle, and his Pan-Africanism was always qualified by the recognition that those communities designated *black* were never homogeneous—as in San Domingo, where that grouping was composed of slaves, freed blacks, and mulattoes—but fractured along the lines of class and caste.

The class-race debate, an insoluble conundrum to be sure, was one to which James never developed a coherent approach. Instead, he negotiated between the two ideologies, and often inverted the hierarchy between them, emphasizing an attention (and attentiveness) to context.

The importance of context is nowhere more evident than in James's examination of the role of African Americans within the body politic of their society.[30] James argued that African Americans formed an unusual political community, or class, if you will, that was grounded solely in their race. Although African Americans constituted a marginal grouping within their society, James recognized that they had the potential to exercise a political influence on American life vastly disproportionate to their status as a numerical minority. The African-American capacity for effective action was a result of their racial cohesiveness; their experience of violence at the hands of white America had molded this community into a distinct political force.

African Americans represented the unique conjuncture of race and class: a race-based social grouping that had transformed itself into a class because their history made it clear that the only way to construct an effective political community was on the platform of physiognomy and the common experience of slavery and oppression. Despite his often-uneasy grappling with and his inability to resolve adequately the race-class question, James was able to produce out of individual contexts creative theoretical conceptualizations and political uses of both social categories. James's work attends to the possibility that race or class, both, or various combinations of the two could be used to mobilize human beings to take actions capable of reconfiguring their society, such as the San Domingo slaves had done, as African Americans had in various moments done and continue to do, and Africans across the continent were poised to do just months before the World War II broke out.

As James learned through his work with the IASB, the emergent tendencies for independence in Abyssinia belonged to the same drive for independence that had characterized the San Domingo slaves' revolution. *The Black Jacobins* performed the vital political task of mapping a trajectory of independence that Padmore, Nkrumah, and Kenyatta could use as a handbook for their nationalist campaigns. James, however, was providing more than a battle plan or a theoretical outline for the leadership of the IASB and their growing constituency, though he was doing that particularly well. By recovering the San Domingo insurrection as an epic moment of anticolonial struggle, James imagined the possibility of a successful revolution in Africa and the Caribbean in the face of massive repression by the European colonial powers.

Researching the history of the San Domingo revolution as it had not been done before, James reconstructed the achievement of the national Haitian state as a triumph of the colonized peoples over their European rulers. In recreating Toussaint's victory, James established the independent Haiti as a precedent for Ghana and Kenya and Trinidad. At a juncture when colonialist discourse premised itself on the inability of the colonized to rule themselves, James created through Toussaint a critique of that discourse: Haiti represented an enabling moment in the history of resistance to colonialism, because it culminated in the establishment of the postcolonial state. Toussaint and the slaves became symbols for African and Caribbean liberation and nationalism.[31]

The Black Jacobins stands, in this regard, as a text with genuinely Afro-Caribbean roots. Not only does it grow out of James's critique of Mussolini, but also is the maturation of an earlier undertaking, James's essay "The Case for West Indian Self-Government." First published in London in 1933, the essay traces the history of resistance and the commitment to Trinidadian independence through the biography of the leader (a method later repeated in the San Domingo work), in this case that of the creole captain Arthur Cipriani. *The Black Jacobins* is more expansive in its ideological scope and sharper in its critical tone, but "The Case for West Indian Self-Government" is as effective a statement against colonialism and its racist underpinnings. In the essay, James argues convincingly for the rights of Trinidadians, and therefore implicitly the entire Caribbean peoples, to govern themselves. James recognizes that the conditions of colonialism had been irrevocably changed by developments in military technology, making resistance of the San Domingo variety more difficult to succeed: "Britain will hold us down as long as she wishes. Her cruisers and aeroplanes ensure it."[32]

The Trinidadian people, however, proved they were equally committed to the process of national independence as their Caribbean neighbors had been almost two centuries earlier. The San Domingo uprising's efficacy as a twentieth-century revolutionary model may have rendered it inimitable to the Trinidadians, but Toussaint's struggle served ideological functions beyond the military so that it could, in different ways, be historically inspirational both in Port-of-Spain and Nairobi: Toussaint and the San Domingo slaves provided a sense of historical possibility and an example of successful resistance for Padmore and his colleagues at the IASB that was not theoretically available prior to the publication of *The Black Jacobins*.[33]

Remarkable for a text in which reconstructed history doubles as revolutionary primer, however, *The Black Jacobins* is characterized by a problematic lack: a critical self-blindness, an inability to think beyond late-eighteenth-century San Domingo, to recognize the postcolonial failures that marked post-Toussaintian life for the newly enfranchised *sans culottes*, and, moreover, the inability to convert the retrospective prescience into a prospective one—to project from the anticolonial mode into its postcolonial (Dessalinian) futurity. Having read the Toussaintian moment of anticolonialism so deftly, should James not have been more alert to the possibility of (post-)modern, postcolonial failure, violence, and socioeconomic upheaval? In its conclusion, *The Black Jacobins* marked the inauguration of the postcolonial state as a repressive apparatus, a condition (of postcoloniality) foreshadowed by Toussaint's "extradition" to France.

The Black Jacobins also shows, more disturbingly, how the deposed Toussaint's faith in modernity is implicated in—if not directly responsible for—the autocratic Dessalines' ascension to power. From the anti-post/colonial locale James had crafted in the text, Dessalines' assuming power signals more than the replacement of Toussaint: in that succession the atrocities that the various Duvalier regimes would later commit against the Haitian people were spawned. Dessalines' campaign against the white plantocracy marks nothing so much as the inauguration of a system of leadership that would be practiced, with brutality and impunity, against internal black opposition. Dessalines introduced a style of postcolonial rule that, in the last half century, has become all too familiar in the Caribbean, Africa, Latin America, and Asia.

Through Toussaint and Dessalines, James became acquainted with the shortcomings of postcoloniality, with revolutions that not only went wrong, but had devastating, long-lasting consequences for the black populace of Haiti. Because of how the Dessalines model has proliferated in the postcolonial world, *The Black Jacobins* is, its prescience notwithstanding, symptomatic of a much deeper failure. James's study of the San Domingan revolt ascribed an unprecedented agency to the anticolonial subject, but it did not think beyond the founding of the postcolonial state. James read Toussaint's inability to produce a democratic Haitian society as the consequence of personal shortcomings (especially his "misguided faith" in the project of modernity), not as representative of larger structural failure.

Because James's work was conceived in an anticolonial milieu, because he did not comprehend the historical significance of Dessalines as metaphor, as portentous historical signifier, he could not produce the full rendering of postcoloniality that his reading of this event positioned him to offer. James's version of Haitian history represents a singular blindness, since both his research on the San Domingan revolt and the lessons offered by Trotsky's *A History of the Russian Revolution* were implicit warnings of the postcolonial/postrevolutionary failure that was Dessalines. James's prescience, his reservations, his anticipations, so sententious in *The Black Jacobins*, did not find its possible postcolonial resonance because he did not comprehend the textuality of history. James remained, in this text, a radical thinker curiously blind to his own hermeneutical insights. He did not fully understand how he had interpreted history, nor was he able to think history more than one step beyond its moment: Toussaint was instructive as the anticolonial primer, but Dessalines could not be transformed by James into a metonym for the (past and future) failure of postcolonial leadership.[34]

Turning Away from *Modern Politics*

As much as *The Black Jacobins* marks the construction of the international proletariat, so *Beyond a Boundary* represents the reclamation and the reimagining of his local Trinidadian community for James thirty years after he had first left it as a young man for England. It is entirely appropriate that James should, having demonstrated his problematic relationship to the Trinidadian working class with his choice of Maple, attempt to theorize his position through the medium of cricket with the intention of relocating himself within that community. However, the publication of *Beyond a Boundary* in 1963, the year following Trinidadian independence, is noteworthy because it indicates more than James's effort to inscribe himself within the Shannon community. *Beyond a Boundary* and *Modern Politics: A Series of Lectures on the Subject Given at the Trinidad Public Library, in its Adult Education Programme* (1960) were conceived out of the same disturbing recognition that the attainment of Trinidadian sovereignty held not promise, but tremendous dangers for the society's working class. The concerns that James had not addressed in *The Black Jacobins* began to make themselves manifest.

In *Beyond a Boundary* James dynamically refashions his intellectual profile by turning, after three decades of real political activism on as many continents, to the vernacular, to the cultural practice of cricket as a means of critiquing the newly installed leadership of Dr. Eric Williams of the People's National Movement (PNM). *Modern Politics*, a collection of talks, represents James's first strategy of attack on the PNM after he was dismissed as editor of its media organ, *The Nation*, following a disagreement with Williams over what became known as the "Chaguaramas incident."

Martin Glaberman, an American Marxist colleague of James in the Johnson-Forest tendency, provides an explanation of the Chaguaramas events in his introduction to the 1973 edition of *Modern Politics:*

> Williams began a massive retreat from the objectives of the PNM, especially in relation to concessions to American imperialism. The retreat was embodied in the dispute over the Chaguaramas Naval Base, a piece of

Trinidadian territory which the British, with their usual generosity, had given to the United States on a long-term lease. A major demand of the independence movement had been the return of Chaguaramas to the people of Trinidad. When Eric Williams abandoned that demand it was a sign that his struggle against colonialism would not go beyond the acceptance of neo-colonialism and the trading of British for American imperialism. That was a direction James refused to go and the break between the two old friends very quickly became complete.[35]

The *Modern Politics* lectures were presented by James at the Trinidad Public Library less than a month after the split with Williams (a former student of his at Queens Royal College), attracting a mostly educated, enthusiastically middle-class audience "crowded into two halls and attended in almost equal numbers outside."[36] At this crucial juncture in Trinidad's history, however, James was not reaching the political constituency that had the longest and most radical history of resistance to British imperialism, the Trinidadian workers. In the same vein as *Modern Politics*, James's 1962 text *Party Politics in the West Indies* failed because it confined itself to a small constituency. While *Modern Politics* was addressed to the Trinidad Public Library crowds, *Party Politics* was a critique of the PNM leadership directed at the general membership of the party but circulated mostly among the ranks of the disaffected that attended the party convention.

Despite the difference in audience, *Modern Politics* and *Party Politics* can be considered part of the same unsuccessful critical strategy—attacking Williams and the PNM through formal political channels. (It would be remiss not to note how the two titles, even, duplicate key words so that they end up mimicking each other.) It should be added, though, that however much the 1962 *Party Politics* is thematically a simple extension and amplification of its predecessor, it is marked off from *Modern Politics* by a distinct change in tenor and an increased analysis of the specificities of Trinidadian politics. *Party Politics* is, within its limitations, an incisive, multilayered document: an extended letter of resignation from the editor of *The Nation* in which James explains his decision; a handbook for the organization and day-to-day management of a political party and all its organs; and finally, a scathing and unbridled attack on Williams and the PNM's leadership's alienation from not only the Trinidadian workers, but the party's rank-and-file membership itself.[37]

As James concluded in *Modern Politics*, only a radical working class could effectively counteract Williams's "acceptance of neo-colonialism and the trading of British for American imperialism." Once the "break between the two old friends [was] complete," James was politically alienated in Williams's newly independent Trinidad since he could depend on neither the middle-class public library audience nor the disaffected PNM membership for support for a program of radical action. Furthermore, James recognized that formal action of the protest variety that had achieved independence would be inappropriate for a context in which the first black Trinidadians had just assumed the reins of authority, in the process acquiring the kind of ideological legitimacy available only to the first colonized class that replaces its colonial rulers—the comprador class or the Fanonian national bourgeoisie. James, working out of the unprecedented Caribbean situation in which Trinidad had just secured national sovereignty, was compelled to reconsider the intellectual means by which he could conduct his struggle against the PNM government. As an intellectual whose primary skills were reading and providing public commentary on politico-ideological situations, James knew he would have to produce a piece of writing that articulated and accentuated the radical history of the Trinidadian workers. At this juncture, this moment of ideological crisis borne out of political isolation, James turned toward the vernacular. The constituency James had tentatively aligned himself with in *Minty Alley* was the group he now recognized as the most critical to the future—and the writing of the past, *The Black Jacobins* project—of Trinidad. In the moment of crisis, vernacularity offered James a way of out of his usual—and most unsuited—political modalities.

When this constituency was confronted by a new form of exploitation, James recognized the importance of the workers not being rendered voiceless. *Beyond a Boundary* was not addressed, as such, to the Trinidadian masses, nor did James claim to speak in their name. The text, however, did produce a profile of a group that was culturally and politically radical with a long history of resistance to colonialism, a point that would not have been lost on the newly installed government. With virtually all the formal political spaces in Trinidadian society closed down by the first flush of independence (which produces a unique kind of loyalty to the postcolonial state), James adapted his favored form of political critique—the didactic Marxist essay, such as *Modern Politics* and *Party Politics* were—to the demands of cricket in order to secure a space in which he could construct a vernacular critique of Williams's neocolonialism. Through this process, James sought to achieve for himself a rare organicism with the Trinidadian working class—the integration into barrackyard life desired but not attained in *Minty Alley*, the kind of location within subalternaeity that the boy at the window, as Lamming recognized, so deeply wanted.

Real versus Cultural Politics

In *Beyond a Boundary*'s most memorable lines, James distinguishes cricket, as a form of cultural politics, from what he understands as real politics and, simultaneously, identifies the roots of his politics in the game. With a richly entangled lyricism, he writes, "Cricket had plunged me into politics long before I was aware of it. When I did turn to politics I did not have too much to learn" (61).

Through the phrase "cricket had plunged me into politics," James both misrepresents and foregrounds cricket's role in his ideological development. In this formulation, James portrays the game's influence as largely the consequence of unconscious, if fortuitous, action. Cricket's politics is visceral, keenly felt but resistant to traditional political articulation and difficult to translate into a movement for social transformation. Cultural politics is unreflective about and unaware of its own agency, a politics where the subject is plunged into positions—of resistance, support—without any real forethought or choice. In James's formulation, it is an act of passion rather than the considered intervention of a traditional political agent. Because it is a form of recreation, its preoccupation with pleasure rather than recognizable political concerns obscures and undermines its capacity to articulate resistance.

As social practice, cricket has a "structure of feeling" because it produces both political effect, as the Shannon-Maple rivalry shows, and psychological affect. Spectators and supporters experience pleasure, disappointment, euphoria, and even despair, depending on the outcome of the game. But it does not, in this Jamesian conception, have an ideological structure, a political significance external to the result of the game or the way in which cricket is played; nor are its capacity or strategies for resistance, its political expressivity, immediately available. Cultural politics lack the requisite vocabularies, the organizational mechanisms, the traditions and practices of institutions such as a political party. Cultural politics constitute a politics that is not conscious of itself as a political practice. It plunges the subject into politics; it is not a contemplative or rational mode of political action. Cultural politics can only be grasped and mobilized as a practice of resistance post–ipso facto: after it has been translated and rendered recognizably political through the discourse of conventional politics. Real politics extracts the political elements from cultural practices, revealing the cultural practice's politics to itself as a politics. Real politics is to cultural politics as the Freudian Ego is to the Id. The real (Ego) is self-knowing, completely conscious, and fully agential; cultural politics (Id) is not.

And yet, *Beyond a Boundary* represents both the mapping and the invalidation of the distinction between real and cultural politics. The text marks the process by which James comes to recognize that culture is constructed by political agents in social practices pivotal to Caribbean life. As *Beyond a Boundary* reveals, not only did cricket immerse James in Trinidadian politics since he was a young boy watching his neighbor Matthew Bondman bat, but its vernacularity had equipped him with a real political vocabulary and consciousness. James was introduced to the politics of class, one of his two foremost categories of social analysis, through Bondman's standing as cricketer. A superb strokeplayer, the ne'er-do-well neighbor Bondman was, James's puritan grandmother declared,

"'Good for nothing except to play cricket'" (15). The Bondmans rented from the educated, lower-middle-class James family, locating them in adjoining households but different classes. For James's puritan, Victorian grandmother, matriarch to a family that included several teachers, cricket signified shiftlessness and unemployment. The sport was symptomatic of working-class pleasure at the expense of more worthy moral (and economic) pursuits. To be good for cricket meant, for her, to be good for little else. Bondman could be good at cricket because, in an overdetermined paradigm of representation (shaped by Victorian morality), it showed that he was useless at everything of consequence. Cricketing excellence was a sure sign of nothing so much as a broader social and moral failure.

Unlike his grandmother, James understood that for the Trinidadian working class cricket represented more than simply a leisurely form of weekend recreation. The politics of culture, what it meant to be a talented cricketer, afforded working- and lower-middle-class individuals such as Bondman and Constantine a status routinely denied them in all other walks of life; two of *Beyond a Boundary*'s main cultural icons, Bondman and Constantine, were superb cricketers both, although the former failed to fulfill his potential or match the latter's accomplishments on the international cricketing stage. In *Beyond a Boundary* the allusively named Bondman functions as analogue for the chasm between St. Hill's (another iconic figure in the book) and Constantine's cricketing skills and their status as disenfranchised colonials.[38] Bondman was, as much for James's grandmother as for all of Maple society, a truculent sign not only of the Caribbean's enslaved past but also its colonized present. The neighboring cricketer was a crude reminder of black bondage in the Caribbean, a society in which gradations in skin tone counted for a great deal. Bondman was black; James and Constantine belonged to the browner, more privileged classes. Bondman's behavior made him unacceptable in Puritanical society, but the political resonance of his name impressed upon the colonized blacks the fact that their servitude had not yet been rendered anachronistic, that it continued to have consequences in the present as it had in the past. More important than his transgression of class lines and his disregard for codes of black civility, Bondman was an inverted symbol of democracy: all of the black Caribbean remained colonized; they were all equally unequal before colonial law. Bondman stands as the repressed within James's grandmother's Puritan psyche, the unspeakable incarnation of her own political disenfranchisement. It was only on the cricket field, within a transient game (but a permanent cultural practice), that site where Bondman was a master exponent, that anything approaching a genuine social equality existed. Bondman was a daily emblem of black inferiority within the colonial paradigm, a(n immoral,) walking symbol of the fact that the Bondmans and the Jameses were—despite their class differences—bound (bonded) together; this, regardless of the lower-middle-class James's reservations, antipathies, and tenuous sense of social (and moral) superiority. These two families, landlord and tenant, were all unequal together, all products—in their different ways—of British imperialism.

Unlike James's grandmother, Bondman exalted in his limited opportunity—and that restricted space, the cricket oval—to express himself an equal. On the cricket oval the black tenant would not be bound by social conventions, of either the black or white variety, or the colonial racial hierarchy. Bondman demonstrated to James, as much as any international Caribbean cricketer he later met or watched (Bondman never represented the West Indies or even Trinidad, for that matter), that to be a good cricketer had affirming social consequences. The game's political impact registered sociologically because it transformed colonized subjects from economic subalterns into cultural superiors, and sometimes even icons. Talented batsmen and bowlers gave voice, through their cultural actions on the cricket oval, to a black (male) agency that colonialism denied the colonized. Frequently, the cultural was not simply the political; it was the only articulation of black agency. James did not have to wait for his involvement in conventional political movements to learn the nuances, strategies, and intricacies of politics. Cricket provided him with an elaborate, politically encoded paradigm that was embedded in a series of highly stylized social practices.

Resistance was articulately encoded within the vernacular, that most enduring form of black opposition in Caribbean society, and the only political modality in which resistance was simultaneously firmly embedded and sufficiently malleable to be able to speak in the anticolonial and anti-postcolonial registers. Batting, as it were, in the socially invisible but culturally all-too-visible vernacular, Bondman speaks not so much *in* as *from* the lowest Ellisonian registers: Bondman demonstrates how the vernacular makes itself heard across a range of (discordant, dissonant) historical epochs, how the politics of the popular refuses to be silenced. The vernacular, in *Beyond a Boundary*, not only is the dominant political mode, but constitutes the only politics that cannot—and will not—be co-opted, by whatever hegemony is in place. The vernacular contains within itself a kind of integrity, morality, and virtue that James's puritanical grandmother prized so highly but could not—or would not, devout Victorian that she was—identify in cricket.

As he acknowledges in *Beyond a Boundary*, James learned a considerable amount from the impacted, complicated, textured nature of politics from his engagement with the sport. "Cricket is," James writes, "a game of high and difficult technique. If it were not it could not carry the load of social response and implications which it carries" (43). While James had always understood that cricket was a "game of high and difficult technique," he did not grasp until he wrote *Beyond a Boundary* the array of "social responses" contained within it. Through this text he recognized cricket as a signal form of vernacular intervention, even—or especially—if cultural politics' exponents are ne'er-do-well neighbors. In *Beyond a Boundary* the cultural is not only insistently political, particularly within the context of colonization (and postcolonialism), but frequently the most complex, unrecognized (by the colonizer and the colonized elite), ideologically embattled mode of politics in a society in which repression is rife in all other forms of human activity.

Text of Last Resort

James's turning away from the realm of formal politics to continue his struggle in the arena of cultural politics in *Beyond a Boundary* signals a minor disruption of his political trajectory but the major accomplishment of his cultural activism. As a document of cultural politics that takes cricket as its point of departure for sociopolitical investigation, *Beyond a Boundary* constitutes an aberrant, though not unique, development in James's intellectual life. It is aberrant because it represents the only full-length treatment of cricket as a subject of study (other projects, such as a book of photographs and commentary on cricketers in action, never came to fruition, while *Cricket* is simply a collection of essays on the game), and it is not unique because its antecedents can be traced to years of cricket journalism and its subsequent use as a form of cultural politics by James as he explained the remarkable achievements of great West Indian exponents of the game, most notably in his essays on Gary Sobers (Barbados) and Rohan Kanhai (Guyana).[39]

Beyond a Boundary stands as a deviation from but not a dramatic break in the line of the events that followed James's 1932 departure from Trinidad to England to pursue a career as a writer. Shortly after arriving in England he gave up his ambitions to be a writer of creative fiction and instead dedicated his energies to studying Hegel, Marx, Lenin, and Trotsky, fashioning himself as a Marxist thinker. *Modern Politics* is a part of this Marxist continuum and belongs to the dominant mode of James's work. While it failed to create the conditions for mobilizing against the PNM, the text does not mark the end of an intellectual phase. Neither does *Beyond a Boundary* inaugurate a new mode of Jamesian discourse. James's outstanding achievement in *Beyond a Boundary* is rather that it interrupted the dominant Jamesian discourse, though continuing to subtly and incisively utilize that discourse's class-based, materialist analysis, while simultaneously drawing on what we might call the secondary James discourse, the politics of cricket on which he had written as journalist for (among others) the *Manchester Guardian* and the *Glasgow Herald*.

Before *Beyond a Boundary*, James's various intellectual pursuits had existed in different texts as discrete pronouncements on Marxism or cricket or literature; before this work the discourses of Marxism and cricket existed side by side, in relative comfort but in isolation from each other. The signal accomplishment of *Beyond a Boundary* is that here the two modes, seasoned by James's interest in literature (we can recall here his pronouncement that "Thackeray bears the heaviest responsibility for me, not Marx"), are integrated to produce to a rare sociopolitical critique that takes a sport as its starting point, its metaphorical axis, and as a site of radical cultural opposition.

Beyond a Boundary is undoubtedly James's definitive work, remarkable for its ability to bring together, for the first, and only, time a voracious literary appetite, cricketing passions, and ideological commitments in a single text. *Beyond a Boundary* weaves these divergent discourses into a single narrative that rendered the characteristics of all three modes recognizable, though somewhat distorted, in creating out of them a hybrid that went beyond all generic boundaries. Out of *Beyond a Boundary* James produced an unprecedented form, one that constituted—like he proclaimed that the "Greek drama was *new*. The Elizabethan tragedy was *new*"—(227, emphasis in original) a "new" genre. In attempting to locate himself within the Trinidadian working class, James had already exhausted the two modes, the Marxist essay and fiction, with which he was familiar. Ultimately, the 1963 work was more than part autobiography, part cultural history, part political history, and part cricket commentary. *Beyond a Boundary* transgressed and transcended formal generic conceptualizations in the process of creating a new genre.

James had to produce a new form because he recognized the limitations of the ones available to him. A history of Caribbean cricket would not have sufficed because the game itself could not be comprehended, as James insisted, without attention to the fact that the "cricket field was a stage on which selected individuals played representative roles which were charged with social significance" (72). The "cricket field," the game's "social significance," and its effects on the various players had to be accounted for within the Jamesian sociopolitical model because they were all intimately and intricately connected. But no political tract could have captured the passions, the tensions, the multiple ideological investments concentrated in the game; no Marxist essay could convey the enthusiasm, the aesthetics of the sporting spectacle, the rare intimacy the game afforded both participants and spectators, and the pleasure involved in playing in the Caribbean for at least eight months of the year, every year.

The genre that could most easily be made to accommodate *Beyond a Boundary* as a project was a significantly reconfigured autobiography. The major adjustment to the autobiographical mode was that it would have to tell more than James's story. At their most engaging, autobiographies draw on, represent, and re-create the lives of their community. In working partially within the autobiographical mode, with the intention to exceed it, James could easily make reference to Bondman, Constantine, and St. Hill, to mention but three members of the Trinidadian community. *Beyond a Boundary*, however, located these individual cricketers, and several others, their interactions, and even their personal histories at the center of "James's" text. The work, integrating as it did the discourses of history, culture, and politics, can only be construed as an autobiography as it is the one moment where James recounts so fully the details of his personal life, most notably the pivotal place cricket occupied in that life. These two features precisely, the deeply personal investment and the broad integration that *Beyond a Boundary* achieves, explain why James, despite several drafts and much encouragement from associates, never completed his autobiography. He did not need to. *Beyond a Boundary*, his "last major work," stood in its stead, rendering a more formal autobiography redundant.[40]

The context in which the text was conceived throws *Beyond a Boundary* into relief as an artifact of literary and cultural originality: it was a text of last resort. It was produced out of a moment of extreme political crisis in which James faced isolation from Trinidadians, his community, whose causes he had championed relentlessly from the 1930s on. Paradoxically, at the very moment that independence was achieved, when James should automatically have located himself in Trinidad, he was displaced to the political margins by Williams and the PNM. *Beyond a Boundary* is considerably more than a new writing of the colonized's experience at the moment that postcoloniality was achieved.

It represents James's last effort to return, in both the most immediate and nostalgic sense of the term, to his intellectual, political, and cultural roots in Trinidad. This text of last resort is informed but not characterized by political desperation.

James shaped *Beyond a Boundary* so that it can be read as an antidiasporic text that speaks determinedly of the diasporic intellectual's efforts to overcome constant dislocation, remove, and alienation from her or his originary community. *Beyond a Boundary* is deeply concerned with the (re)creation, maintenance, and consolidation of substantive links between the diasporic, cosmopolitan intellectual and the originary community. Political involvement and ideological underwriting are important markers of those ties. Finally, however, James sees engagement with the cultural life of that community as the means that not only secures the links, but the intellectual's place in that community and the new postcolonial nation itself. The antidiasporism of *Beyond a Boundary* is a phenomenon that proposes that cultural participation by the intellectual in the activities of the postcolonial community can coexist with the cosmopolitanness of the intellectual—mobility between various sites, most notably the (metropolitan) center-periphery axis.

Antidiasporism facilitates negotiations between cosmopolitanness, at the most banal level an enlarged sense of the world that was an inevitable by-product of colonialism (a historical contingency James himself embraced), and cultural engagement, which metaphorizes the intellectual's increased political enfranchisement in the new nation. As a practice, cultural engagement may in fact act as a guarantee against a more general disenfranchisement (such as James experienced) if the intellectual's cosmopolitanness is such that she or he spends very little time in the originary community. Antidiasporism is more than simply a code word for the intellectual's longing to return home: unlike the exile who cannot return home, the postcolonial intellectual has the choice of relocation but is specifically concerned with the process by which secure cultural connections rather than the physical occupation of a single site enable integration into the postcolonial community. Within the paradigm of the antidiasporic, Trinidad is a place to which James can return, both symbolically and literally, rather than representing the last site to which he must resort because of historical links that have long lapsed into the cultural category of the residual.

In *Beyond a Boundary* James returned to Trinidad via the tiny town of Tunapuna, where as a young boy he watched cricket and mimicked his mother's voracious reading habits—"She was a reader, one of the most tireless I have ever known. Usually it was novels, any novel . . . and as she put them down I picked them up" (26). *Beyond a Boundary* serves to register the extent to which James, after almost forty years and several international political campaigns, remade himself intellectually. The cultural memory of the Maple cricketer is now moved to account for his decision to join that club. Through the act of historical explanation James is able to recognize, and claim, the Shannon constituency as the one ideologically natural to him. In addition to the generic boundaries that are transgressed, James also charts the autobiographical ones that he has crossed.

The bourgeois intellectual has become, for the most part through his transformation into a Marxist (in this text particularly we learn because of his involvement with the sport), a vernacular intellectual who foregrounds the significance of cricket as cultural practice and site of "his" community's most radical expression of political agency. The physical parameters of the game, the "boundary," functions as the political metaphor with which James engaged this process. It was Shannon, however, and not the game of cricket per se, that taught James to treat the notion of boundaries with skepticism. James accepted that boundaries were never simply artificial constructions, designed to exclude; boundaries could not be disregarded or arbitrarily transgressed. As a cricketer he knew that the game could be conducted only within a finite space. By engaging "Shannonism," which "symbolized the dynamic forces of the West Indies," James was encouraged to step beyond the boundary, and into the crowd, as it were: to move from the traditional through the organic toward a vernacularity (64). Shannonism called for a critique of the political and cultural forces and tensions that existed among those who were spectators, or, as importantly, those deprived of even the role of direct observers.

James encountered the latter phenomenon when he went to play a match in rural Trinidad. He was initially mistaken for the Shannon batsman St. Hill, for whom the spectators made evident their passion. What is remarkable about this incident is, as James reports, that "[n]one of them had ever seen St. Hill. But they worshipped him.... One said weightily: 'You know what I waitin' for? When he go to Lord's and the Oval and make his century there! That's what I have to see.' I have to repeat: It took me years to understand.... It was the instinct of an oppressed man that spoke" (97).

In its hopes for victory, the Shannon community exceeded the scope, boundaries, and depth of political commitment that James himself had not even contemplated. This incident is significant in that the political impulses invested in St. Hill's anticipated success at Lord's (the headquarters and symbolic home of the game in London) in this remote corner of the island was consistent with those in Port-of-Spain, the capital. We are dealing here with Shannonism: the political and ideological commitment to the experience of the Trinidadian working class, both the proletariat and the rural workers. Shannonism transcends the rural-urban split (much like the French masses–San Domingo slaves axis) and symbolizes the possibility of an imaginatively unified Trinidadian working class. To amend our understanding of the terms slightly, the metropolitan crowds at the Queens Park Savannah were one in their commitment to Shannonism with their peripheral counterparts in the Trinidadian hinterland.

James's deep-seated belief in the capacity of the working class to organize itself and direct social transformations, which he regarded as a universal phenomenon, finds passionate expression in this encounter with the rural Shannon fans. The passion, however, emanates not from James, whose pronouncements undercut the excitement of St. Hill's supporters, but from these cricket enthusiasts. James's intervention into this scene ("It was the instinct of the oppressed man that spoke") is politically didactic beside the unbridled support of the rural fans for the cause of St. Hill and Shannon. It is as commentator, in the role of revealing and unpacking the codes for those not directly party to the event, that James thrives, not as participant. *Beyond a Boundary* provides readers with an inimitable portrait of the proletariat primarily because of James's commentating skills: the ability to initiate the unfamiliar by defining cricket's codes as deeply embedded in, and expressive of, sociopolitical events, thereby reencoding the codes simultaneously as sites of pleasure, resistance, and ideological reinscription; and the commentator re-created for the familiar in terms disconcertingly unfamiliar. In the game's collo-quial, it "wasn't cricket" to reconstruct so radically this sport of the colonial empire; cricket was a game of extreme propriety, immunized from politics—discussions of or references to class, a tension so central to the game's history in England, race, or ethnicity. In this regard, James's commentary is especially disruptive to the sport's initiated because the speaker is as well trained to pronounce on developments within the boundary as he is to make the connections with the history beyond.

By reinventing the role of the commentator, to which James was preeminently geared by his marginality, James was able to profile the radical potentialities of the Caribbean proletariat with an insight and brilliance that is matched only by his portrait of Toussaint and the slaves in *The Black Jacobins*. Shannonism, *Beyond a Boundary* reveals to us, stands as the articulation of a radical politics with an impassioned cricketing face, one not only belonging to the spectators who worshiped St. Hill, but shared by James as well. Despite the extent to which James's own fondness for the game is vitiated by his sometimes too-bald politics, he is nevertheless excellent as author of the larger social passions that are invested in Caribbean cricket. James's critique of the game in *Beyond a Boundary* produced a very particular understanding of community, its establishment, its composition, and its historical contingency.

Aptly, it was Shannon, its players, its fans, and the interactive rela-tionship between the two, that provided the catalyst for James's imagin-ing of the concept of community. The "old Shannon club," James says of *Beyond a Boundary*, "is a foundation pillar of this book" (63). The cultural forces that Shannon encapsulated were such that James could conceptualize community by simply focusing on the boundary as a signifier that contained within it notions of inclusion/exclusion as well as class and racial distinctions.

Through unexpected exchanges such as the one in rural Trinidad and those involving the urban Shannon crowds more directly, James came to consider how crucially those outside the field of play participated in the Caribbean game. As a man who fielded, bowled, and batted against Shannon, he recognized that the interplay between their players and spectators was a fundamental dynamic that had to be accounted for if the game itself was to be comprehended anywhere, but especially in the colonial Caribbean:

> All of us knew our West Indian cricketers, so to speak, from birth, when they made their first century, when they became engaged, if they drank whiskey instead of rum. A Test player with all his gifts was not a personage remote, to be read about in newspapers and worshipped from afar. They were all over the place, ready to play in any match, ready to talk. (68)

The relationship between the West Indian spectators and players James describes resonates with intimacy. James conveys this familiarity by revealing to us how the minutiae of everyday Caribbean life inform the spectator's appraisal of the person as batsman or the bowler, the "Test player" representing their country. A cricketer's preferred drink or when he became engaged are details as important as when he achieved a remarkable feat on the field, such as scoring his first century (to score one hundred runs in a single inning, a remarkable score in a cricket game). The player is "not a personage remote" but firmly located within the same community as the spectator and, what is more, he was "always ready to talk" and maintain the social links. The intimacy of player-spectator relations, within the confines of the Caribbean islands, made it is easy for the community to claim the players' performances as a more general Trinidadian or even a specifically Shannon achievement.

The close links between player and community enabled the Trinidadian crowd to insert itself into the proceedings on the field and to redraw the boundaries of the game. The crowd became, in James's reading, the twelfth player, a sociopolitical agent who assisted in marking the Caribbean game as black and working-class. Even as the crowd and the players observed the physical limits of the playing field, the masses showed the white picket fences—which marked the boundaries—to be porous and the game subject to their intervention at crucial moments. In any event, the working class knew that even as it stood and watched from beyond the boundary, that they could never be excluded from the game because they were already embodied on the field, vernacularly inscribed in the person of Wilton St. Hill (or his like):

> I know that to tens of thousands of coloured Trinidadians the unquestioned glory of St. Hill's batting conveyed the sensation that here was one of us, performing *in excelsis* in a sphere where the competition was open. It was a demonstration that atoned for a pervading humiliation, and nourished pride and hope. Jimmy Durante, the famous American comedian, has popularized a phrase in the United States: 'That's my boy.' I am told that its popularity originates in the heart of the immigrant, struggling with the new language, baffled by the new customs. . . . Wilton St. Hill was our boy. (99)

St. Hill's batting articulated the ambitions, dreams, hopes, and future shapes the Trinidadian working class wanted their lives to take. St. Hill, the man who spoke so cryptically, even acerbically, according to James, was eloquent and expressive with his batting. He performed, *"in excelsis"* delicate cuts and glances, cricket strokes of great difficulty, which easily found their way to the boundary and into the psyche of his fellow oppressed Trinidadians. In St. Hill the masses that watched the game, and even those denied access to the spectacle, as we have observed, saw a vision created in which anger and resentment at the "pervading humiliation" they suffered was distilled into a finely tuned batsman.

St. Hill performed so brilliantly in the only democratic forum in colonial society that he "nourished hope and pride" for a subjugated people. His Saturday afternoon stroke-making displays represented a victory over the forces that held sway over this community's life in all other walks of life. Despite the regularity of the Shannon cricketing triumphs (on an almost weekly basis), working-class successes were still a rare phenomenon in colonial Trinidad. By embracing St. Hill with such deep-rooted enthusiasm and locating him within their community, the Trinidadian working class could celebrate his batting feats as theirs, could metonymically claim his centuries as theirs. He would always belong to the "tens of thousands of coloured Trinidadians" who reveled in the "unquestioned glory" of his batting, he would always be nothing less than their boy. (St. Hill's belonging was a communal experience, a transcendent affiliation constitutively different from the way in, to recall Mr. Roach, the Maple boys identified narrowly with each other, and their class.)

The analogy between the experience of the (American) immigrant and the Trinidadian colonial, contained in the Durante's "That's my [our] boy," is a particularly provocative one. The immigrant community considered the achievements of their boys as markers of partial integration, the acquisition of fluency in the new language and cultural literacy in the new customs; the colonized community saw St. Hill's feats as a potent metaphor of their equality; if they could compete as cricketing peers they could participate fully in any sphere of Trinidadian life if there was an even playing field. The learning of these new skills, however, also created the possibility that the recently adopted language and customs would come to dominate the old, relegating the original to secondary, if not residual, significance. A fissure, drawn mostly along the lines of generation and class, opened up between the boy and his (it is seldom her) community.

There is an anxiety contained in the enthusiasm with which the immigrant community claimed the boy as theirs. He could very easily become someone else's boy, which indicates not only an alienation from the immigrant community, but also a dependency on (usually in an economic relationship) someone else, so that the diminutive applies all too pejoratively to the immigrant male adult. The public embracing of their boy by the immigrants is thus both an effort to secure links with that community and a recognition that the original language and customs will have to adapt to new conditions by creating a new understanding and functioning of community if it wants to retain, albeit in qualified form, its boys.

St. Hill was firmly grounded in his working-class community, in some measure due to the fact that, unlike his immigrant counterpart, he had little prospect of material advancement in colonial society. The anxiety that riddled the Shannon community relationship to their boy was a very different one. Relieved of the pressures of individual alienation through assimilation or upward mobility, the Trinidadian workers were concerned with the potentiality that their cultural and political enfranchisement could be contained to "performing *in excelsis*" on the cricket field. Secure in the knowledge that St. Hill would always be their boy, the Shannon community was confronted with the historical reality that in every other social sphere they lived the experience of the political diminutive: they were, in the most disenfranchised and infantilizing sense of the term, the "boys" in and of colonial Trinidad.

The most important struggle that this community was engaged in was the one against the boundedness of the conditions in favor of a space—a "sphere where the competition was open"—that made St. Hill's achievements possible. *Beyond a Boundary* is salient in the Jamesian corpus for its ability to demonstrate the concentration of political and ideological social forces within the game and to give voice to the political import of cricket. This text is most remarkable for its ability to recognize that it would be culture, West Indian cricket, not real politics, which would announce the maturation of Caribbean politics. As important as the founding of sovereign states from Jamaica to Trinidad and Antigua was to James, the key moment in the struggle for national sovereignty predated the formal independence of Trinidad. This event occurred not at the lowering of the Union Jack at the inauguration of Anglophone Caribbean independence, but on the faraway shores of

Melbourne in 1961. It is a moment James identifies as that occasion when the Australian cricketing public turned out in the hundreds of thousands to bid farewell to Frank Worrell, the first black man to captain the West Indies, and his team:

> I caught a glimpse of what brought a quarter of a million inhabitants of Melbourne into the streets to tell the West Indian cricketers good-bye, a gesture spontaneous and in cricket without precedent, one people speaking to another. Clearing their way with bat and ball, West Indians at that moment had made a public entry into the comity of nations. (252)

Frank Worrell and his "boys" stripped the term of the pejorative references it had held for St. Hill and transformed the victory of a cricket tour into the symbolic enfranchisement of the Caribbean people. Worrell had not brought down British imperial rule in the Caribbean, but for James his cricketing triumph in Australia made Trinidadian and Guyanese independence inevitable, if not a formality. Through Worrell, James was able to do more than finally make that metaphorical journey home by inscribing himself into—and as—the vernacular intellectual. He was able to grasp cricket's import, to understand what Bondman was resisting, to comprehend what Wilton St. Hill and George Headley were expressing in their strokes, to appreciate how Shannon, not Maple, represented both the future and the radical past of Caribbean society. The signal event that was Worrell's departure from Melbourne after drawing (tying) a five-match cricket series 2–2 made, with lasting consequences, a Shannon cricketer of James the Maple player.

Through writing *Beyond a Boundary*, James grasped both the value of and his desire for location within the vernacular: through this text he not only understood his marginality, but was able to imaginatively—if transiently—transcend it and realign himself symbolically, lending a cultural substance and sporting passion to his lifelong ideological commitment. It was through Shannonism that James discovered the popular as a vernacular politics: Shannonism functions, in *Beyond a Boundary*, as the most dynamic articulation of the vernacular: the politics of popular

resistance is grasped and represented as a viable series of political practices, the accumulation of several "high and difficult" expressions of
oppositionality. Encoded in Caribbean cricket is the desire for anti-
(post)colonial resistance, revealed through it in *Beyond a Boundary* is the
very process of coming—through a rich and circuitous intellectual, philosophical, and ideological meandering—(in)to vernacularity.

CHAPTER 3

Stuart Hall, the Scholarship Boy

> The move away from the singularities of "class" or gender as
> primary conceptual and organizational categories, has resulted in
> an awareness of the subject positions—of race, gender, generation,
> institutional location, geopolitical locale, sexual orientation—that
> inhabit any claim to identity in the modern world.
>
> —Homi Bhabha, *The Location of Culture*

Making a Metropolitan Intellectual
out of a Caribbean Thinker

C. L. R. James was, like Stuart McPhail Hall is, nothing if not an inveterate internationalist. James, whose life span encompassed the major
moments of twentieth-century colonialism, witnessed the beginning and
end of the Cold War, anticipated and was entangled in the problematics
of postcolonialism, and stands as an intellectual committed to a struggle
that is global rather than local in scope. A veteran of several deracinations, James was a man who experienced a deep (but never debilitating)
alienation from the black majority who inhabited his native West Indies.
He was able to conduct an ongoing, dynamic, and animated conversation
between his Caribbean roots and the various metropolitan locations, of
which London held the greatest purchase, he inhabited in his life.

Stuart Hall's preeminence as an intellectual owes a great deal to
his ability to work from within the context of postcolonial Britain while
inflecting his writing with an international usability. His groundbreaking writing on cultural studies, Marxist theory, and the politics of
identity has found a receptive audience in Britain, the United States,
Europe, his native Caribbean, and beyond, communities that all find in
his work strategies, critical insights, and a vocabulary for addressing
the complexities of their own historical conditions. In works such as
Po-licing the Crisis, *The Hard Road to Renewal*, and countless essays, Hall

has consistently taken up these and other questions. Over some two and a half decades he has expanded considerably both his subject matter and his critical audience. While still grounded in British politics and culture, he has gone on to explore, inter alia, questions on race in the United States and popular cultural practices in Jamaica. All these projects are undertaken in a Marxist-inflected discourse at once theoretically nuanced and politically incisive, lending his work a distinct contemporaneity and an interventionist edge.

Hall and James share a great deal in terms of class status, education, ideology, cultural background, and intellectual accomplishment, but the different historical moments into which they were born required them to confront markedly distinct political questions, from geographical locales at variance with one another. Hall was born in February 1932, thirty-one years after James; the sociopolitical conditions in the Anglophone Caribbean of Hall's youth were vastly removed from those of the Trinidadian's. Growing up three decades apart, Hall and James shared little except for the common experience of British colonialism, and even this political preoccupation was viewed through different historical lenses because independence for the islands was more clearly within sight for Hall than James. The anticipation and achievement of Caribbean nationhood coincided with the first stirrings of an emergent black Caribbean culture, a subject that James took up just as Hall was making his mark as a New Left intellectual in Britain.

Hall is separated from James by the pronouncedly metropolitan trajectory of the former's intellectual career. James remained in the Caribbean until his early thirties, time enough for the political workings of the Caribbean to be indelibly stamped into his consciousness. Hall, on the other hand, left for undergraduate study at Oxford immediately after graduating from high school. While James's ideological critiques, Marxist theories, and cultural vocabularies were reconceptualized and refined in metropolitan centers, his understanding of how the world functioned—especially in terms of race and class—was primarily the product of his Caribbean upbringing. The autobiographical tenor of *Beyond a Boundary*, its metropolitan inflections notwithstanding, reflects a work saturated with the spirit of West Indian life. But Hall, whose tenure at Oxford as an undergraduate and graduate student between 1951 and 1958 coincided with the formation of the British New Left in England's elite universities, was shaped by the politics of the metropole. As an Oxbridge student, Hall was deeply immersed in the colonial power's national politics. Within the space of a few short years, the young Jamaican quickly carved out a space for himself in some of the key political institutions of the metropolitan left. He became a leading member of the New Left, an innovative teacher in English universities, and a supporter and an incisive critic of the Labour Party.

Hall's commitment to the metropolis, his immersion in English ideology, would only years later reveal its political costs. His construction as a metropolitan figure would later, more tellingly, show how his intellectual trajectory was characterized by a dynamic, debilitating silence about his Caribbean past, by a complicated antinationalism (of both the anticolonialist and the postcolonialist variety), and a problematic subsumption into English life. It would be two decades before Hall's intellectual life, initially mediated by class, and thereafter the colonial and the postcolonial projects, was seriously complicated by race. This ambiguous relationship to England is not unusual for a member of the last generation of Caribbean scholars who came to intellectual maturity in the metropolis before independence. In his own words, Hall is a thinker trained from his Jamaican childhood to be a "member of a colonial intelligentsia;"[1] he was a colonial subject critical of British imperialism while being solidly schooled in European philosophy and culture. This ambivalent immersion in metropolitan life required Hall, after postponements that were unusually protracted, to rethink more than that always-vexed relationship between race and class. He also had to reflect on how differently, and at such distinct conjunctures, these categories of analysis impacted his formation as an intellectual.

Hall is an intellectual transplanted from a colonial site, where he belonged to a second-tier, native elite, to a metropolitan location with which he was familiar. Highly literate in the norms of the metropolis, Hall found that London's political economy, racial hierarchy, and spatial arrangements were not dissimilar from Kingston's. The small Caribbean middle class in the metropolis shared a cultural outlook with their English counterparts (with whom they were in frequent contact in institutions of higher learning), so Hall was easily drawn into the ranks of the metropolitan culture. Ruth Glass makes exactly this point in her work on the experience of first-generation immigrants in Britain. Because of the "awareness of differences of origin, social class and colour accompanies the West Indian migrants to Britain," Glass argues. "In many respects the West Indian middle classes have far more in common with their English counterparts than with the West Indian working class."[2] Hall shared a cultural and political outlook with his Oxbridge fellows and his New Left colleagues, an experience that was alien to working-class Jamaican immigrants. As a middle-class metropolitan intellectual, Hall's identity coincided precisely with the elevated status he enjoyed in Jamaican society. Hall's metropolitan location mimicked his Caribbean privilege, an approach he maintained until he engaged the racial dimension of class divisions in 1970s England. So salient a critical lack is race in the Hall corpus that the moment in which he addresses it, most fully in *Policing the Crisis*, signals a major transformation of his work.

The Caribbean diaspora compelled Hall to engage directly the ways in which empire, race, black immigration, economic disparity, ideological shifts, and culture conjoined to disrupt and reconfigure popular cultural practices and the English nation. Hall is a unique "Anglo-British"[3] intellectual not so much because of his Anglo-bias—though that is undoubtedly pertinent—but rather because his preoccupation with the affairs of the white metropolitan community long postponed his revisiting of colonial origins and the postcolonial experiences of black immigrants.[4] Hall's formation as a distinct English intellectual is key to understanding the postponement of his engagement with race. His dislike, unlike James's empathy, for nationalist formations of the anti- or postcolonial variety was at once a theoretical and political position and, as ironically, a marker of his integration into English "national" life. In the anti- and postcolonial metropolis the nation came into view only in a moment of crisis, an occasion that would prove especially—

if idiosyncratically—true for Hall. In addition, Hall missed out on the nationalist struggle in Jamaica (although he would retrospectively have to engage its psychosocial consequences), a process in which issues such as race and ethnicity invariably manifest themselves.

Race will constitute the pivotal category in this study of Hall's formation as an intellectual, mediated through the complicated links between his implication in the English national popular and the ways in which that political commitment delays, informs, and lends ideological shape to his relationship to the immigrant Caribbean community. Because of its centrality, Hall's coming to racial consciousness will be shown to rely on more than a chronological charting of the process, crucial as the transition from those early historical moments in which Hall fails to make connections with the diasporic Caribbean community and the later ones in which he identifies with the diasporic struggle is in his intellectual career. This chapter will engage race as an embedded problematic, an issue that demands reading against the grain of chronology. The acquisition of a racial consciousness is not only an uneven process, but also a development that has to be understood as the outcome of an ideological crisis, a process contained within the very title of the text, *Policing the Crisis*, that marks the moment of upheaval and transformation. Hall's exploration of this issue often finds articulation in different texts, sometimes in works that are produced in different historical moments but speak to, amplify, elucidate, and clarify each other across the chronological divide. For example, a modest 1970s essay on race, "Black Britons," one of Hall's first forays into the issue, raises questions that are only fully addressed in his 1988 work *The Hard Road to Renewal*.

However, Hall's trajectory cannot be understood without mapping his complex construction as an intellectual. Hall is a thinker who learned, however belatedly, how to negotiate between the unspeakabilities of his Caribbean past from a disjunctive locale: an intellectual formed in the cauldron of 1950s (and beyond) white British politics. Unlike James, who thrived on the margins of British and American political life, Hall situated himself at the center of metropolitan political life. For this reason, as much of this chapter demonstrates, Hall is a figure whose work can only be understood in relation to the several political, intellectual, and social movements of the 1950s–1990s—the British New Left, *New Left Review*, cultural studies, identity politics—to which he contributed, and which, of course, in turn shaped his profile as a complex diasporic thinker. Hall's propensity for the collective intellectual enterprise is also borne out by the fact much of his work—which is chiefly interventionist in nature (speaking to, critiques of, specific political events or trends, a tendency that characterizes *The Hard Road to Renewal*)—is collaborative, from his earliest work, *The Popular Arts* (cowritten with fellow New Lefter Paddy Whannel), to *Policing the Crisis* (coedited with several of his colleagues at the Centre for Contemporary Cultural Studies).

But Hall was, as the chapter's title and dominant metaphor suggest, a scholarship boy, a thinker geographically dislocated, an intellectual who learned his own past, his history, only after he had become immersed in metropolitan politics; Hall is the intellectual who became a vernacular postcolonial figure through discomfiture, through unlearning and reclaiming his Jamaican past. This process of turning from and then toward his past produced in Hall an understanding—articulated through the kind of questions he pursued rather than a reneging on the work he had done before—of how his personal profile was incommensurate with that of the hegemonic left institutions in Britain.

Present at the Birth of the New Left:
Inserting Culture into Politics

The well-educated son of middle-class colored parents from Kingston, Hall read Marx, Lenin, and Freud at an elite local high school staffed by white Oxbridge graduates. The nineteen-year-old Hall arrived in England in August 1951 as a Rhodes scholar at Oxford's Merton College, duly completing his B.A. in 1954. An undergraduate active in anticolonial politics, Hall remained at Oxford to pursue a Ph.D. in English. Four years later, he abandoned his graduate studies on the work of Henry James. (As a dissertation topic, Henry James is a telling choice because the American's self-exile echoes the kind of trajectory that would mark

Hall's life. Hall's later negotiations between the metropolis and the periphery, the immersion in the metropolis, and the inability to return "home" are all issues that James's fiction—from works such as *Portrait of a Lady* to *The Europeans*—grapples with repeatedly. These Jamesian conceits, not fully engaged or resolved because he never completed his dissertation, nevertheless articulate themselves in Hall's reconstitution of himself as a postcolonial thinker.) Hall's decision to forgo his research on Henry James was made largely because of the massive upheaval caused by the events of 1956, a year of signal political events. Between February and October of that year, Khrushchev denounced Stalin, the Soviet Union invaded Hungary, and an Anglo-French naval force set out on an abortive invasion of the Suez Canal. In the next couple of years, in large measure because of his participation in Oxford political debates and the Aldermaston marches (a cross-section of the British left protesting the proliferation of nuclear weapons and arguing for the nation's unilateral disarmament), Hall became formally associated with the British New Left, a movement that would remain central to his political identity.

The New Left was born, in the main, out of a rebellion against Stalinism and the Soviet Union and Britain's neoimperialist forays of 1956. The British New Left was a political formation that took its ideological cue from disillusioned ex-Commmunist Party (CP) members, such as Raymond Williams, E. P. Thompson, and John Saville. In "Outside the Whale," Thompson's famous reflection on the origins and future of the New Left, he offers a stinging indictment of the movement's predecessor. "The old Left, because it refused to look evil in the face," Thompson writes, "because it fudged the truth about Communism or suggested that human nature could be set right by some stroke of administration, appeared mechanical, 'bullying,' de-humanised: it could only speak in the language of power, not of socialised humanity."[5] The New Left was founded on a commitment to reconstitute the left as a deeply moral and unmistakably socialist endeavor, a cause that few championed as vigorously as Thompson.

Because of the shared anti-Stalinist proclivities, ex-CPers made common cause with middle-class radicals from Oxbridge and London and with certain sections of the Labour Party. According to Michael Kenny, for these constituencies the New Left marked a collective "response to the problems facing the dominant traditions of the left in Britain—the reformist social democracy of Labour, which had tried in vain to build a 'new Jerusalem' after the war, and the Marxist-Leninism of the Communist Party."[6] This response initiated a series of ideological exchanges that produced a very particular brand of socialist humanism.[7]

The rethinking of socialism represented a significant break with pre-1956 Marxism because of its singular "preoccupation with 'culture.'"[8] The New Left was preoccupied with "culture," a crucial element for Hall, as a means of challenging and reconceptualizing the dominant understanding of social practices in British society. This conception of culture encompassed a broad sphere of human existence: music, sport, leisure activities, youth culture, morality, and articulations of national identity. The articulation of the New Left's cultural politics marked a crucial transition in British intellectual life. The emergence of the New Left represents the moment in which the *Scrutiny* (and Bloomsbury) tradition of highbrow literature as culture was critiqued (and tentatively replaced) by a more popular understanding of the practices of everyday life. For all the ostensible differences between these two cultural modes, however, the fledgling 1950s movement that would mature into an as-yet-unnamed practice called cultural studies was as much an evolution of the Cambridge University–based journal as it was a commentary on *Scrutiny*'s ideological shortcomings.[9] In *The Moment of "Scrutiny"* Francis Mulhern briefly (and, quite unintentionally) delineates the similarities, differences, and intellectual links between the two movements: "Anti-fascist, anti-war, anti-capitalist, and yet unable to accommodate itself to socialism, even in the latitudinarian popular-frontist version of the late thirties—*Scrutiny*'s eventual recoil from socialist politics was indicative of its general failure to make the practical connection between 'culture' and organized politics."[10]

Although many of the New Left's leading first-generation intellectuals, among them Williams, Hoggart, and Hall, were products of a Leavisite training steeped in "'moral seriousness'" and were sympathetic to

Scrutiny's "opposition to the mechanical/reductionist versions of Marxism," serious ideological differences remained between the interwar defenders of elite British culture and the postwar generation of nascent cultural studies proponents.[11] The crucial, and informing, tenet of the New Left's attack on the *Scrutiny* tradition was its unprecedented regard for the historic achievements of working-class culture. In his "Conclusion" to *Culture and Society*, a founding text of both the New Left and cultural studies, Raymond Williams speaks directly to the movement's proletarian concerns. In this work Williams insists that it was necessary to "say something about the idea of 'working-class culture'" because those practices constituted the "key issue in our time."[12] The movement's exploration of working-class culture, and the notions of proletarian agency and resistance encoded within it, developed into a "key issue" because of the democraticizing effects of the welfare state on British higher education. Nevertheless, this constituency's difference from the traditional tertiary student meant that the New Left had a fledgling community whose background and history spoke of different cultural resources (and the lack thereof) and agency. Appropriately, the key issue of working-class cultural history was taken up in the three pivotal texts of the early New Left.

Produced within the embryonic phase of the New Left, Williams's theoretically astute reading of the Romantics, *Culture and Society*, Richard Hoggart's autobiographically inflected contemplation on prewar Yorkshire working-class culture, *The Uses of Literacy* (1957), and Thompson's groundbreaking study of the nation's formative institutions of labor, *The Making of the English Working Class* (1963), contributed to the movement's growing political ascendancy within the universities.[13] Between 1964 and 1966 the New Left was able to secure a space for itself in the English academy, beginning in 1964 when Hoggart and Hall were appointed, respectively, director and assistant director of what would become the renowned (but not, at that time, considered groundbreaking) Centre for Contemporary Cultural Studies (CCCS) at Birmingham University. In this same year John Saville and Ralph Miliband launched the *Socialist Register*. In 1966 Raphael Samuel started the History

Workshop at Oxford University, a project that followed hard on the heels of the Centre for the Study of Social History at Warwick University, which Thompson had founded in 1965.

Within the wider public domain, however, the Aldermaston marches for nuclear disarmament marked the origin of the New Left. The Campaign for Nuclear Disarmament (CND) produced what Alasdair MacIntyre dubbed in the movement's first major collection of essays, *Out of Apathy*, the "Aldermaston generation": a political constituency opposed to the "twin crimes of Suez and Hungary, the premeditated crime of nuclear warfare, and moreover the apparent deadness and dull cynicism of official politicians in the face of these things—these launched students along with other adolescents into the world of political questions."[14]

For thinkers such as Hall, who participated in the Aldermaston marches, CND stands as a formative New Left moment. Even though it was not conceived as such, the campaign marks the development of a broad-based cultural struggle as a political strategy. As the first (and only, some would argue) instance of New Left popular politics, CND was a single-issue organization galvanized by the proliferation of Cold War nuclear weapons and the attendant specter of an atomic holocaust. While CND marked the political initiation of the movement, the alliance included within its ranks not only New Leftists but also old leftists such as Bertrand Russell (who played an important role on the Committee of 100) as well as Thompson, and to a lesser extent Williams and Hall.[15] Within the history of New Left protest, the antinuclear campaign is distinguished by its ability to elevate the way in which "popular imagination ha[d] seized upon the gesture of renouncing the bomb"[16] and organized it into highly visible mass protests. Utilizing and molding the sheer force of anti-bomb sentiment in Britain, CND organized several public events—rallies, meetings, marches—to register the left's protest against nuclear weapons. Among these marches, which began in 1958, the most successful was the 1961 march in which 100,000 protestors walked from Aldermaston (the English missile base) and Wetherfield to Trafalgar Square. CND is a salient New Left event because it redefined and provided a working model of what counted as political activity and how political structures could be built without the formal bureaucracy of a party, of any ideological stripe.

CND was prescient within the New Left because it gave impetus to the protest culture of the 1960s and anticipated (and facilitated) the new social movements of the 1970s and 1980s, all of which were to some extent or another single-issue campaigns in which Hall would be a key intellectual figure. The CND phase of New Left politics lasted only five years, 1957 to 1962 (ending with the Cuban missile crisis), but its revisioning of British culture and ideological interrogations of an imperial nation in decline made a lasting impact on the left.

The New Left Review and the First New Left

The CND moment coincided with what is now known as the "first New Left," a period that also saw the founding of the *New Left Review* in 1960 under Hall's editorship.[17] The *New Left Review* was the result of the merger of two left journals, the *Universities and Left Review* (of which Hall had been an editorial board member) and the Thompson and Saville–edited the *New Reasoner.* Hall's tenure as editor was a brief (1960 to 1961) but vital one because he oversaw the birth of a major international left publication, one to which he would contribute for decades after his short editorial spell. He and his colleagues in the first New Left[18] produced a journal premised on an expanded conception of socialist politics. "We are convinced," Hall wrote in the introductory issue's editorial, "that politics too narrowly conceived, has been the main cause of the decline of socialism in this country, and one of the reasons for the disaffection from socialist ideas of young people in particular. The humanist strengths of socialism—which are the foundations for a genuinely popular socialist movement—must be developed in cultural and social terms, as well as in economic and political."[19]

The journal's very first editorial reads as a succinct manifesto for Hall's political approach: socialism was a political struggle that had to be waged on several fronts—economic, parliamentary, and cultural, at the same time. These three terrains all enjoyed, in Hall's paradigm, equal import and status.[20] The highlight of Hall's tenure was undoubtedly the publication, in the fifth issue, of American sociologist C. Wright Mills's "Letter to the New Left." Mills, a sociologist at Columbia University in New York, was a key supporter of the movement and its youthful adherents. In an article that reads like the New Left's declaration of political intent, Mills's faith in the movement is ebulliently evident: "Who is it that is getting disgusted with what Marx called 'all the old crap'? Who is it that is thinking and acting in radical ways? All over the world—in the bloc, outside the bloc and in between—the answer's the same: it is the young intelligentsia."[21] Wright Mills's letter was a ringing endorsement of intellectuals such as Hall and Perry Anderson, the editor who became *New Left Review*'s second editor.[22] Post-1961 the journal's cachet in the ranks of the academic left[23] grew as Anderson and the new editorial team crafted the publication into a truly international review.[24]

For the British New Left, the dynamism of the 1960s extended well beyond the countercultural protests. During this decade the movement engaged in a concerted rethinking of the role of intellectuals inspired by theoretical invigoration from Europe. According to Tom Nairn, "Translating Gramscian, Althusserian and other ideas into British terms, a new and less conformist intellectual class certainly arose in those decades."[25] Also, serious attention was paid to national specificities; there was the development of a critical vocabulary that could address the phenomenon of youth and popular culture and the emergence of the women's movement; there was also periodization of British history, a *New Left Review* project spearheaded by Anderson.[26] Most important for (this rendering of) Hall, the period inaugurated a serious engagement with the effects of large-scale black immigration to the metropolis.

All of these issues were initiated during the 1960s counterculture, but they assumed critical importance in the following decade. In the 1970s the previous decade's debates about culture as a "sphere in which social meanings and values are generated" came to fruition.[27] The 1970s, according to Chun, represented the apogee of the movement because the "most creative ideas of the British New Left were actually formulated in that particular decade"; debates "about culture, cultural revolution and cultural politics; about the peculiarities of the English; about the working classes, the minorities, youth, the intelligentsia; about emancipation, either in pursuing 'the liberation of desire' and 'democratic participation' in the west, or in the liberation causes in the third world," occupied the New Left in this phase.[28]

One of the abiding ironies of the movement in the 1970s was that it achieved its intellectual maturity in the same decade as its slow demise; one of the historic saliencies of the decade was that the trajectory of the New Left coincided so precisely with that of the welfare state. By 1978, a mere ten years after the radical intensity and rambunctious optimism of Paris, both the British New Left and the welfare state were in serious decline, if not eclipse. The end of the 1970s foreshadowed the disarticulation of the historic Keynesian pact between labor and capital, an agreement administered by successive Labour and Tory governments for more than two decades. While certain aspects of Keynesianism survived the defeat of Labour, the Tory ascendancy of 1979 marked Thatcherism's programmatic onslaught on the institutions of the welfare state.

In the 1970s the issues of "emancipation" and "liberation causes in the third world" had a real purchase on and consequences for British society as a whole—in particular for those working-class white communities who shared neighborhoods, places of employment, and social spaces with them. For the resident, though shallowly rooted, Asian, African, and Caribbean communities, the 1970s represented an important conjuncture. In this decade the second generation of postcolonials—the first postwar generation to actually be born in the metropolis—grew up and came to sociopolitical consciousness. During the 1970s black immigrants' distinct racial and cultural status in Britain was confirmed. These immigrants from the ex-colonies represented, Nairn argues, the "new (disenfranchised) stratum" of British society and as such they "soon occupied the worst housing, concentrated in the most decaying inner-city areas."[29] A community that had seen its ranks grow from thirty thousand in 1950 to over one million in the early 1970s,[30] diasporic blacks undertook the process of crafting a space for themselves in the metropolis from a precarious material position.

The Scholarship Boy

Black migration to England compelled Hall to realign himself on the metropolitan landscape. Unlike the majority of his fellow Caribbean immigrants who came to Britain as menial laborers, to be "employed in public transport, in the post office, and in the service of local authorities,"[31] Hall arrived in Britain as a scholarship boy. The "scholarship boy," according to Richard Hoggart, lives "at the friction-point of two cultures."[32] Writing autobiographically of his Yorkshire upbringing, Hoggart could not have had the Jamaican Hall, later his research assistant and successor as director at CCCS, in mind when he described the peculiar difficulties of the scholarship boy's location in English society in *The Uses of Literacy* (a text that influenced his protégé's early work). The "scholarship boy," *The Uses of Literacy* makes clear, was conceptualized by Hoggart as a specifically male, white, British, working-class phenomenon. As Hoggart saw it, the "two cultures" that grappled with each other in the intellectually gifted boy were indigenous to Britain. There was, on the one hand, the scholarship boy's working-class background and, on the other, the middle-class world he was tentatively ascending into by virtue of his unusual academic prowess.

A son of the colored Jamaican middle class, Hall does not conform in three of the four crucial aspects to that of the archetypal scholarship boy. Only in his maleness is he commensurate. However, in some important respects Hall's profile is consistent with the Yorkshireman's formulation. As a product of elite Jamaica College in Kingston, Hall was familiar with black and other colored Jamaican boys who gained entry into these institutions through scholarships. The scholarship system was a "merit-based" process that sought to remove the handicaps of class for an intellectually talented working-class boy. There is a shared recognition among the communities of the mining towns of Yorkshire and those in the barrackyards of Kingston that one of the few means to transcend your own class is via the acquisition of education, all the more so if that education is obtained at the preeminent institutions of the dominant class.

By attaining prestigious scholarships, both Jamaican and British scholarship boys break ranks with their class. In Hall's case, the break was compounded by his relocation to the metropolis. In Jamaica, his links with the black populace were strained, if not severed, because of his class status, and in England his links with the diasporized Caribbean were subjected to the same pressures over a longer period.[33] In Hall the condition of the scholarship boy and the colonial boy conjoins, revealing the striking similarities and dissimilarities of their trajectories. Hall's position is so unusual that the customary distinction between the scholarship and the colonial boy, their hugely different experiences of England, does not apply. Usually, the former is "English" in England while the latter lives at a geographical and ideological remove from the metropolis, all the while in possession of a contingent "Englishness." The Rhodes fellowship transplanted Hall to England, transforming him into a unique scholarship-colonial boy hybrid.

It is appropriate that the pivotal characteristics, Englishness, class, race, and culture, that distinguish Hall from Hoggart's scholarship boy coincide precisely with the primary questions that the Jamaican has undertaken in his intellectual career. Salient, however, is the way in which Hall's approach to and engagement with these issues have changed over the course of almost three decades. Nowhere is the difference more marked than in his writing on culture, which of course serves in Hall's work as the lightning rod for all the other questions. Hall's earliest work on the subject, his 1964 *The Popular Arts* (written with Paddy Whannel, an education officer of the British Film Institute and a fellow member of the New Left), bears little resemblance to his later, more developed, writing on cultural matters in a text such as *The Hard Road to Renewal*, a collection of essays published some twenty-four years later. *The Popular Arts*, inspired by Hall's and Whannel's experiences as secondary school teachers, is a study of the disjuncture between formal education and the everyday experiences and interests of British youth. British education is, in their opinion, unable to address the "conflict between the norms and expectations of formal education and the complexities of the real world which children and young people inhabit."[34]

The focus of *The Popular Arts* is on that "real world" and the postwar youth's relationship to popular culture, particularly the movies and jazz. Hall and Whannel's commitment to the study of popular culture emerges through a complex model, one that speaks of the history of British cultural studies. The New Lefters draw on the "work of Richard Hoggart and Raymond Williams," and a spirited admixture of Matthew Arnold and New Criticism (15). In a work spiced with abundant quotes from F. R. Leavis, Q. D. Leavis, and T. S. Eliot, Hall and Whannel's contemplation on how the concept of "discrimination"—the discernment of literary taste—can be applied to the popular culture of their day, is highly evocative of Arnold's *Culture and Anarchy:* "A true training in discrimination is connected with pleasure. It places its emphasis on what can be gained from the best that is available. It is careful not to define the best in narrow terms" (39) Immersed in the Arnoldian paradigm of the best that's been said and written, Hall and Whannel are, however, seriously attempting to, if not break the mold, then certainly make it fit their late-1950s to early-1960s experiences.

For all of the philosophical preoccupation of *The Popular Arts* with the "sweetness and light" (a phrase that is never used but saturates Hall and Whannel's work) ethic, the book is dedicated to reading 1960s popular culture in a vocabulary that extends beyond "narrow (literary) terms." This break with Arnold and Leavis owes much to *The Uses of Literacy* as a study of working-class Yorkshire life. Hoggart's work is uniquely autobiographical, rooted in his own experiences as a young boy growing up in 1930s Yorkshire, and quasi-sociological contemplation on the effect of industrialization on the cultural practices and community structures of postwar England. When Hall and Whannel describe how the "rhythms of work have been permanently altered and the enclosed small-scale communities are vanishing," they recall the communities described in Hoggart's post–World War I Yorkshire small towns rather than evoking Arnold's Victorian Rugby (39). However, despite Hoggart and Williams's impact and the attention to the cultural practices of the working class and their consciousness of and uncharacteristic (British) appreciation for 1950s and 1960s American popular culture, *The Popular Arts* is beset by the limitations of *Scrutiny* criticism. Embedded in a

Leavisite discourse founded on aesthetic values such as judgment and discrimination, Hall and Whannel recognize social problems but advocate only the least organized form of political activity—that is, "individual" action. Even when the New Left authors acknowledge that the "changes that education can effect are fundamental," they put their political faith in a more esoteric place:

> No system can guarantee either freedom or cultural health. Ultimately it is our quality as individuals that will count. This is not to say that we can neglect social action, only that It must spring from the capacities for sympathy and understanding and the powers of judgement and discrimination it is the purpose of education to develop. (384)

The failure to critique the elitism of traditional British education reveals the lack a political vision in which both "freedom" and "cultural health" are attainable goals, shortcomings that Hall's later work would more carefully engage. In *The Popular Arts* Hall and Whannel are also unable to make the connection between formal education and the production of "understanding" and "judgement and discrimination," rendering it the most politically restrained—and therefore unrepresentative—of Hall's work.

The political reticence that mar(k)s this first book is obvious when the Hall-Whannel work is set alongside the culturally dynamic *Resistance through Rituals: Youth Subcultures in Post-War Britain* or the insistent political articulations of his 1978 and 1988 works, *Policing the Crisis: Mugging, the State, and Law and Order* and *The Hard Road to Renewal: Thatcherism and the Crisis of the Left.* However, while there is a wide ideological gulf between *The Popular Arts* and Hall's later work, his first book established the primary terrain—English and American popular culture—in (and from) which he would work. After *The Popular Arts*, Hall would radically amend his approach to cultural issues, bringing to it, inter alia, questions of race, diasporic relocation, and postcolonialism. The basic commitment, however, to viewing the world from the paradigm of cultural production, only increased over the decades.

The Birmingham Years: CCCS and Gramsci

Collectively, Hall's three later books and the numerous subsequent essays reflect not only how he refashioned his approach to culture, but also how his thinking on culture has been reshaped by his tenure as, first, assistant director, then director of the CCCS. During his early years at Birmingham, a period that coincided with the translation of Gramsci into English by Quintin Hoare and Geoffrey Nowell Smith (friends of his, so he was privy to early drafts of the work), Hall started exploring cultural frameworks beyond those offered by *The Uses of Literacy* and *Culture and Society*. The Birmingham scholars,[35] working in the Williams-Hoggart New Left tradition, developed "cultural studies" as a means of opening up the "debate about the nature of social and cultural change in postwar Britain."[36] Birmingham's CCCS represents, foremost, an engagement with the cultural production of communities traditionally excluded from the academy. Under the auspices of CCCS, Hall and his colleagues procured an academic environment in which they could study marginal cultures that traditionally had been neglected by universities. When CCCS was founded in 1964, "Contemporary cultural forms did not constitute a serious object of contemplation in the academic world. And the political questions, the relationships, complex as they are, between culture and politics, were not a matter considered proper for study, especially for graduate students."[37]

Hall and other members of the CCCS at Birmingham, including Chas Critcher, Tony Jefferson, John Clarke, and Brian Roberts, all of whom collaborated with Hall in individual essays in *The Hard Road to Renewal* and coauthored *Policing the Crisis*, made the Centre a space that addressed the question of youth culture/s, working-class culture/s, subcultures, and later black immigration and settlement, and the effects thereof for traditional British communities. *Resistance through Rituals*, edited by Hall and Tony Jefferson, was one such CCCS project in which a range of issues on marginal cultural groups was covered. However, whereas *The Popular Arts* was imprinted with the signature of literary figures such as Leavis, Eliot, and Arnold, Hall's cultural studies work at Birmingham is more indebted to the insurgent sociology traditions of that moment. The writings of sociologists such as Albert Cohen on deviancy, delinquency, subcultures (invaluable theoretical tools in the later work of CCCS graduates such as Paul Willis, Dick Hebdige, and Paul Gilroy, all of whom could be conceived of, in moments, as sociologists), and moral panics (a key concept in *Policing the Crisis*) served as pivotal texts for CCCS work.[38] The Birmingham era marks the transition in Hall's work from a literary modality to a cultural-sociological one as CCCS sought theoretical tools more appropriate to the political project he and the Centre was undertaking.

In the process of "sociologizing" cultural studies it is ironic, however, that as the Birmingham model's influence spread within Britain and then across the Atlantic to the United States, it found its most ready— if not most hospitable—reception in English departments (or their fringes, more precisely). Struggling from the mid-1970s on with issues of the political relevance of literature (especially of the canonical variety, its authority challenged as it were by ethnic minorities, women, and working-class students), the impact of European theory, a couple of waves of feminism, and a growing inter- and transdisciplinarity, language departments on both sides of the Atlantic found themselves grappling with the very issues with which Hall and his colleagues were working.

Hall's uncompleted thesis on Henry James returned to situate him, however unintentionally, sometimes squarely, sometimes disjunctively, as central to the very discipline he had abandoned almost three decades earlier for more direct involvement in political struggle. So much so that through his work in cultural studies Hall made the "relationship ... between culture and politics ... a matter for proper study," provided it with hybridized disciplinary theoretical apparatus, and offered the insights, critiques, and a reconceptualization of disciplinary boundaries that the Birmingham school had pioneered as an alternative model for the study of literature in English, romance studies, and comparative literature departments. The debate about culture, so crucial to work of T. S. Eliot, Leavis, and I. A. Richards, mutated through cultural studies into a form unrecognizable to the ambitions of those modernist scholars; in truth, however, in their more populist moments, Leavis (particularly) and Eliot would have understood the impulse that shaped and sustained the CCCS project.

Such was Hall's impact on the U.S., British, European, and Australian (among others) academy via cultural studies, mainly through a range of essays he published during the 1980s, that by the 1990s he became one of the preeminent intellectuals in the world. In truth, because of the international rise of cultural studies, Hall came to be regarded as an academic star, an intellectual celebrity, and a philosophical guru: he became the incarnation of cultural studies, first in Britain and then in the United States, widely anointed as the spokesman for the politics—and the endemic politicization—of the popular, the theorist in the forefront of politicizing (all) identity. His audience proliferated as his work became increasingly available, the impact of his work was acknowledged—appropriately—across a range of disciplines, causing a sudden boom in cultural studies that came as a surprise, a development that spun out of control (Hall was especially wary of the political, or lack thereof, turn that cultural studies took in the United States), to one of its original—in both senses of the term—thinkers.

Whatever Hall's reservations about his standing in the international academy, it is precisely because of his originality—his capacity to attend to the demands of the ever-changing intellectual times with a recognizable sense of project and politics—and his longevity—the scholar who was there at the moment of cultural studies' conception and continues to shape the field—that he has achieved such status. Hall's work is, in a fundamental way, the metonymic articulation of cultural studies: the road from Suez to Aldermaston, from the first engagements with European theory to identity politics, from the earliest CCCS writings to the several cultural studies readers to which he either contributes or in which he is voluminously cited, can be mapped through his oeuvre. Not least among Hall's accomplishments has been his capacity to vernacularize cultural studies. Writing with a remarkable clarity, he is significantly responsible for the international proliferation of cultural studies; he has made this discipline without an ostensible methodology a popular discourse, a field that attends to developments in the popular

realm always capable of revealing—critically—the ways in which popular cultural practices are encoded with crucial, or not so profound, political import.

Originally conceived as a series of *Working Papers in Cultural Studies* published by the CCCS, *Resistance to Rituals* includes essays by Tony
Jefferson on the Teddy Boys, by John Clarke on the Skinheads, and by
Angela McRobbie on women and subcultures. Inasmuch as the Birmingham thinkers were geared toward an academic recounting of the experiences of nontraditional groups, their work was always underwritten
by a dialectic conception of working-class and marginalized communities' social practices. The subordinate groups were always considered in
relation to the dominant culture and the ways in which these two cultures interacted with, informed, and shaped each other. In the introductory essay, "Subcultures, Cultures and Class," written by the two editors
and Clarke and Jefferson, this process of cultural exchange is described.
Unlike *The Popular Arts,* the essay provides a clear sense of the political
stakes involved in all cultural contestations. Dominant culture, according to this particular CCCS group,

> tries to define and contain all other cultures within its inclusive range. *Its
> views of the world, unless challenged, will stand as the most natural, all-
> embracing, universal culture. Other cultural configurations will not only
> be subordinate to this dominant order: they will enter into struggle with
> it, seek to modify, negotiate, resist or even overthrow its reign—its *hege-
> mony*. The struggle between classes over material and social life thus
> always assumes the forms of a continuous struggle over the distribution of
> "cultural power" (emphasis in original).[39]

The contestations around the "distribution of 'cultural power'" are
struggles over resources and representation, part of a campaign of political resistance by subjugated communities. The struggle for cultural
recognition is simultaneously a fight for political enfranchisement and
part of subordinate cultural formations' battle to find a voice for themselves, to challenge the ubiquity and combat the "natural-ness" of the

dominant culture; or, as Hall would describe the phenomenon in his later work, it was a critical engagement with the production of a hegemonic "common sense." The opening chapter of *The Hard Road to Renewal* reveals the deeply ideological characteristics of common sense, arguing that "common sense, however natural it appears, always has a structure, a set of histories which are traces of a past as well as intimations of a future philosophy."[40] A struggle over culture, a key terrain for the solvency of a society's "common sense," becomes an "all-embracing" one because it is constituted out of a variety of social sites and it includes a range of political and ideological battles.

Hall's engagement with the salience and centrality of cultural politics and his popularization and careful definition of terms such as *hegemony* and *ideology* originate during his involvement with the second New Left, are explored carefully during his involvement with the CCCS, and find their most incisive articulation in the *Hard Road to Renewal* years (1978–1988). It is a mode of politics for which Hall is deeply indebted to his study of Antonio Gramsci. The *Hard Road to Renewal* phase, undoubtedly the dominant Hall moment and mode from the conjuncture of 1978 to the present, is characterized by an astute advocacy of the Gramscian approach and a thoughtful dissemination of the Italian theorist's vocabulary. Over the course of some two decades, Hall has explicated the nuances of Gramsci's work, advocating the values of adopting a "war of position" as opposed to a "war of maneuver" (or vice-versa), he has drawn on this discourse to craft Thatcherism as an instructive instance of "Caesarism," and he has deployed the Gramscian vernacular to represent the 1980s Tories, rule as a peculiarly punitive (and racist) "authoritarian populism." Hall's immersion in Gramsci's work was a gradual process, stretching over roughly a decade and a half, which fundamentally impacted his entire intellectual career.

Keenly affected as both New Lefter and postcolonial subject by the political upheavals of the late 1960s on both sides of the Atlantic (the European student movement of 1968 and the black militancy in the United States), a moment that coincides with his appointment to Birmingham University, Hall began the arduous project of constructing for himself an unprecedented role. Stuart Hall: the prototypical Gramscian intellectual, the thinker who studies the Italian's writings of the 1920s so that he can use it efficaciously in contemporary postcolonial, if reluctantly postimperial, Britain.

In the initial period of Hall's engagement with the Turin-based intellectual, from the mid-1960s to the early 1970s, Gramsci's writings in *The Prison Notebooks* was especially attractive to the New Lefter. Committed to a vigorous, dynamic, and nondoctrinaire Marxism (a radical approach to politics that engaged material conditions while recognizing "civil society" as a vital terrain of struggle), Gramsci provided an approach to politics that was simultaneously firmly grounded in specific historical conditions and theoretically astute. Gramsci's philosophical bent, girded as it was by an innovative vocabulary, was a particularly critical attribute to the second New Left, a generation more theoretically inclined than their predecessors and a constituency with whom Hall collaborated in the pages of the Perry Anderson–led *New Left Review*. In Kenny's view Anderson's essay in the 1965 collection *Towards Socialism* (which he coedited with Robin Blackburn), "Origins of the Present Crisis," owed much to "Gramsci's concept of hegemony."[41] Of all the New Lefters, Hall pursued the Gramscian line most vigorously. By the time he embarked on the *Hard Road to Renewal* phase of his career, his adoption of a Gramscian political ethic was patently clear and his work saturated with the Italian's mode of thinking. "Many of the concepts," Hall acknowledges in the introduction to the book, "which I use to think the 'specificity of the political' in relation to the present crisis I owe to my reading of Gramsci."[42]

Produced by Gramsci while he was incarcerated by Mussolini's regime for his role as political agitator and union organizer, *The Prison Notebooks* represented both an intellectual and a political challenge to Hall. Increasingly cognizant of the changing racial composition of late-1960s British society, Hall could no longer rely solely on the New Left discourse that had previously guided his thinking. He recognized that he had to fashion himself into an intellectual who possessed an ideological vocabulary and a mode of political thinking that would enable him

to make efficacious interventions into a society undergoing major transformations—the loss of Empire, the Cold War had reduced Britain to
America's chief European satellite, the economy was in serious decline,
and British society was just beginning to confront its own postcoloniality. This period was a crucial one for Hall, a moment in which his work
as New Left thinker evoked (and demanded a confrontation with) his
colonial past and anticipated his future as postcolonial intellectual.
Gramsci facilitated an engagement between these (problematically) discrete phases of Hall's life; Gramsci enabled Hall to grapple with the political (and, to a lesser extent, psychic) tensions between these moments
and to situate himself as a black intellectual figure within the metropolis. Gramsci's firm grounding in the (cultural) popular was crucial in
enabling Hall to grasp the import of the vernacular.

Appropriating the Gramscian Model

In his seminal essay "The Formation of the Intellectuals," Gramsci is
less concerned with distinguishing between traditional and organic intellectuals than in emphasizing the organicism at the core of both.
"Intellectuals of the rural type are for the most 'traditional,'" Gramsci
writes, "they are linked to the social mass of country people and the
town (particularly the small-town) petite bourgeoisie, not as yet elabo-
rated and set in motion by the capitalist system."[43]

Raised in a nonmetropolitan context, albeit one with strong and
direct metropolitan "traditions," Hall was in possession of a singularly
contingent organism. In both Jamaican and British society he had only
a limited access to the "social masses" whose causes his work advanced.
He was only conditionally integrated into his native Caribbean because
of class and caste (a member of the educated local elite and in the imperial center his interpellation into the ranks of the metropolitan left
was qualified by his status as black intellectual. Valuable as the Gramscian paradigm may have been for Hall in all other respects, it offered him
too little in the way of an intellectual model. Except, of course, that for
a thinker who came to political maturity and full racial consciousness
in the moment of postcoloniality (with its attendant deracinations, the

rapid making and remaking of community/ies, and uneven and unpredictable shifts in identities), Hall grasped the material dimension of organicism. It was never an innate or essential condition, but was always an achieved and highly contingent condition.

By rethinking his own status as intellectual in a Britain that was being racially reconstituted, Hall was able to effectively deploy, reconceptualize, and translate Gramsci's notion of the organic into his own historical terms. He was able to convert, through his work in cultural studies, the Gramscian organic into the Hallian vernacular: this process turned on his identification with and advocacy for the struggles of postcolonial black Britain through his historicized understanding—originating in his 1950s New Left phase—of how (popular) culture constituted its own efficacious brand of politics. Grounded in Hoggart, Thompson, and Williams (who each had their own critical appreciation of the vernacular as, respectively, autobiography, history, and literary criticism—and fiction, in Williams's case), Hall fashioned out of his New Left theoretical legacy a vernacularity inspired by Gramsci and his own discomfited location within British intellectual life. Hall is the (black) colonial who came to understand race and how it impacted him, and others like him, through struggles around political and cultural battles in which he was engaged not as black intellectual but as intellectual activist; this was the case when he campaigned against the extreme criminalization of mugging during his directorship at CCCS in Birmingham, an engagement that produced *Policing the Crisis*.

Hall came to the vernacular unevenly and, most importantly, historically: through an understanding of how his role shifted over time, in response to changes in conditions, and sometimes by initiating new conceptions and theorizations of current political and popular developments; he melded the vernacular out of his work on cultural studies and his determination to renovate Marxism. Hall adopted the vernacular because he recognized that the popular, "common sensical" notions of race had to be opposed because of the consequences that hegemonic British "common sense" had for black, immigrant, and other minority communities. He grasped, in response to the ontological, ideological, and epistemological crisis spawned by the Handsworth events (making *Policing the Crisis* Hall's signal text in the way that *Beyond a Boundary* is James's), that he could no longer work in his usual modalities. The colonial-cum-British (New Left, as a composite position) intellectual realized that he had to remake himself in order to address the crises that his work had not, up to that point, engaged with any sustained theoretical rigor. Vernacularity, which pivots upon the centralizing of race within the Hall oeuvre, did not require the unmaking of the New Left thinker or the unlearning of his intellectual privileges: it meant retooling his critical skills, relocating himself on metropolitan society's intellectual landscape, prioritizing (however temporarily) one set—those one constituency—of concerns above others; at worst, it meant integrating the issue of race into his work on the popular, cultural studies, or his Gramscian hermeneutics.

Because of the upheaval provoked by *Policing the Crisis,* Hall is reconstructed as intellectual by his attending to race. This development not only enables him to make connections, however difficult, tenuous, or mediated, with the resident black population and their concerns in Britain, but also lends his work its especial resonance among scholars of color from the United States to Africa to diasporic European communities; it is precisely because of race that Hall is, after some four decades, able to turn his intellectual focus (back on/) to his native Caribbean. His attending to the condition of blackness allows Hall to "postcolonialize," to demonstrate how his writing might be critically useful in the Caribbean or sub-Saharan Africa, his work in cultural studies. Whereas for James vernacularity is achieved by returning (after the barrackyards of *Minty Alley*) to the cricket ovals of the savannah, Hall achieves vernacularity by turning for the first time to/ward blackness, making his work speak to the one constituency whose popular experience had been absent from the body of his work. For Hall the vernacular signifies that moment when the popular becomes inclusive of the unacknowledged, repressed self, that moment when the black self begins to speak—however tentatively—the self's (relocated, previously ignored, now metropolitanized, postcolonialized) past in its new siting/citing. The vernacular also means,

in Hall's case, a location within a community that is—unlike the organic—substantively new and unknown. In his affiliation with postcolonial
British blackness, Hall had to acquire both a historical and a popular
(colloquial) racial identity. It is, for this reason, inevitable that the
process of racial reaffiliation that began in Birmingham would have to,
at some crucial conjuncture, make its way back to—and confront the
repressed history of—Kingston.

For Hall, the vernacular is where Gramsci and Marx mediated
the popular, where Gramsci and Marx were enjoined in the campaign
against racism, where the organicism that Gramsci valued so highly had
to be recalibrated through the prism of race, where the politics of the
New Left had to be reconfigured by the demands—and harsh realities—
of black postcolonial life in postimperial Britain. Hall undertook the
process of reconfiguring the organic by, much like Gramsci, turning
to Marx in order to address the specific demands of his own context. In
the "Eighteenth Brumaire of Louis Bonaparte" Marx writes, "Men make
their own history, but they do not make it just as they please; they do not
make it under circumstances chosen by themselves, but under circumstances directly encountered, given and transmitted from the past."[44]

Understanding his "own history" is crucial to the way in which
Hall has fashioned himself as a Gramscian intellectual. Like James, he
conforms completely to the model of neither the traditional nor the
organic intellectual. Instead, Hall creates a historic and transformative
hybrid out of Gramsci's categories in the process of assuming a singular
vernacularity. Deeply rooted, like the Trinidadian, in the cultural norms
and customs of the metropolis (so that for Hall vernacularity can sometimes be understood as the articulation of the politics of the cultural
popular), Hall is an intellectual who recuperates and reclaims the traditions of the erstwhile periphery from within the European capital itself
—albeit some two decades after his physical departure from the Caribbean. Intellectually domiciled within the metropolitan left, his organicism there was nevertheless a tangential one, a condition qualified and
complicated by race and his subsequent efforts to relocate himself as a
diasporic thinker affiliated with the Caribbean intelligentsia through his

interventions into questions of culture and politics. Hall has to, in a critical sense, remake Gramsci in order to construct himself as a diasporic intellectual; Gramsci's focus is too "narrow." Regardless of the efficacy of the traditional-organic model, it does not account for the intellectual who cannot be easily identified with national classes. As a psychically alienated and dislocated thinker, culturally hybridized, committed to and in the forefront of a new political formation (the New Left), Hall could not be readily accommodated by a model that—as much as it favors one class over another—is still deeply embedded within the paradigm of the nation. Unlike the organic or the traditional intellectual who has an a priori location within the nation, Hall had to translate Gramsci in such a way as to transcend the limitations of national identification while still working—disjunctively, but never uncommitted—within the political structures of the (metropolitan, post/colonial, diasporized, racially reconstituted/ing) nation. Hall had to make Gramsci usable, and in the process he offers his trajectory as a different, conceptually complex, and derivative model for intellectual work.

Hall represents the most considered representation of a dialectic within the Gramscian paradigm, the negotiation between intellectual model and historical moment (and the demands of that conjuncture). Hall is the post/colonial figure who resuscitates a European philosopher, historicizing the Italian's mode of radical oppositionality. Hall synthesizes select(ed) qualities of the Gramscian paradigm into a distinct ideological discourse and political approach, one informed, animated, and articulated by that of the Italian Marxist, aware of its conceptual limitations and theoretically adept in adjusting them to the demands of his own moment and particular historicity. Hall is the intellectual who, through critical reflection, intervenes in (often through the disruption of conventional Marxist approaches) contemporary political debates through culture as much as ideology, through theory as much as through direct involvement in political struggle. Hall is the figure who takes the project of socialism (and the politics of the left that will secure a socialist future) so seriously that his work is dedicated to continually looking at new shifts in the ideological landscape, always with an eye to "renewing" the left—a Gramscian concept upon which the title and intellectual thrust of *The Hard Road to Renewal* turns. (*Crisis*, as can be gleaned from its usage in two of his titles, is a term to which Hall repeatedly turns: *crisis* represents an opportunity for Hall to think his way through an ideological dilemma and into a new paradigm, an alternate, imaginative left way of an engaging a problematic.) Hall has never simply rotely applied Gramsci's philosophies; he has consistently tailored them into a particular vernacularity or amended the lessons of *The Prison Notebooks* to match the conditions in which he works. Through Hall's dissemination, Gramsci has become an intellectual template for cultural studies scholars, diasporic communities, constituencies of the postmodern left, and, most importantly, for postcolonial thinkers.

The Burden of Overrepresentation

Located at the core of the role of postcolonial intellectual, a position that Hall and others like him have had to learn to occupy, is the burden of overrepresentation. Postcolonial intellectuals are imaged as both typical and atypical of the newly arrived community, constructed by the dominant bloc as one of the few members of the marginalized community able to give public voice to immigrant experiences and qualified to speak in its name at important junctures. They are, on the face of it, the minority representatives par excellence: articulate in the dominant discourse while remaining identifiably Other. Command of the hegemonic vocabulary, sophistication in the dominant culture, and the level of and propensity for academic achievement render these figures unrepresentative of their community. Meanwhile, their race, native culture, and mutant national identity, or what is often perceived by the hegemonic culture to be either an attenuated or a severe lack of a national identity, fits them squarely in the mold of their diasporic "compatriots." However, inasmuch as the elite immigrant constituency that the Oxbridge-educated Hall belonged to was skilled in the dominant discourse, so this group was also traditionally one from which the political vanguard of the marginalized community emerged. While the colonial project engendered class divisions in the ranks of the colonized, it also traditionally provided the native elite with the education and bicultural sophistication to resist colonialism.

Hall belonged to a generation, if not to a class, marked by the condition of postcolonial interstitiality. All the Caribbean immigrants of Hall's generation were caught in a unique moment of anti- and postcolonial in-between-ness. Their arrival in the metropolis pre-dated the birth of an independent Caribbean, while the composition of a settled immigrant black community was only in its infancy. More specifically, their generation consolidated those communities in London and Birmingham as well as contributing to the independence campaigns in the Caribbean. Hall's was an immigrant generation that had to make a space for themselves in English life without an independent national identity, a status that implied a symbolically, if not de facto, altered relationship to British society.[45] This generation possessed an interregnum-like political identity because of their fluid ideological location, a position rendered tenable only by their ability to maximize their cultural resources. These first-generation immigrants' adaptation of their Caribbean cultural practices sustained them in the initial stages of their diasporic experience. Unlike Hall, most first-generation working-class immigrants were not primed for integration into English society and they quickly debunked the concept as a colonialist myth. They "silently abandoned 'integration' as a practical aspiration," and instead "turned to other things—like making a living and a tolerable life for themselves, among their own people in their own areas."[46]

As an interpellated, nonnative intellectual grappling with the special challenges of the interstitial moment, Hall's position straddled the poles of the interregnum. The interregnum, however, is a moment that symbolizes neither a complete historical separation nor an unproblematic connection, but a complicated mix of the two—that moment where the old (colonial) is dying all too slowly and the new (postcolonial) bears all too many traces of the old. As a well-trained, erudite thinker from the periphery, he was a colonial intellectual shaped by the preindependence dynamics in addition to being an intellectual who engages the problematic of the postcolonial era in the reconstituted metropolis (as well as the erstwhile periphery). To explicate the interregnum in Raymond Williams–like terms, Hall bears (and embraces) several residues of the dominant power complex (colonialism), while grappling astutely with the emerging condition of metropolitan postcolonialism.

As an anomalous immigrant and intellectual, Hall is in unexpected ways representative of the complications, unexpected positionings, and variations within the anti- and postcolonial immigrant community. The effects of postcolonialism in the metropolis on Hall were such that he had to develop from scratch a political vocabulary that could account for the experience of immigration and the transition from colonialism to postcolonialism. In the metropolis, marginality is at the core of these events; immigrants, having made the journey from the colonies to the center, constitute a minority that have to adapt to a new environment, a new climate, and conditions of physical and psychic existence. The latter, of course, was a source of great concern to Hall because his residency in the postcolonial metropolis was overwritten by a series of critical issues.

All Identity Is Political

Hall has always attributed his initial postponement of his return to the Caribbean to his participation in the New Left. In an interview with Kuan-Hsing Chen, aptly entitled "The Formation of a Diasporic Intellectual," Hall reiterates this position:

> I would have gone back, had the Caribbean Federation lasted, and tried to play a role there. That dream was over at the moment in the 1950s when I decided to stay, and to open a "conversation" with what became the New Left. The possibility of the scenario in which I might become politically active in the Caribbean closed at the very moment when personally I found a new kind of political space here. After that, once I decided I was going to live here rather than there, once Catherine and I got married, the possibility of return became more difficult.[47]

This explanation is, of course, a post–ipso rationale—for a decision that was equal measure personal and political. Hall's leading role in the New

Left was the main political reason for his remaining in England; a future career in the Caribbean did not, clearly, depend on the survival of the federation. In fact, the failure of the federation only created more intellectual possibilities for an intellectual such as Hall, a thinker renowned for his ability to offer imaginative, nondoctrinaire solutions to ideological conundrums. The collapse of West Indian unity at a crucial juncture in Hall's own intellectual development functions as an overburdened shorthand political explanation for his continued residency in England. The Caribbean Federation also, as significantly, doubles as a metaphor for the personal: it enables the incorporation of the personal dimension— his marriage to the social historian Catherine Hall—so that remaining in England assumes an emotional nuance, a decision that cannot be reduced to a simple ideological choice between the metropolis and the Caribbean.

However, the decision not to return permanently to Jamaica does not pivot only on Hall's political commitment to the New Left. A telling, and painful, aspect of that narrative resides in other aspects of his autobiography, a personal history that has only since the late 1980s begun to find expression in Hall's work. Until 1988, Hall's work is characterized by the omission of autobiographical information. The barely told personal history is a matter of deliberate concealment: in the decades of intellectual engagement leading up to the mid-1980s, Hall publicly repressed the painful memories of his Jamaican past. Hall engages his Jamaican background through a mode of writing and interviewing that is often confessional, revealing how those first eighteen years of his life in Kingston shaped his work indelibly. Growing up in Kingston as a middle-class colored in a colonial society had a profound impact on Hall's life and work. For decades afterward, those years determined his relationship to Jamaica and the Caribbean diaspora in Britain. Hall's Jamaican upbringing disabled, except for rare moments, an engagement with race and distorted his own identity, politically and psychically.

It is apropos that Hall should take up the matter of his past within the context of identity politics, a burgeoning field of political inquiry of the mid-1980s to which he was making a significant contribution.

Identity politics, more than any other mode of intellectual (and psychic) engagement, enabled Hall to overcome the painful silences that had distanced him from the black diaspora in Britain. Identity politics made it possible for a Marxist intellectual to rejuvenate his political thinking where previous leftist approaches to the issues of race and ethnicity had failed; identity politics facilitated the careful thinking together of class, race, and ethnicity, each assigned a place, an ideological and psychic import, and a role commensurate with the subject and the community's understanding of itself. Identity politics offered a difficult but imaginative way out of the zero-sum game of race or ethnicity or gender versus class so endemic to conventional leftist thinking. It enabled, most importantly for Hall, a reconciliation between his racialized, silenced Caribbean past and his diasporic present, between his New Left past and his "hard road to renewal" present, between—reductively phrased—his intellectually "white" past and his racialized, vernacularized present.

Identity politics is an articulation of how, in the post–*Policing the Crisis* Hall modality, the vernacular derives from the politicized personal. It is a critical project that enables Hall to narrativize his past, to cast his past as a political, yet deeply personal, experience. It is also, of course, through identity politics that Hall's attention to (his) race (/racialized identity) comes full circle: the project of engaging the politics of race in the metropolis that began in Birmingham in the mid-1970s returns, in the mid-1990s, to the site of origin (which is also the site of the original traumatic encounter). In order to deal fully with race, Hall has to, in a fundamental sense, undertake that most onerous of tasks for the displaced, relocated diasporic intellectual: he has to return, however briefly or metaphorically, "home," to the periphery, the place of origin where the first encounter with the raced, racialized identity took place—where racism was, however retrospectively, as in Hall's case, initially experienced, forgotten, or repressed as that encounter may be. By retrieving his Caribbean past, Hall is simultaneously laying claim—however tentatively or reluctantly—to that (traumatized) past and situating himself within the vernacular experience—of his fellow West Indian immigrants. They may not share the same psychobiographies, but their trajectories are also, in their different ways, journeys from the periphery to the metropolis. By locating himself within the vernacular, Hall is able to confront a personal crisis and render common his experience. Through the vernacular Hall can, however belatedly, qualifiedly, and problematically, overcome his status as scholarship boy and assume a shared, politicized identity rooted in—and routed through—a "common" Caribbean past.

The Hallian personal had considerable political purchase during the Thatcher years because identity was an urgent issue for several marginal communities; postcolonial subjects in both the metropolis and the sovereign states of the erstwhile periphery, women, gays, lesbians, bisexuals, blacks, South Asians (another diasporic British constituency for whom Hall's work had enormous significance), and in the United States. Identity politics enabled Hall to renegotiate his own self-construction in a vocabulary that could accommodate an admixture of psychic contradiction and ideological linearity. This mode of writing allowed Hall to engage in public self-analysis through a paradigm sympathetic to narratives of default, contingency, unconscious processes as well as conscious ones, and personal memories long repressed. Hall's forays into identity politics from the late 1980s to the mid-1990s provided him with the opportunity to clarify, rethink, and amplify issues about his Caribbean past that had been latent in his work for more than two decades. In a Britain that had been politically and culturally reconstituted by its resident Caribbean, Asian, and African populations for three generations, Hall was able to map for a receptive audience his psychological trajectory from Kingston to London, a process that we retrospectively learn had been occupying him ever since he left Jamaica.

In his 1988 essay "Minimal Selves," Hall condenses his decision to remain in England after leaving Oxford into a cryptic sentence. It is a reduction, however, that is not only revealing but psychically a world removed from his earlier New Left explanation. "Migration is," he states definitively, "a one way trip."[48] However, he then goes on to reveal the profoundly personal undergirding of this gnomic statement. Hall explains: "I am here because it's where my family is not. I really came here to get away from my mother. Isn't that the universal story of life? One is where one is to try and get away from somewhere else. That was the story I could never tell anybody about myself."[49] Within the Hallian corpus, "Minimal Selves" marks the introduction of the phase in which he publicly (re)engages his relationship to Jamaica. Insistently personal, pseudo-Freudian psychoanalysis, and quasi-confessional, the 1988 essay set the terms for this period of Hall's life: Hall the public intellectual and the private (post)colonial were in dialogue about the personal consequences of the Caribbean's caste, color, and class system. The repressed private self found rare and liberating voice in public forums unaccustomed to this type of Hallian disclosure. The introduction of autobiographical material into his theoretical explication complicated, personalized, and enriched public understanding of Hall's work. The new access to—and admission of—the autobiographical Hall invalidated the disjuncture between the public and the private.

In and of itself, "Minimal Selves" discloses tantalizingly little personal information. It merely initiates a highly politicized autobiographical process that culminates in Chen's "Formation of a Diasporic Intellectual," an exchange published in 1996 but conducted some four years earlier. Even as Hall takes the audience into his confidence in the 1988 essay, there is still a considerable guardedness about his articulations—the most obvious example of this is when his rationale for escaping his mother slides easily into psychoanalytic generalizations. Hall's broad Freudian question, "Isn't that the universal story of life?" is evasive and deliberately decontextualized, a moment that draws attention to itself because it is unusual for a thinker characteristically given to historical specificity.

However, when Hall does offer the full account of his escape from his mother and Jamaica, his reticence is patently understandable. It is an intensely personal story, a tale in which Hall recalls (and tells publicly for the first time) how his middle-class family's interpellation into the racist hierarchies of colonialism destroyed his sibling and psychically disabled him. In this account Hall offers a painful history of a colonized young man coming to racial consciousness:

> When I was seventeen, my sister had a major nervous breakdown. She began a relationship with a young student doctor who had come to Jamaica from Barbados. He was middle-class, but black and my family wouldn't allow it. There was a tremendous family row and she, in effect, retreated from the situation into a breakdown ... It was a very traumatic experience, because there was little or no psychiatric help available in Jamaica, at that time. My sister went through a series of ECT treatments given by a GP, from which she's never properly recovered. She never left home after that ... But it crystallized my feelings about the space I was called into by family. I was not going to stay there. I was not going to be destroyed by it. I had to get out.[50]

This is the "story" of multiple losses and a teenage boy's helplessness that Hall "could never tell anyone about," not in 1988 or for a long time before or after that. It is a tale of psychological repression, of "traumatic" memories that indelibly marked a life, but which has concertedly been hidden from public view. "The Formation of a Diasporic Intellectual" stands as the overcoming of autobiographical taciturnity and elusiveness and his entrée into postcoloniality.

In this interview and this essay Hall theorizes the vernacularity of his intellectual trajectory by translating the experience of psychic loss—a moment that proved key to his intellectual formation (without the traumatic encounter he would, ostensibly, have returned to the Caribbean to become a very different kind of intellectual)—into a popular idiom. In these two articulations Hall enters the vernacular through the "confessional." Unable to explain his continued residency in England after Caribbean independence in a theoretical vocabulary (neither Gramsci nor Marx were of much use here), Hall turns to the vernacular: a popularly accessible (to both the British left and the diasporic community), explicable, and painful narrative of the self. Transformed by racial and ideological crises into a vernacular intellectual, Hall uses the language of identity—the personal as the profoundly, resonantly political—to explain his political career and personal decisions. Through the vernacular Hall accounts for how the (Caribbean) personal produced the (British, New Left, postcolonial) political.

Hall's narrative vividly lays bare for us the complex psychic roots of migrancy; he sketches a mental map of his own journey's tortuous routes. The 1996 interview makes clear that relocation from any one place to another is a process grounded as much in history, ideology, and economics as it is in the autobiographically unmentionable. The act of leaving one home in order to avoid self-destruction and of making another, however transiently, precariously or even permanently, is over-written by a personal background that is barely mentionable. Arguably, Hall's scarred psychobiography demonstrates that his personal history bears a greater responsibility for his nonreturn to Kingston than the lack of political will. His investment in the British New Left and the journal he edited are thrown into sharp relief against the background of this tumultuous psychic canvas—a full portrait that includes its condensation into the figure of his mother, "I really came here to get away from my mother," as well as his sister's failed love affair. It is historically fitting, though not without a certain paradox, that Hall should take up these psychological issues that are so rooted in colonialism in the metropolis itself. The product of colonialism's psychic violence, Hall has, as it were, returned to the source in order to address the matter. A concern, we might assume, that goes far deeper than his sister's story; in fact, his sister's experience is perhaps only the most articulate vehicle, or screen memory, for a collection of earlier or more jagged or rawer psycholog ical scars.

The devastating experience suffered by Hall's sister is, more than anything, an indictment of the colonial project and the internal racism it nurtured in the colonized. The indigenous form of colonial racism was, as we see, a brand more potent and vituperative than its European variety. The Hall family illustrates this point sufficiently because it is not class that disqualifies the Barbadian suitor but his color—"My parents wouldn't allow it." Earlier in the interview, Hall recalls his own experience of how blackness was considered a mark of racial unsuitability among middle-class Kingstonians: "I had the identity in my family of being the one from the outside . . . the one who was blacker than the others, the 'little coolie.'"[51] This section of the Chen interview is propelled by a resonant subtext: the racism of the colonized alienates Hall from his class and drives him out of his homeland. The racist tendencies of the Jamaican colored elite, a constituency in training as the nascent postcolonial ruling class, estranges Hall from his society and makes his life there psychically untenable. In the metropolis Hall would have to work his way (back) to racial identification with the displaced Caribbean community, negotiate his path to "blackness" through ideological crises and culture.

Against the background of these recollections (with all the complications attendant to retrospection and hindsight), it is striking that race should have been, until his participation in the *Policing the Crisis* project, *the* political category that is substantively absent from his work—the 1978 book on the Handsworth events represents the undertaking that signals his (re)integration into the black Caribbean community. How could a Caribbean thinker surrounded by racialized and racist discourse in the formative years of his life not have turned his intellectual attention to race earlier in his career? How could a child of familial racialized violence, witness to the traumas of racialized social practices, have averted the issue for so sustained a period? Or, was race an issue to which he could only return, rather than confront head-on upon his arrival in the metropolis, once he had established himself psychically in Britain? Hall has provided sound historical and demographic reasons (to which I turn shortly) for the omission of race in his early work, but it is now clear that these questions cannot be considered without attending to the repression that shaped his writing.

Acquiring a Race Consciousness: The Theory of Occupancy

By the early 1970s Hall had started to address these questions—even if he did not have the discursive strategies to confront them more fully—through his involvement with the working-class Caribbean community. There is, of course, a certain paradox to this. The Jamaican scholar who could not make a home for himself in the Caribbean because of middle-class racism was making common cause with proletarian-class black West Indian immigrants struggling to secure a place for themselves in metropolitan English society. Hall's writing about this constituency in a short 1970 essay, "Black Britons," could easily be construed as a self-referential text. "I do not believe," he argues, "that the vast majority of black immigrants to Britain are going to return to their countries of origin."[52] Like them, though for very different reasons, Hall is not going back. To express it more poetically: he could go "home," he just could not stay. Over the last forty-five years Hall has visited Jamaica several times, but a permanent return has been impossible since 1951. He may have left only subconsciously knowing that he had no intention of going back, but it is a decision that he has never seriously reconsidered. In truth, by departing from Jamaica Hall did not so much leave a home as he did a "country of origin." He was a self-proclaimed member of the initial diasporic generation ("I turned out to be in the first wave of the diaspora"), and his life has been about transforming the impossibility of return into the process of making a home in the metropolis.[53] The redi-asporization of the Caribbean to Europe has been the historical factor most crucial in facilitating that project. Without a psychic "home" (a safe and unviolated space) in the Caribbean, he has turned his attention to securing such a locale (no matter how embattled) within the metropolis itself. Unable to go home, Hall has struggled to make a home.

"Black Britons," which marks an important step in the process of making that home, also emphasizes another significant feature of Hall's work: his theory of occupancy. Hall's work on racism is founded on the premise that a discourse about discrimination depended on black immigrants' residency. A critique of racism required black occupancy, a manifest presence, because it was a phenomenon Hall claims that he could not contemplate in the abstract. Consequently, Hall's writing on race develops only at that moment when Caribbean immigrants have established a sufficiently large and permanent presence within the metropolis—a critical Caribbean mass, as it were. Occupancy signifies the cultural, economic, and political settlement, that conjuncture which brings black West Indians into confrontation with the British establishment and the white public more generally. The late 1950s represents the earliest moment in this trend, but the black presence is really established in the late 1960s and early 1970s. (Before "Black Britons," race is an issue rarely present in Hall's writing.)

Hall's argument that his critique of race hinged upon a resident, and substantive, Caribbean constituency within the metropolis represents a problematic conception of settlement. Indeed, it is a theory that Hall is already rethinking by the mid-1970s. In "Racism and Reaction," his contribution to a BBC-TV program on multiracial Britain, he comments laconically on this matter: "To hear the problems of race discussed in England today, you would sometimes believe that relations between British people and the peoples of the Caribbean or the Indian subcontinent began with the wave of black immigrants in the late forties and fifties."[54] Before the early 1970s, however, Hall's work does not register the long tradition of black West Indians in England. The Caribbean presence in the metropolis, as Hall points out in "Racism and Reaction," is an established one, almost as old as the English presence in the West Indies. Of equal vintage is the narrative of conflict between West Indian blacks and white Britons that arose out of Caribbean, Asian, and African settlement. British history post–World War I is especially riddled with incidents of racial strife.[55] During this decade of rapid Caribbean immigration[56] blacks in Britain "came to experience considerable racial hostility,"[57] a process that culminated at the end of the 1950s with the Notting Hill riots and the murder of Kelso Cochrane in May 1958. Cochrane, a thirty-two-year-old West Indian carpenter, was murdered "near the railway bridge at a sordid street corner in Kensal New Town."[58] No one was arrested for Cochrane's murder even though there were widespread suspicions that one of the white supremacist groups operating in the area, Sir Oswald Mosley's Union Movement, the White Defence League, or National Labour Party, were responsible.

August 23 of that same year marked the most dramatic turning point in race relations in postwar Britain. The Notting Hill riots, as they have popularly been dubbed, broke out in the Midland city of Nottingham after an altercation between a black and a white man. The riots inserted the discourse of race relations permanently, if not constantly, into British public life. The interracial scuffle between the two men took place in a part of Nottingham known as the Chase, an area described by Ruth Glass as a "decaying district where a considerable number of coloured people are concentrated."[59] A few days later, the impact of the Nottingham racial disturbances reached London. The conflict in the capital, centered around Notting Hill (a largely West Indian area), generated more tension and lasted considerably longer than that in the Midlands. The riots disrupted, as Hall and others would later fully realize, the notion of Britain as a homogenous, white nation by drawing attention to the ways in which colonialism and European economic expansion were reconfiguring the British ideological landscape. For the first time, race established itself as a crucial, contentious factor in metropolitan life, one that would continue to influence the civic affairs of Birmingham, Glasgow, London, and Nottingham for decades to come.

The result of the Notting Hill furor was a barrage of calls from the white conservatives and reactionaries for the control of black immigration, a "polite term for some sort of colour bar."[60] The "colour bar," of course, was a "polite term" that would soon degenerate into Enoch Powell's call for the repatriation of blacks, a constituency the Conservative Party Wolverhampton Member of Parliament labeled the "Enemy Within."[61] More important was the silence of the black community in this debate about race relations: in the "assessment of race relations in this country [Britain], their [black immigrants'] side of the story is often rather strangely—or perhaps not so strangely—neglected."[62]

The lack of a black immigrant narrative about race relations, not only in the dominant discourse but by the immigrant community, Hall, and the British left, constitutes a telling and instructive omission. The exclusion of the black immigrants' response(s) to the violence of 1958 from the official narrative is understandable, even if it is unjustified. They were regarded by the white establishment as a marginal constituency, a(n electoral) bloc alien to the British body politic. Since they were conceptualized as a transient labor force, not a community establishing permanent residence, they were presumed not to have local spokespersons who could take up their cause. In fact, it is significant—and no less offensive—that resident black voices were excluded from the debates about Notting Hill and Kelso Cochrane while the British government cooperated with the Jamaican authorities to found the British Caribbean Welfare Service. Established in 1956, the Welfare Service was designed to help black immigrants find housing and employment in the metropolis. It was "under the control of a welfare liaison officer, Ivo de Souza, who was a civil servant seconded from the government of Jamaica."[63]

By setting up the Welfare Service, the British government conferred authority on colonial blacks in their employ; the state thereby explicitly refuted the right of representation of those blacks in their metropolis. Britain was identified as a white political arena, a terrain unavailable to Caribbean immigrants. Black authority was positioned as having control only outside the metropolis, they were not enfranchised to speak in Britain itself. Blacks were at once racially Othered and politically disenfranchised. Their status as Commonwealth citizens, which guaranteed their right to live in Britain, did nothing to ameliorate their conditions of internal racial exile. The rhetoric of repatriation, which reached a vitriolic crescendo in Enoch Powell's 1968 "Rivers of Blood" speech, was based on the notion that blacks were little more than temporary sojourners, a sort of acculturated, racially distinct Gastarbeiter.

While the white authorities' response to these developments was expected, it is more problematic that the immigrant community and the British left were not able to impact the discussion about racial disturbances in the late 1950s. In this regard, Hall's silence in this moment deserves special attention. Inasfar as it was possible at that conjuncture, he symbolically bridged the gap between the immigrants and the New Left. Unlike most members of the West Indian middle class, a constituency removed from the experiences of their working-class compatriots in places like Kensal New Town because they were materially advantaged, Hall was involved with the disenfranchised immigrant community. (There were other figures positioned like Hall in relation to the immigrant communities. Tariq Ali, for example, performed much the same function for south Asian migrants as Hall did for the Caribbean community.) As a secondary school teacher in London from 1958 to 1960, Hall escorted black students to their homes because of the threat of white violence.[64] Hall's actions speak not only of personal courage, but also of his commitment to the inner city's immigrants: it demonstrates an understanding of the very real physical dangers of racism in metropolitan life. Hall's bravery as a teacher complicates his status as symptomatic New Left intellectual. The immigrant activist is divided from the New Left theorist.

In the late-1950s (and much of 1960s) Britain, the interests of these two communities did not overlap sufficiently so that one—in Hall—could volubly and publicly support the other's struggles. Able to effect an ideological unity only through personal intervention, Hall straddled the division between the postcolonial immigrants and the New Left uncomfortably. Although such a separation was paradoxical, since the New Left derived in considerable measure from the anti-imperial experience of Suez, this aporia is explained by the conception of the postcolonial as an external paradigm in the postwar British political imaginary. Hall describes this phenomenon as "historical forgetfulness—what I want to call the loss of historical memory, a kind of historical amnesia, a decisive mental repression—which has overtaken the British people about race and Empire since the 1950s."[65] Racial conflict and anticolonial tension are presumed to occur outside the metropolis, not at its very core.

Hall's silence about 1958 speaks of a newly relocated intellectual. Ideologically divided and politically torn, he was not yet at the point where he could translate his (and the immigrant community's) experiences into a written critique of British race relations. The collective effect of his investment in the New Left, the lingering effects of his middle-class Jamaican past, and the still-unarticulated decision to remain in England effected a split between his immigrant community activism and his "public" political critiques. As a political forum, the predominantly white New Left could neither engage nor provide a political vocabulary for Hall's activism in the black community.[66] The immigrant question was in its "infancy" and there was no public discourse that could facilitate a debate about the issues of race at variance with, and conducted in terms independent of, the government's. Neither Gramci's organicism nor his own vernacularity was yet available to Hall.

The lack of an alternate public discourse produced a critical disjuncture between the postcolonial expression and actual experience of immigration. There was a time lag because articulation followed long after physical settlement. Immigrant issues became a part of the broader British consciousness only when the Caribbean community was already in place and had been subjected routinely to white racism. In 1958, ten years after the *Empire Windrush* (the vessel that brought the first postwar Caribbean migrants to Britain) had docked, black West Indians may not have constituted a settled community, but they were certainly a group of immigrants making a place for themselves in English society. The place the immigrants were crafting for themselves in the metropolis was, however, substantially different from that of a middle-class Kingstonian scholarship boy. Hall was not only ideologically split between the two communities in which he was invested, he was separated by class from the one with which he shared a racial affinity. Hall could give critical public voice to the tensions, stresses, and precariousness inscribed within that process only retrospectively, once he had been able to resolve the issue of class and reassumed his identity as a black post/colonial.

Mugging, Policing, and Birmingham Racism

The condition of the immigrant and the vulnerabilities to which that community's members are subjected by the dominant order constitute the focus of *Policing the Crisis*. A 1978 project on which Hall collaborated with Chas Critcher, Tony Jefferson, John Clarke, and Brian Roberts, it announces Hall's entry into the politics of immigration in the metropolis. The 1978 work was conceptualized by Hall and his colleagues as an "intervention in the battleground of ideas"[67] about "mugging," racism, and the British state's deployment of its judicial apparatus against black immigrant youth. Inasmuch as Hall understands "interventions" as political engagements made with a view to transforming ideological and material conditions (*The Hard Road to Renewal* in the introduction is described as a "series of interventions" with a "cutting edge"), the arena of contestation for him is consistently that of "ideas"—and the

terrain where they are produced. In privileging the philosophical engagement over, say, an activist one, Hall is simultaneously redefining
his relationship to the immigrant community and marking out the space
on which he would conduct his struggle against the racist machinations
of the British state. The attention to ideas in *Policing the Crisis* resolves
the community activist–metropolitan intellectual bifurcation Hall experienced during the Notting Hill riots; here Hall takes on the task of representation, of speaking for the experience of the immigrant. In 1958
the activist Hall was completely disconnected from the theorist Hall.
But in *Policing the Crisis*, Hall's acknowledgment of permanent black occupancy, he is actively committed to challenging the dominant portrayals
of the immigrant community in the media from his institutional base at
CCCS, offering counterrepresentations of the black diaspora. His work
at CCCS during the Handsworth crisis established Hall as a spokesperson for black British communities and their struggles against the white
authorities.

If the intellectual is, as Edward Said argues, an "individual endowed with the faculty for representing, embodying, articulating a message, a view, an attitude, philosophy to, as well as for, a public,"[68] then
the Handsworth intervention signals a moment in which Hall does
not so much change "publics" as expand (and conjoin) them. Handsworth represents the moment when the New Left intellectual converts
Gramsci into postimperial praxis: Hall transcends his 1958 mode of
(unarticulated) activism and not only achieves an organicism—a linking
with the black immigrant experience—but also acquires a popular sense
of the workings and consequences of everyday racism—and its effects for
immigrants from Handsworth to Notting Hill. Moreover, Hall now
addresses the dominant public differently with a new message and from
a changed philosophical perspective. Hall, in this moment, seeks to
embody for the British media and the country's left the experiences of a
community subjected to routine harassment. Intervention has become
for Hall a matter of utilizing his professional training in the cause of the
immigrant community he is attempting to integrate himself into. Hall's
work as a cultural theorist and member of the political left is a means of

overcoming his historic alienation from the Caribbean community in order to refashion himself as a vernacular intellectual. Although Hall had been incapable of publicly mapping the contours of the black immigrant experience in the late 1950s, in the 1970s he was able to adapt his work to fit the demands of the postcolonial paradigm—first, like James, as an organic and then as a vernacular intellectual—that was being established in England. In the process of reconstructing himself as an intellectual Hall became a spokesperson—in the academy, in the British left—for the experiences, expectations, visions, and struggles of the community he had so long been racially from (even if only nominally so), but only partially and contingently of. The vernacular Hall had come to represent the black British community, to speak for them, in their name, as he slowly identified with them more than he did with the predominantly white New Left.

In acquiring his blackness, Hall also came to speak for a condition that had long been alien to him. By breaking with the "ritualized" intellectual tradition he was situated in and by publicly championing the cause of the black diaspora, Hall self-consciously aligned himself with a political constituency he had slowly, but surely, come to embrace, and a community where he ideologically and metaphorically, if not literally, belonged. The constituency he had not known in Kingston, the community he had only transiently embraced in Notting Hill, these were the people for whom he now spoke. It was through their presence, through representing them, that Hall publicly and vernacularly assumed his blackness. Handsworth marks the initial stage in Hall's vernacularity, an intellectual identity that he would fully develop in the next decade through his work in cultural studies, identity politics, and the cultural struggles he advocated, recognized, and supported in *The Hard Road to Renewal*. In accepting vernacular responsibilities, Hall conceived himself differently as an intellectual. His work now spoke differently because it spoke from a different place and for a different (or additional) constituency.

In both James's and Hall's cases, vernacularity emerges out of the crisis in and of black life that cannot be addressed by these intellectuals in prevailing left paradigms. Vernacularity is, for both these figures, founded on the need to relocate the left intellectual self: to explore new theoretical possibilities, take up new positions, and, most importantly, to recognize the increasing inefficacy of the current political modality. In Hall's case it also produced a congealing of developments. Through and because of the Handsworth crisis, Hall set in motion his reconstruction as an intellectual: he brought together his New Left intellectual base (CCCS), his theoretical rethinkings (Gramsci, Althusser), and then began the process of overcoming his alienation from blackness. Seeking an unprecedented (Gramscian) organicism, Hall acquired—not in its stead but because of it—the beginnings of a resonant, efficacious vernacularity. Hall became not only a black postcolonial intellectual, but a postcolonial black intellectual who understood the politics of the black popular. The New Left's cultural studies had prepared him to appreciate the politics of the popular, but Handsworth inflected these insights with race, the crucial component his work had heretofore lacked.

Hall cowrote *Policing the Crisis* in order to combat the unexpectedly harsh sentences for mugging handed down against three teenagers, Paul Storey, Mustafa Fuat, and James Duignan, from Handsworth, an inner-city Birmingham community. Of the youths, Storey and Fuat had "immigrant" profiles, the former's father was a West Indian and the latter's family had "Cypriot connections," while Duignan lived on a street deemed a "'Mini United Nations.'"[69] Hall and his coauthors, who never lose sight of the painful experience suffered by the elderly mugging victim Robert Keenan, offer no doubt as to why they are conducting this analysis of mugging. "We *are* concerned with 'mugging,'" they argue, "as a social phenomenon, rather than as a particular form of street crime. We want to know what the social causes of 'mugging' are.... More important is why British society *reacts to mugging*, in the extreme way it does, at that precise historical juncture—the early 1970s."[70] The CCCS collective's concerns focused on the phenomenon of mugging because it recognized that the extreme criminalization of this act can only be grasped by locating the vituperativeness of the dominant public's response within the moment of the "early 1970s." *Policing the Crisis* is an engagement with the "moral panic" mentality that was being generated by the local politicians and the mainstream media around the Handsworth youth. The moral panic was, in the collective's understanding, the media/state/police's exaggeration of the threat of mugging so as to legitimate a disproportionately punitive reaction to not so much the crime but the perpetrators, young black immigrants.[71] The call for increased policing of this "new" form of street crime coincides with the emergence of the second generation of immigrants in the late 1960s and early 1970s Britain.

The "precise historical conjuncture" that Hall and his coauthors identify is crucial because it marks a generational shift and a radical transition from one form of being an immigrant in England to another. Unable to make a place for themselves in broader British society, first-generation Caribbean immigrants turned inward, resuscitating the memory of island life as a defense against their current alienation.[72] The second generation, however, "emerging from the difficult experience of an English education into a declining labour market were in a quite different mood. The better equipped, educated, skilled, languaged and acculturated they were, the sharper their perceptions of the realities of discrimination and institutionalised racism, the more militant their consciousness."[73] Members of this second generation, Storey and Fuat were not among its "better equipped" or "educated." Rather, as inner-city youths they were studies in the changing composition of the English inner city and the structural disenfranchisement of the area. Handsworth, once the most desirable place to live in Britain's second city, was now home to ethnic minorities, Birmingham's white underclass, and discontented black youth, communities who shared—in varying degrees—the experience of joblessness and hopelessness. There could be no surer index of the neighborhood's 1960s decline. Handsworth was, as Paul Storey's mother acerbically put it, a "lousy area."[74] Although Storey (who did not know his West Indian father) and Fuat did not belong to the upper strata of second-generation immigrants, they were nonetheless representative of their generation's racialized understanding of its place in English society. The "militant consciousness" of these boys was steeped in the "realities of discrimination and institutionalised racism" of their generation; it was their daily experience of life in the English Midlands.

Policing the Crisis, in its most conceptually astute moments, marks a philosophical intervention in the process of immigrant representation. Hall and his colleagues not only are protesting the disproportionately harsh sentences meted out to the youths, but also are intent upon exploring the relations between the rising militancy in the black community and the "moral panic," a process that allowed Hall to make common cause with other black immigrants. The roots and influences of this militancy, however, could not be accounted for simply as an expression of black Britain's anger at its impoverishment, alienation, and disenfranchisement. It was also a sociopolitical force informed in its strategies by an international black revolutionary moment. Paul Gilroy points out that black Britain, because it had a very recent history of immigration (mostly post–World War II), was especially dependent on radical disenfranchised influences from outside. Hall and Gilroy's community was, of course, not unlike other communities in the colonies and the diaspora that needed to borrow from black groups who had longer histories of sustained opposition with numerous occasions of spectacular resistance. This recognition, however, in no way detracts from Gilroy's argument in *The Black Atlantic* that "black Britain has been heavily reliant on the output of black populations elsewhere for the raw materials from which its own distinctive, cultural and political identities could be assembled."[75] Not unlike those other anticolonial and diasporic communities, black immigrants in Britain looked across the Atlantic for "raw materials" and political solutions. "The cultures of black America," Gilroy reminds us, "have also supplied political language to the world-wide black public. First the rhetoric of rights and justice, then the discourse of Black Power crossed the seas and enabled black folks here, there and everywhere to make sense of the segregation, oppression and exploitation they experienced in their countries of residence."[76]

African-American models of resistance were especially useful for black Britons in that they came with a rich history and traditions that were girded by centuries of struggle. African-American 1960s cultural creativity, political resistance, and the Black Power movement spearheaded by the militant Black Panthers provided West Indians with a range of strategies. The various African-American modes of struggle increased the resources available to blacks in Handsworth and Brixton, those communities that had for decades been subjected to "segregation, oppression and exploitation." The "black American rebellions," Hall remembers, gave rise to a "powerful and regenerated 'black consciousness'" among the inner-city Caribbean youth.[77] In varying ways, Storey, Fuat, and Hall were participants in a transatlantic black cultural, political, and ideological movement that provided them with an enlarged sense of community, a process that transcended national boundaries because both were grounded in the material and cultural deprivations of their respective experiences. Ironically, the black transatlantic connection between Handsworth and Harlem proved strangely appropriate because the British police imported the labeling of the crime and definition of *mugging* wholesale from the United States—an attendant racism, of course, in toto.

The rationale for a "law-and-order society" that erupted out of the mugging crisis and concentrated itself around the three inner-city youths was a response to a more profound crisis in British society, a crisis about the failure of the Keynesian welfare state and "'social authority.'" "The degree of success in the exercise of hegemony—leadership based on consent, rather than the excess of force—has to do, in part," Hall writes, "precisely with success in the overall management of society; and this is more and more difficult as the economic conditions become more perilous."[78] In a Britain where a depressed Midlands region—with its outmoded industrial base—typified the nation's "perilous" economic conditions, it was clear that the postwar Keynesian pact was being renegotiated in a Britain that had become a second-tier economic power.

The Changing Culture of the Diaspora

The socioeconomic crisis that marked the decline of Keynesianism produced its response, using as its basis the 1960s and 1970s racist, anti-immigrant Enoch Powell rhetoric, in Thatcherism. Thatcher's was a political philosophy that strove for hegemony even as it took as a founding principle the exercise of state-sponsored coercion against those constituencies—immigrants, gays, those sections of the working class it could not co-opt or silence, and so on—who challenged its Powellian conception of the British nation. Black Britons would come to bear the brunt of this increased state-sponsored repression. The police brutality during the Tottenham riots of 1985 was such that one could easily have been in a South African black township where there was an insurrection going on at the very same moment. "The water cannon and the plastic bullet," favorites of the South African police, had "quietly take[n] their place in the repertoire of normal policing." Enoch Powell may have been personally defeated, but Powellism succeeded "because his official eclipse was followed by legislating into effect much of what he proposed ... [and] because of the magical connections and short-circuits which Powellism was able to establish between the themes of race and immigration control and images of nation, the British people and the destruction of 'our culture, our way of life'"[79] Powell privileged the discourse of nation above class, a strategy refined by Thatcherism, so that he could invoke Britain as an unfissured white "nation"—rather than as an economically stratified society—under attack by immigrant hordes.[80]

The Handsworth mugging of Keenan demonstrated how the demographics of England's cities were rapidly changing. Handsworth was symbolic of how immigrants were forcing the historic inhabitants of England's urban areas to seek refuge in suburbs beyond the city limits. Handsworth became the story of how England's inner-city neighborhoods were no longer safe for their traditional inhabitants. Expunged from the Powellian narrative during the 1960s and early 1970s and inserted into the Hallian one in its most incisive form in the critiques of Thatcherism was the relationship among economic and imperial decline and anti-immigrant racism. Writing on the early 1980s Falkland crisis, but relevant to the Handsworth moment, Hall reflects on these connections: "As the country drifts deeper into recession, we seem to possess no other viable vocabulary in which to cast our sense of who the British are and where they are going, except one drawn from an inventory of lost imperial greatness."[81] Powell's vocabulary fit Hall's description exactly, relying on an all-too-easily-recalled memory of "lost imperial greatness." At the Handsworth conjuncture, the danger of Powell's bleached logic was that his racist national profile—and his struggle to preserve the national identity—became a lightning rod for appeals for increased coercion. Law and order as it existed in the late 1960s and 1970s was outmoded, suited to conditions when "'our [homogeneous] way of life'" was the only way of life. Now, however, law-and-order practices needed to be brought into line with the new heterogeneous urban realities. Handsworth 1972 was symptom enough of a nation distorted, wrenched out of racial shape, culturally bastardized.

August 1972 brought home to Hall, his colleagues, first- and second-generation immigrants, if not to the Labour Party and the British left in general, how deeply Powellian logic had permeated the nation's psyche. This particular moment marked not only the Handsworth mugging, and the subsequent outcry, but also the intensification of the anti-immigration campaign. The targets of the campaign were a group of British subjects—African Asians—who were being persecuted on racial grounds by the rulers of newly independent African states. "Without pressing the conjuncture too far or too hard," Hall argues, "it is worth noting that the beginning of the panic about a new 'deluge' of Ugandan Asians and the panic about 'mugging' occurred in the same month: August 1972."[82] August 1972 constituted a major crisis for the immigrant community, and the magnitude of that crisis can be measured in terms of the dramatic shift toward race it effected in Hall's work.

Hall's ability to produce a public critique of race depended heavily on the impact of postcoloniality in the metropolis. In fact, besides his admiration for the second-generation immigrants' determination to claim a space for themselves in English life as a whole rather than confine themselves to their urban ghettoes, the multiple ways in which the black community committed itself to the postcolonial metropolis accelerated Hall's achievement of a critical racial consciousness. The immigrant settlements in London and Birmingham made imperative updated socio-political readings because the experiences of the new arrivals barely cor-responded with any of the paradigms that Hall had used in his earlier work. The Leavisite approaches to culture, a Marxism without a racial component, and the Anglo-centered politics of the New Left were all inappropriate models for engaging postcolonialism in England. Within the paradigm Hall had been developing, the conditions under which working-class immigrant communities adapted themselves to English life could be analyzed most incisively by the theorizing of race and post-colonialism through culture. After Handsworth, and its theorization in *Policing the Crisis*, cultural studies located the question of race within the context of social practices. Racism could be investigated in terms of how cultural traditions enabled immigrant communities to position themselves on the English landscape, to survive the hostilities, preju-dices, and marginalizations they were subjected to, and how immigrant communities transformed themselves from ghetto alienation into viable political blocs.

While alienation and disenfranchisement are but two of the chal-lenges endemic to a marginal position within the body politic of the metropolis, it is not a condition approached uniformly by different gener-ations of immigrants. Within the immigrant community, first- and second-generation members had markedly different conceptions of their Eng-lishness, so that a major contestation ensued about the place of blacks in English society. The first generation's children were instrumental in the process by which race found critical expression in Hall's work, because he recognized that this group took on the challenge of living, physically and psychically, as blacks in England. The second-generation immi-grants are the urban colony's "first true progeny. They have no other home. Their parents are the bearers of that double consciousness com-mon to all migrant classes in the period of transition; the second gener-ation is the bearer of the exclusive consciousness of the black 'colony.'"[83]

The new immigrant generation's preoccupation with racial consciousness, as opposed to their parents' reliance on a "cultural double consciousness," manifested itself as a challenge to entrenched modes of racism, to confronting white England with its colonial past and how the colonial project had resulted in the deracination and resettlement of colonized peoples. However, Hall writes soberly of the risks this generation runs. "Sooner or later," he says, "the front line troops, with their superior weapons and sophisticated responses, will corner some of our young people on a dark night along one of those walkways and take their revenge for Tottenham."[84] Issued in the 1980s, Hall's caution to the newest (third) generation of immigrants is premised upon his embracing of the immigrant community: he has situated himself fully within the community so that the protesting Brixton youth have become "our young people." Although Hall has always been critical of "their" "front line troops" and "superior weapons," in this instance his iteration marks less an antimilitarism than a commitment to the black community; this is what motivates his concern for the violent retribution Caribbean youth can expect if they challenge the system. The lessons of Handsworth, the acquisition of a new, solidifying organicism and a growing vernacularity, articulate themselves in the discourse of a black postcolonial intellectual. The Jamaican colonial has, in an ontological sense, come home—he has relocated himself, albeit with difficulty, within the black immigrant experience. Hall is, in Derrida's sense, finally able to speak his name as black, diasporic, interpellated postcolonial subject. Having "iterated" his (new) name, he can now inhabit the metropolis as a disjunctive—with a rooted "white" political history that is critically transcended through his participation in the *Policing* project—vernacular intellectual—the black subject with a New Left past.

Unlike the initial Caribbean generation, which sought to counter English racial exclusivity with an enhanced cultural inclusivity of their own, their children and grandchildren are determined to live an unabbreviated Englishness even while in possession of a racially qualified national identity. The urban colony's offspring were prepared to demonstrate the full effects of what happens when (post)colonialism's chickens claimed the entire metropolitan roost, and not just the small coop allotted to them, as their home. The children (and grandchildren) of a community compelled into an alienated ideological and spatial settlement, they resist the replication of the old but not outdated colonial paradigm in the metropolis even as they are made to live out its geographical arrangements. While the hegemonic group seeks to (dis)qualify the second generation's national identity with their race, its very structures of domination (education, the media, electoral politics) school them in the practices of Englishness. Every time the education system, the courts, the Enoch Powells, or the media remind young blacks how their Englishness is "truncated," they inadvertently conceptualize a national ideal against which the Handsworth youth define their relations to England. Immigrant youth are black in the British nation, sometimes culturally constitutive of it (frequently imitated for the ability to function as cultural trendsetters), but only rarely fully accepted by the ruling bloc.[85]

Meanwhile, the "'native quarter' at the heart of the English city" constituted a training ground in immigrant cultural and political assertiveness, a site that provided the "material and social basis for a new kind of consciousness—an internally integrated black cultural identity. Black people were struggling to make ends meet, permanent migrants in a land not their own—but they were no longer apologetic for being what they were: West Indian people, with a homeland and a patrimony, and black with it."[86] In *Policing the Crisis* Hall positioned himself so that he could cross and recross the divide that at once separated and connected parents and children across the barriers of experiential difference and common heritage. Indeed, in mapping the trajectory from the first to the second generation Hall inadvertently duplicated his own route from the outskirts of colony life to a fuller interaction with that community. As a first-generation immigrant, he was atypical of that community. Removed from the ordinary West Indian immigrant of his generation by class and academic training, Hall wrote *Policing the Crisis* as an attempt to align himself with the difficulties of the second generation, to observe and possibly emulate their strategies for finding their own place in English society, a project he was himself embarking upon anew. *Policing the*

Crisis marks Hall's difficult path toward black vernacularity through (cultural and political) organicism.

He writes admiringly of the "fact that young black people in London today are marginalized, fragmented, unenfranchised, disadvantaged and dispersed. And yet they look as if they own the territory. Somehow, they too, in spite of everything, are centered, in place: without much material support, it's true, but nevertheless, they occupy a new kind of space at the centre."[87] In precisely this spirit of immigrant assertion and under conditions where "young black people"—despite their historic deprivations and material impoverishment—and other marginal communities are energetic, culturally dynamic, and politically aggressive Hall fashioned *The Hard Road to Renewal* as an ideologically creative rewriting of his relationship to the center.

Rethinking Class

If the New Left and *The Popular Arts* represent a Hall preoccupied with working-class culture, and *Policing the Crisis* marks his first serious engagement with race, black organicism, and vernacularity, then *The Hard Road to Renewal* stands as a text that simultaneously brings together and transcends the previous two paradigms. Comprised of a series of essays over ten years, 1978 to 1988, it records the struggles and achievements of an intellectual who is attempting to speak to and for both the working-class and immigrant blacks, but is also committed to rethinking the efficacy of "class" and the de-essentializing of "race" as political categories. (It should be said, however, that the accent in this collection of essays—three of which are cowritten—is more on the former than the latter, though race remains a vital and vibrant mode of analysis.) *The Hard Road to Renewal* is "predicated on the end of conventional wisdom that there is a simple, irreversible correspondence between the economic and the political, or that classes, constituted as homogeneous entities at the economic or 'mode of production' level, are transported in their already unified form onto the 'theatre' of political and ideological struggle."[88] In a postindustrial, technologically advanced, global economy, the classically economic understanding of class on its own cannot explain the (often unexpected) ways in which structurally disenfranchised or dispossessed or marginal persons act.

For Hall (as for James), class is a political category that can assist in that explanation, but not the single mode of critical analysis. Hall, however critical he is of class reductionism, never abandons the category. Not only do material conditions dictate that class be understood in its complex, anti-economistic manifestation, but the ideological terrain in Britain necessitates such an approach. Thatcher's ideology produced a remaking of the political landscape in Britain that led to the "recomposition and 'fragmentation' of the historic relations between classes and parties." One of the consequences of Thatcherism's "shifting boundaries between state and civil society, 'public' and 'private'" was that it opened up "new arenas of contestation, new sites of social antagonism" and introduced "new social movements, and new subjects and political identities in[to] contemporary society." With this reconfiguration of political constituencies, it is important to forge alliances with the "new social movements"; those groups who organize around race, sexual orientation, gender, environmental issues. Hall, borrowing from Gramsci, regards these emerging constituencies as historical "blocs" constructed out of a range of heterogeneous communities. "A social bloc is, by definition, not homogeneous. It does not," Hall argues in "Blue Election, Election Blues," "consist of one whole class or even part of one class. It has to be constructed out of groups which are very different in terms of their material interests and social positions."[89]

Thatcherism's victorious "social blocs" were built out of the disarticulation of traditional loyalties in which the Tories appealed across class lines to the anachronistic and ideologically bankrupt notion of a homogeneous nation, one with a glorious imperial past that was all too easily invoked in the Falklands war. "Empires come and go. But the imagery of the British Empire," Hall laments, "seems destined to go on forever." In "The Empire Strikes Back," an essay that critiques the British invasion of the Falklands, Hall reflects on the powerful residues of the colonial past: "The imperial flag has been hauled down in a hundred different corners of the globe. But it is still flying in the collective unconscious." More importantly, however, is Hall's uncovering of the moral and ideological bankruptcy at the heart of Britain's "collective unconscious." Hall's antipathy toward residual British colonialism is made manifest through an irony that is sharp and acerbic. The country is "going to war for a scatter of islands eight thousand miles away, so integral a part of the British *Imperium*, so fixed in our hearts, that we have not managed to build a decent road across the place or to provide it with a continuous source of power." Race played a crucial role in the construction of Tory social blocs because the "imagery" of nation and empire were premised upon the exclusion of the "alien [black] wedge" responsible for the "dilution of British stock."[90] Thatcherism's ability to create and maintain these political alliances is central to the Conservative Party's repeated electoral victories. "Blue Election, Election Blues," written in the wake of the Tories' third consecutive triumph at the polls (this despite an uncharacteristically sound campaign by then–Labour Party leader Neil Kinnock), is underwritten by an injunction to the left to reflect assiduously on Thatcherism, which resonates throughout this work. Nowhere is that caution more explicitly contained than in the title of the essay, "Learning from Thatcherism."

Hall's reconsidered analyses of class and his reading of the second generation's struggle to overcome racial marginalization, economic disenfranchisement, and cultural degradation prepared him to critique, from the late 1970s on, the phenomenon of Thatcherism from an unusual position on the British left: he vigorously opposed Margaret Thatcher's policies by taking her ideological accomplishments so seriously as to respect them. In "Learning from Thatcherism" he states this position plainly: "Unless the left can understand Thatcherism, it cannot renew itself because it cannot understand the world it must live in if it is not to be 'disappeared' into permanent marginality. It is time, therefore, in the context of rethinking, to make clear exactly what is understood by 'learning from Thatcherism.'" *The Hard Road to Renewal* represents a concerted effort to first execute precisely that political function, to "learn" from it, and then to contest Thatcher's hegemony. Hegemony is constructed out of a number of "different spheres at once—economy, civil society, intellectual and moral life; culture"; the anti-Thatcher struggle is therefore one that has to be equally multifarious.[91]

To contest Thatcherism implies not only the reconceptualization and rearticulation of the very ground on which the left must conduct its political struggle, but a firm grasp of how significantly the conditions of struggle have been changed by the Thatcherism. Hall's reconceptualization of Marxism in this decade frequently brought him into contention with the militant or "classist" sector of the British left. Hall often found himself debating, in public and in print, "hard" left thinkers such as Jessop (one of the essays in *The Hard Road to Renewal*, "Authoritarian Populism: A Reply to Jessop et al.," is, as the title suggests, a direct engagement with one of his critics), A. Sivanandan, and Meiskins Wood. Frequently critiqued for his rendering of culture, Hall became the leading figure of the "cultural" left in its battle with the "hard" left for whom cultural struggle, cultural politics, and identity politics constituted a capitulation to capitalist forces, if not an outright betrayal of Marxism. Hall was frequently taken to task for claiming that he could speak, however complicatedly, in the name of Marxism. However, for Hall Marxism has never represented an orthodoxy but a means of conducting politics, and he was, unlike his critics, less invested in occupying the Marxist (and moral, we might even say) high ground than he was committed to finding the necessary means to understand and oppose Thatcherism. This approach to Marxism often turned on critiquing and issuing ideological challenges to a Labour Party (the main and most viable left organ in British politics—Hall has never sought the Jamesian margins) Hall sometimes considered moribund, often doctrinaire, and all too frequently unimaginative and unwilling to take into account or adapt some of the cultural strategies that abounded in various sectors of working-, lower-, and middle-class British life.

Hall's critique is that the Labour Party–led left, in equal measure despite and because of the struggle over the "soul" of the movement (the purge of the hard left, the rise of New Labour, events in which he was himself involved via his contributions to *Marxism Today* and the "New Times" project), has been found wanting in regard to the cultural struggle. In his view the new social movements and vibrant political organizations such as the Greater London Council (GLC) have taken up the Thatcherite challenge. The GLC represents a particularly energetic forum for political democracy that the Labour Party lacks: "The dingdong, complaint, pressure, pushing-and-response, the negotiation in public forums between the movements and the politicians is the positive sound of a real, as opposed to a phoney and pacified democracy at work. It is also a positive recognition of the necessary tension in the contradictory relations between civil society and the state." The dynamic engagement and ebullient participation by GLC members that Hall celebrates in this essay made the Irish rock star Bob Geldof's Live Aid a politically successful project. Geldof, whose "rock connections were his political credentials," organized a social movement in which the "combination of culture and politics, altruism and fun, was irresistible. The link between rock culture and politics is not, of course, new—it was a powerful element in the politics of the 1960s. Rock Against Racism, the GLC's cultural politics and Red Wedge are more recent examples from the left. But the sheer scale and ambition of Live Aid was unprecedented. Never had 'pop' politics created and shaped a whole movement in this way."[92]

If *Policing the Crisis* marks Hall's entrée into vernacularity, *The Hard Road to Renewal* represents the maturation of that process. In this text, especially the penultimate section, "Crisis and Renewal of the Left," Hall's 1980s vernacularity—by now firmly grounded in and by his affiliation to black immigrant communities—integrates "race" (without ignoring the specific conditions that Afro-Caribbean, South Asian, and African communities face in postimperial Britain) into broader popular cultural struggles. In this moment the vernacular becomes, for Hall, a transcendent category, the rooting of the New Left–trained, newly configured black postcolonial intellectual in a series of contiguous relationships: race and popular culture coexist, attended to not so much in equal measure as with regard to moment, which struggle demands the most urgent attention. Or, how do these various constituencies, as they often did in this period in their battle against Thatcherism, work cooperatively?

How do they inform, remake, or reinforce each other? The narrowly dialectical moment represented by *Policing the Crisis* is supplanted in the later text by the collaborative project. Afro-Caribbean communities and disenchanted white Labour Party members could work together in the GLC, or the latter could support the former in its campaign against police brutality; always, of course, propelled by Hall's sense that the popular is where the most dynamic articulation of politics is taking place. However, as various of the essays of this period demonstrate, Hall's is a strategic vernacularity: he recognizes that in certain moments, the interests of immigrant "blocs" may be more, or not as, important as that of class or generalized cultural struggles. Hall's vernacularity negotiates among the various political demands of the constituencies with whom he is affiliated.

The theoretical and civic grounds prepared by Hoggart in *The Uses of Literacy* melds, in *The Hard Road to Renewal*, with Gramsci's understanding of political struggle—recognizing the appropriate modality of intervention, war of position or war of maneuver—girding much of Hall's text. In the 1980s Hallian vernacular, questions of race and popular continue to jostle each other, always in an intellectually provocative way. *The Hard Road to Renewal* represents the difficult, attentive reconciliation of race, Hall's New Left legacy, his commitment to Marxism, and his investment in the popular: these various elements combine in Hall's intellectual composition to make the vernacular more efficacious, cohesive, and complicated than anywhere else in his writing.

The ability of GLC, Geldof's Live Aid, and Rock Against Racism to renovate and reinvigorate the British left represents the kind of "radical renewal"—"our capacities to reimagine the future"—that the Labour Party so obviously lacks. Inasmuch as *The Hard Road to Renewal* is a critical engagement with Thatcherism, it is also an attack on the ideological inadequacies of the Labour Party. Labour's continued investment in an economistic understanding of class, where it adheres to the belief that there is an "inevitable or guaranteed link between class origin and political ideas," has rendered the party unable to become a truly popular, hegemonic political institution capable of protecting and furthering the interests of the working class or the working poor, to say nothing of its inability to reverse the condition of the unemployed. (Mired in the "Narodnikist" predicament, the unquestioning belief that the working class is always already socialist, that all that is required by the party is that they listen to their constituents and articulate their positions, Labour and its intellectual sponsors cannot—according to Hall—see that conditions have become antagonistic to that form of struggle, to say nothing of its anachronism as an electoral strategy. Conditions have been so altered by global economic restructuring and Thatcherism's capacity to translate those conditions into a conservative hegemony that it is now "inconceivable that the left could ever become a hegemonic historical force again without undergoing a cultural revolution of some kind."[93]

As is consistently the critique in the post-1978 Hallian era, the crisis within the left produced by Thatcherism requires a massive rethinking, the Gramscian "renewal" that will make possible a new alignment of political forces; a new historical bloc, which recognizes how conditions of ideological struggle have changed, must be constructed in order to fundamentally change the way in which the left does politics and, as important, how it conducts the business of governing once it assumes power. Hall, often identified by the hard left as an ideological factor in Tony Blair coming to power (if not as an ideologue for Blairism), confronted this issue in the mid-1990s with the rise of New Labour. Because Blair recognized, and acted on, how Thatcherism had reconstituted the very terrain of British politics (especially the future prime minister's ability to attend to cultural politics and his determination to renovate the party), Hall has frequently been cited as a Blair supporter. However, while Blair may have grasped the import of Hall's critiques of Old Labour (whatever such a designation may imply), Hall has been more wary of the new leader.

Dubbing Blair, with an ideological accuracy and a stinging rhetorical flourish, "The Son of Margaret?" Hall warned in 1995—two years before Labour came to office and maybe four or five years before the effect of Blair's conservatism fully manifested itself—of the consequences of a party not committed to drastic social transformation. While Hall credits the "Blair revolution" for its ability to modernize Labour, he is much more concerned about the Thatcherite influence: "A Labour government that cannot spend an extra penny on health, education, public housing, community, family and caring services, transport and a strategic element of security in the labour market, is not worth voting for."[94] This indictment from an intellectual who, while advocating the renewal of Labour for almost two decades, is here warning about the dangers of a Blair government is telling. Hall's prescience would, of course, prove prophetic—"One law of the Medes and Persians is that Labour is always more cautious, more conservative, in office than before it. What it does not campaign about beforehand, it will be mastered and driven by afterwards"—and it brought forcefully home to him, after his critiques in *The Hard Road to Renewal,* how great the disjuncture between the language of renovation and the implementation of genuinely new policy.[95] The critical imperative of *The Hard Road to Renewal,* after all, is to claim political territory for the left that will enable it not only to contest Thatcherism, on its own grounds and terms, if necessary, but to defeat it and transform left politics in toto. This is the part of the Hall lesson that Blair never took, and never intended to take, to heart.

The Hard Road to Renewal, perturbed as it is by Labour's four consecutive electoral failures, sought—as Hall makes clear in his 1995 essay—to accomplish significantly more than an improvement in Labour's electoral fortunes (mindful though he was of the importance of defeating the Tories at the polls.) He is, however, especially opposed to the left's inability to incorporate the "innovative character of the "'new politics'" of the GLC and the other new social movements into its political platforms. Cultural politics, the expansion of the sites of political struggle and sources of political energy, represents the primary means by which the left can renew itself. Motivated by the same goal, the identification of the failures of the Labour Party in order to re-create and rejuvenate the party and its component constituencies, *The Hard Road to Renewal* reads like a series of individual addresses to the British left, a critique of its inability to comprehend Thatcherism as an ideological formation. The essays (most of which are republications of works that first appeared in *Marxism Today* and the *New Socialist*) are characterized by a directness—"The rising fortunes of Thatcherism were tied to the tail of Labour's failing ones"—and specificity that, while not unusual in the Hall oeuvre, achieve a distillation unprecedented in his work.[96] The sense of urgency about the 1988 work derives from the way in which it speaks to immediate issues—the success and the lessons to be drawn from the Live Aid project, praise for GLC democracy, and strategies for refashioning of the Labour Party. *The Hard Road to Renewal* is Hall at his most interventionist, at his most determined to theoretically conceive of a culturally vibrant, ideologically attuned left politics.

The Hard Road to Renewal stands as the text most representative of Hall's intellectual position. While *The Popular Arts* (a committed but theoretically underdeveloped conception of popular culture) and *Policing the Crisis* (the coming to racial consciousness) focus on individual issues that are central to Hall's work, the 1988 text integrates and amplifies the concerns of the previous two books. The chronological arrangement of *The Hard Road to Renewal* is, in this regard, crucial because it opens with an extract from *Policing the Crisis;* traverses the terrain of black immigration, culture, racial politics, and postcoloniality; and finally emerges as a serious engagement with the politics of identity. By starting with "Living with the Crisis," in which he identifies one of the "four principal aspects of the 1972–1976 conjuncture as the direct interpellation of the race issue into the crisis of British civil and political life," Hall establishes the groundwork that will enable him to attack Thatcher's policy on black immigrants.[97]

The constant refrain from *Policing the Crisis*, "the drift into a law-and-order society," finds a resounding echo in *The Hard Road to Renewal*'s "Cold Comfort Farm," Hall's response to the Tottenham disturbances. The essay makes the link between the two texts and experiences explicit. The British police "have become, as many of us predicted ten years ago," he writes, "Mrs Thatcher's 'boys'—the front line in the crisis of British cities." The connections between Handsworth and Tottenham, Birmingham 1972, and a mid-1980s London are clearly drawn. Conditions of

immigrant life, Hall charges, have changed so little materially and ideologically as to render the two historical moments all too recognizable
to each other. Black Britons still constitute, despite their prolonged
presence and their transformative effects on British culture, an "'alien
wedge'"—at the "bottom of th[e] pile ... the dispossessed, the excluded."[98] As much as *The Hard Road to Renewal* marks a transcendent,
inclusive vernacularity, so the text shows itself to be founded on an un-
shakable commitment to critiquing conditions of black metropolitan life.

The Hard Road to Renewal records the transformations of Hall as an
intellectual. He has become a settled, engaged, metropolitan intellectual
and has successfully negotiated an intellectual space from which he can
maneuver the competing claims of the white metropolitan left and the
black immigrant community. More than that, however, *The Hard Road to
Renewal* maps Hall's reinterpellation into the life of the British left. This
time Hall, through his work in the New Left, at Birmingham, at the
Open University (which he joined in 1980 as professor of sociology), and
as critic of the Labour Party, achieved a public prominence from a very
different position. On this occasion, Hall has claimed an agency for himself that bears little resemblance to his interpellation as a member of
the New Left where he was defined as intellectual—the roles he could
occupy, the groups whose interests he was invested in, the publics he
could address— by the (homogeneous) movement. Hall now approaches
the British left as a fluid collection of constituencies who can all be
engaged—simultaneously or discretely, essentially or strategically, as the
need arises.

Completing the process that was initiated with *Policing the Crisis*,
he made race a central aspect of his intellectual profile so that he positioned himself closer to black immigrants. Hall's investment in the
immigrant community obviously reflects the changing racial demographics of Britain. However, the new demographics also give voice to
the forms in which an increased black presence, and the attendant postcolonial paradigm, renders the colonial scholarship boy more of a native
and less a nonnative intellectual. Since Britain is now a heterogeneous

nation, the notion of native has been radically altered and Hall has become a representative of the competing political energies, cultural practices, and the dueling ideologies that make up the postcolonial metropolis. In the process of engaging all these dynamics, Hall has become a distinct figure: not only a metropolitan intellectual who is black, but a metropolitan intellectual who has come to terms with the political implications of his race, principally through crisis and culture, and emerged into a critical vernacularity.

CHAPTER 4

Bob Marley, Postcolonial Sufferer

Ethiopia, the tyrant's falling,
Who smote thee upon thy knees,
And thy children are lustily calling
From over the distant seas.

—Burrell and Ford, "The Universal Ethiopian Anthem"

The Song Remains the Same

If Stuart Hall came to race through crisis and culture, Bob Marley understood, from his earliest days in their shared homeland, that race was culture. Race and culture were lived indistinguishably in the yards of Trenchtown, where Marley learned about music, history, politics, and religion, a part of Kingston unknown to Hall until he made acquaintance with his countryman's music in London. This was a metropolis where Marley himself spent a great deal of time practicing his craft, a locale from which, during his exile from Jamaica, he became an internationally recognized musician. Dreadlocked and speaking unapologetically in a uniquely black Jamaican patois, Bob Marley introduced the world to reggae, a completely new brand of music. Blended from the mix of traditional African rhythms and drumming techniques (the legacy of slavery), an exaggerated backbeat, black Caribbean musical innovation, and 1950s and 1960s black American soul, Marley's lyrics championed the right of poor people in the Third World.[1] He sang about freedom from economic exploitation, physical degradation, and moral debasement. Reggae's spiritual source was Rastafarianism, a little-known faith that was African in derivation with a small band of loyal adherents in the Caribbean. As a religion Rastafarianism was Coptic in that it held God to be at once both "divine and human."[2] "Mighty God is a living man" is how Marley defined the unique divinity of his faith, one that held God to be the living Ethiopian emperor Haile Selassie I. The great cultural achievement of Rastafarianism was the (re)conceptualization of God as black.

In the process of cofounding (with a host of other Jamaican musicians) and popularizing reggae, Marley became more than just the Third World's first musical superstar—a feat that was of course noteworthy in and of itself. In the second half of the 1970s he became widely recognized as one of the region's preeminent and most highly regarded spokesperson. Writing on Marley as a postcolonial figure, with a particular focus on Africa and a hint of hyperbole, Eusi Kwayama puts this aspect of the reggae star's status in perspective: "Bob Marley's music has done more to popularise the real issues in the African liberation movement than several decades of backbreaking work by Pan-Africanists and international revolutionaries."[3] It is appropriate that in a career filled with stirring shows, from his native Kingston to New York to London, the signal performance of Marley's life should have occurred in the Third World.

At the stroke of midnight on April 18, 1980, the southern African nation of Zimbabwe was born. Prime Minister Robert Mugabe and his people achieved its independence from imperial Britain and liberation from the white minority rule of Ian Smith's Universal Declaration of Independence (UDI) Rhodesia. At this historic event, Marley was not only the headline musical act, but also an honored guest of Mugabe's incoming black majority government. The first words spoken in Zimbabwe, as the Union Jack was lowered and the new nation's flag was raised, were, "Ladies and Gentlemen, Bob Marley and the Wailers!" As Roger Steffens, the Jamaican's unofficial archivist and historian put it, "Bob Marley opened a nation."[4] The reggae star walked out to thunderous applause when he and his band took the stage at Rufaro Stadium in Harare. Following the sonorous bass of the Wailers' Aston "Family Man" Barrett and the "Viva Zimbabwes!" of assorted Wailers, Marley broke into "Natural Mystic":

> There's a Nat'ral Mystic blowing through the air,
> If you listen carefully now, you will hear.

This could be the first trumpet,
Might as well be the last.
Many more will have to suffer,
Many more will have to die.
Don't ask me why.
Things are not the way they used to be.
I won't tell no lie.[5]

One of the Rastafarian anthems from his 1977 album *Exodus*, this overtly spiritual track was greeted with enthusiastic cheers by the vast crowd, which included both visiting dignitaries (such as Britain's Prince Charles and assorted heads of state) and ordinary Zimbabweans alike. Indeed, "Things [were] not the way they used to be." Zimbabwe had just become an independent nation, the fiftieth state to achieve such status in Africa, boasting a newly elected and legitimate black majority government, a black prime minister and a black president.

Marley had barely finished this song and was just starting into the anthemic "Zimbabwe" when the euphoria that had welcomed the Wailers was rudely interrupted by a commotion at the main entrance to the stadium. Outside, the Rhodesian riot police set off tear gas to quell boisterous Zimbabwe African National Liberation Army (ZANLA) guerrillas frustrated at their inability to gain access to the arena. The ZANLA fighters, who had secured the establishment of the new postcolonial state, had been inspired by the Jamaican's "Zimbabwe" during their struggle against the Rhodesian forces. They wanted to witness Marley perform in person and pay homage to him for his commitment to their cause. It was historically ironic that they were restrained by the police during the performance of the song Marley had dedicated to them. Amid this tumult, Marley and the band were hustled off the stage and to safety by their surprised hosts.

After twenty minutes or so, the concert resumed. With a spirit of unease hovering over the proceedings, Marley and the Wailers concluded their abbreviated presentation with "War." Accentuating the now-unexpectedly ominous tone underlying "Natural Mystic" ("Many more will have to suffer, / Many more will have to die"), "War" echoed more loudly the belligerence of the exchanges between the old authorities and the newly installed ones that had disrupted the Wailers' performance. The choice of "War" as the last song is intriguing, betraying at once a resolve and an uncertainty Marley and his band may have been experiencing because of the unexpected hiatus in their performance. The biggest hit from the Wailers' 1978 European bus tour, "War" is Marley's reggae transcription (almost word for word) of then Ethiopian emperor Haile Selassie's memorable address to the United Nations in San Francisco a decade earlier.

Recalling Fanon's injunction about the incendiary nature of neo-imperial race relations, Selassie spoke with passion and eloquence before the United Nations in a moment of global turmoil. The Ethiopian leader suggested that the upheaval could only be stymied and harmonious relations between and within nations restored if racial equality became an international priority. Marley transformed the emperor's script into one of the most extraordinary songs on the double album *Babylon by Bus* (a work that was the product of the Wailers' European tour in support of *Exodus*). The "anti-racism"[6] of "War" is, as is evident from the very first line, its most striking element:

> Until the philosophy
> Which holds one race superior
> And another inferior
> Is finally and permanently discredited
> And abandoned
> Everywhere is war
> Is a war
> Until there are no longer
> First class and second class citizens
> Of any nation
> Until the colour of a man's skin
> Is of no more significance

Than the colour of his eyes

Is a war[7]

"War" is both fitting and incongruous as the grand finale at a postcolonial celebration. The song was an appropriate choice because the event
marked, in one respect, the triumph of Selassie's philosophy—the final
discrediting and abandonment of the racist "philosophy" that girded Ian
Smith's Rhodesia. But it was also, given the context of the performance,
inappropriate because the premise of the song is perennial universal
(racial) conflict—"War in the East, War in the West / Everywhere is war."

However, "War" was arguably less an improper choice than a
muted critique of the brand new postcolonial government's treatment of
its barely enfranchised citizenry. Marley was deeply conscious of the
track's illustrious African and postcolonial history, so his decision to perform it prevents the song from being dismissed as simply an anachronistic battle cry. Instead, its presentation stands as a commentary on the
night's disconcerting events. Moreover, through the last line of the chorus—"Everywhere is war"—Marley issued a warning that bespeaks a rare
and insightful political prophecy. Although it did not resonate as such
on April 18, 1980, "War" was a prescient closing song because it anticipated the ideological repressions of Zimbabwe's postcolonial future.
The maintenance of the Rhodesian model, dividing the nation into first-
and second-class citizens along strict racial lines (with minor accommo-
dations for the new black elite), would give ample pause to reflect on the
musings of "War" in the postcolonial nation; the conditions of race-as-
class separation was exacerbated by the fact that within a few years there
would be "an internal power struggle" (to invoke a phrase from the song
"Zimbabwe") that would further accentuate cleavages in black Zimbabwe.

This time the fault lines were both ethnic and class-based in
character—pitting Mugabe's Shona majority against Joshua Nkomo's
Ndbele minority and poor, black Zimbabweans against the oligarchical
state. From the mid-1990s on, political life in Zimbabwe became even
more fractious as Mugabe's ideological expedience set black citizens

against other blacks, poor black war veterans against wealthy white farmers, and the state bureaucracy against gays and lesbians. The longer Mugabe has stayed in power, the more ubiquitous "War" has become in Zimbabwe. Marley was more prescient in the target of his critiques than he might have imagined—war has proliferated in Zimbabwe decades after Marley's death.

The exchange between the police and the ex-guerrillas is now long forgotten, meriting little more than a footnote in postcolonial history. At best, the episode is remembered as a mere skirmish on a rambunctious evening. However, as a moment in Marley's political career, this one incident is significant because it is so representative of the ambivalence—so absent in Ali's thinking on and conceptualization of postcolonial Africa—that marked his thinking on the postcolonial state. In Zimbabwe Marley was temporarily and awkwardly located between the hype of postcolonial celebration—and the compromises inherent to that condition—and his endemic suspicion of political leaders the world over. As an artist who self-consciously crafted himself throughout his career as a Rastafarian with an intense attachment to Africa, and as a guest and an international champion of Zimbabwean liberation, Marley could not comment directly on the disturbances even if he harbored misgivings about the situation. He could not state publicly the reservations he had about the unsettling and antidemocratic trends he feared would result. As he left the chaos of the Rufaro stage he cryptically remarked to the I-Threes (his all-women backing band), "Now we'll find out who are the *real* revolutionaries" (emphasis in original).[8]

This skepticism is a remarkably unguarded moment of political commentary for Marley. In this, the "postcolonial" (post-1977) phase of his career, the Wailers' leader very seldom allowed himself the luxury of full frontal attacks on the political institutions he opposed. Rather than engage in direct confrontation with the state, in its Babylonian (the Rastafarian metaphor for Western and colonial wickedness, immorality, and corruption) or postcolonial (though these distinctions did not always hold) manifestation, Marley's critiques were more subversively coded. Even in this instance, telling as it is, he relies on his lyrics from

"Zimbabwe" to register his political displeasure rather than making a direct intervention. For this reason the songs he performed and the order in which they were presented bear the burden of the critiques he could not deliver; his music enunciates the political reservations he could not articulate more forthrightly. It is critique through lyrical nuance, a feature of Marley's songwriting that is frequently overlooked. His choice of song was iconoclastic, but historically apropos. "War" and "Zimbabwe" compel us to examine closely the Marley performance at Rufaro Stadium in 1980. This event shows how Marley, as a radical reggae musician, is simultaneously a singularly empowered and disenfranchised cultural spokesperson in the postcolonial world. Precisely because he is venerated by the Zimbabwean leadership and its subjects, in crucial ideological moments, Marley is publicly "silenced" by his own status as postcolonial spokesperson.

The Zimbabwean independence celebrations are regularly invoked in this chapter on the reggae star as a point of postcolonial reference because they mark the apogetic moment in Marley's transformation from Jamaican Rasta to critical—in both senses of the term—Third World icon. This chapter maps that process by tracing Marley's radicalism not only to Trenchtown, that all-too-frequently romanticized Kingston locale, but to his birthplace in the parish of St. Ann's. Marley's notion of postcoloniality, his commitment to blackness as an incorporative, racially girded, transatlantic epistemology, derives from a rich Jamaican tradition of opposition to European colonialism and postindependence neocolonialism in both the Caribbean and sub-Saharan Africa. Historically Marley was heir to the legacy of Marcus Garvey, the dominant figure in preindependence Jamaican political life who had given black people in the Caribbean and the United States a powerful sense of ideological affiliation with the African continent. Garvey celebrated African history and culture and was the first black Caribbean leader to grasp the significance of Rastafarianism, forging the earliest imaginary links between a black theocracy and its symbolic importance in the diaspora.

This chapter also explores the complicated relationship between Marley and the political leadership in Jamaican society of his day. The

Rasta's vexed affinity for Prime Minister Michael Manley, the similarities and differences between these contemporaries (two of the most dominant Jamaicans of their day), are examined here within the context of a Caribbean society negotiating between the racialized residues of the colonial past and the struggle to relocate blackness—as a cultural and ideological construct mobilized in Rastafarianism—in the Jamaican public imaginary. However, while the relationship between the national and the postcolonial is crucial to this rendering of Marley as a vernacular intellectual, this chapter also offers an extensive reading of the Rasta man's music because his politics finds its most eloquent articulation there. Key to constructing Marley's vernacularity are, of course, his lyrics. Since the mid-1970s Marley's songs (and the Wailers' hits) have woven themselves indelibly into the fabric of popular music and cultural expression the world over, and so this chapter focuses on Marley as a pop postcolonial poet. As the events in Rufaro Stadium demonstrate, he is a postcolonial griot who possesses an acute sense of moment and a firm grasp of his oeuvre, a collection of albums that mark a changing, ideologically conflicted relationship to pivotal Rastafarian concepts such as Africa, Zion, and Babylon. Marley's corpus is marked by identifiably different phases, the most salient and lyrically developed of which is his criticism of postcoloniality.

The Sly Rasta: Subtle Postcolonial Poet

The Zimbabwean incident is instructive for a reading of Marley's career since it marks that moment when he starts to confront postcolonialism on an international scale. The postcolonial era was inaugurated by the 1977 album *Exodus* and coincided, not accidentally, with the two periods of exile from Jamaica Marley was forced to endure between December 1976 and his death in May 1981. Marley produced five LPs during these years, and his sociopolitical critiques started to rely less on narrative conflict than on lyrical guile and skeptical phrasing, almost always hidden beneath the anti-Babylonianism of his Rastafarian faith. Marley's lyrics have been received consistently as a popular endorsement of Africa, a glorification of the continent's past as much as an expression of hope for its (postcolonial) future. While this perception has a considerable validity, Marley's musical oeuvre is far more complex and nuanced than that. His songs are often an admixture of the politically subtle and the unnuanced, songs in which catchy refrains of social protest often conceal a deeper ambivalence or critique. Marley skillfully accomplishes this delicate political balance in many of his songs. Eschewing political diatribe without undermining the popular understanding of him as a Rastafarian crusading for African freedom (a poetic balance Ali was unable to strike), Marley embedded his message deep—and often in the most disguised forms—in his music. Zimbabwe 1980 is an object lesson in how Marley was not silent at a pivotal political moment. What may have been construed as silence or reticence is instead a triumph of Marley's lyrical subtlety.

Invited by Zimbabwean cabinet minister Edgar Tekere to participate, Marley had come at his own expense to sing the praises of postcolonial Africa and, by implication, its leadership. However, through his music Marley had long fashioned himself as a spokesperson critical of postcolonial elites, such as Mugabe's Zimbabwe was soon to become, the Jamaican Labour Party (JLP) of Hugh Shearer had long been, and Edward Seaga's would soon become. The Jamaican People's National Party (PNP) of Michael Manley, with which Marley was loosely affiliated ideologically, had tried valiantly (it ultimately unsuccessfully) to resist this mode of politics. His own history as a Jamaican, even in the midst of postcolonial euphoria, situated Marley ambivalently in relation to Prime Minister Mugabe. Much like the truculent ZANLA forces, Marley's musical career had been characterized by his disruption of the dominant discourse: Marley challenged the public representation of the postcolonial nation. As a reggae musician who spent his teenage years as a sufferer in the Kingston ghetto of Trenchtown, Marley understood the alienation from and structural disenfranchisement of black subjects by the postcolonial state; *sufferer* is a colloquial term for the "suffering," impoverished, and physically vulnerable inhabitants of Jamaican ghettoes from Kingston to Montego Bay, and all the counties in between. The boisterous behavior of the ZANLA guerrillas, which preempted these

developments in the southern African nation, was in sync with the inter-
rogative girdings of "Natural Mystic." The din of the independence celebrations was too resounding for the critical reverberations of the song
to be heard that evening. If any misgivings were audible, they could only
be received on the Ellisonian "lower frequencies"—on those obscure,
hard-to-tune-in-to channels of political discourse.

More than anything, the celebrations shrank the distance between
the sufferer from Trenchtown and the Zimbabwean masses in the
audiences—and beyond the celebrations going on in the capital that
memorable night. April 18, 1980, was an instance in which geographical
distance was overcome, demonstrating how the experience of being a
sufferer in Trenchtown had enabled Marley to forge ideological links
with Third World sites such as Ethiopia and Zimbabwe.

From the Garden Parish to Trenchtown

Marley arrived in Trenchtown in 1957, a twelve-year-old fresh from
the Jamaican countryside. Like his intellectual progenitor, Marcus
Mosiah Garvey, Nesta Robert Marley was born in the "Garden" parish
of St. Ann. Nestled in the Jamaican hinterland, this rural parish is
nationally renowned for the rich abundance of its fruits and vegetables
and the "special, somewhat fiery quality of its people." St. Ann is also
acknowledged as the "spiritual center of the island nation." Marley would
go on to exhibit the "fiery qualities" that distinguished his parish within
the island and which Garvey, more than any other parishioner before
the reggae artist, embodied so proudly. But at birth, what was most "special" about the future high priest of reggae was his parentage. Born in
Nine Miles on February 6, 1945, Marley was the product of a fleeting
inter-racial dalliance between a black woman and a white man. This
union dissolved after a brief marriage. Marley's mother was an eighteen-
year-old black woman, Cedella Malcolm, the daughter of respected Nine
Miles village elder Omeriah Malcolm. So esteemed was Marley's mater-
nal grandfather, a "man of property and some authority in the district,"
that he was regarded as the local "custos"—a man of social standing and
influence.[9]

Bob's father was fifty-year-old Norval Marley, an itinerant white captain in the British West India regiment. Norval Marley, from an old Kingston family, abandoned his wife and son soon after Bob was born. He would have no contact with his father again except for a brief moment when he was about six years old. Under the pretext of providing good schooling for his son in Kingston, Norval Marley successfully entreated Cedella to send Bob to him in the capital. Instead of educating the boy, however, his father farmed him out as a house servant to Mrs. Grey, an infirm old friend of the Marley family in Kingston. For almost a whole year Bob, who had briefly started his primary education in Nine Miles, was kept out of school so that he could assist the elderly white woman with her daily chores. During his time in the city, Marley never once saw his father after Norval Marley had deposited him with Mrs. Grey at Heywood Street. He would not see his father again after that. Norval Marley died in 1955 when his son was only ten.

As a single parent living in rural Jamaica, Cedella Marley saw few prospects for herself. However, out of loyalty to her family (and her father in particular), Cedella did not migrate from her country village to Kingston for a long time. She waited until her son was almost a teenager before she moved to Kingston. Cedella left Nine Miles first, waiting almost two years before sending for Bob. Her experience was, as Anthony Payne describes it, typical of the plight of the postwar rural Jamaican poor: "Under the dual pressure of modernization and the market, many peasants were forced off the land, emigrating to Kingston where they swelled the ranks of the poor and the unemployed. Wage levels for many casual workers and domestic servants within the urban economy were such that even employment did not lead to an escape from poverty."[10] An impoverished casual worker, Cedella took up a room in a Kingston government yard, a run-down public housing unit. Despite the squalor of the government housing, the living conditions there were decidedly better than those in Trenchtown, the impoverished ghetto on which the yard bordered. The proximity to Trenchtown would prove crucial to Bob because it gave him access to the communities that would prove formative within his life.

After being deracinated for the second time in his young life, Marley found much more than just a home in Trenchtown. He discovered the community that provided his youthful political consciousness with a fledgling cultural form and a precise ideological content. Largely because of Marley's music, Trenchtown has become both an international metaphor and metonym for the collection of poor communities located on the western fringes of the Jamaican capital. In countless Marley songs, among which "Trenchtown Rock," "Belly Full," and "No Woman No Cry" number most prominently, Trenchtown is the community directly invoked and described; any number of other tracks, from the mournful "Johnny Was" to the apocalyptic "Small Axe," are informed by the Trenchtown experience. The West Kingston settlements first grew up around the turn of the century, consolidating around the 1930s. The urban geography of Kingston, planned without a sense of historical irony, literalized the disempowerment of the Trenchtown dwellers through both their physical location and the names they acquired. Of the three shantytowns, the actual ghetto of Trenchtown was "built up over a ditch that drained the sewage of old Kingston."[11] The other two, Dung Hill (also known as the Dungle) and Back O'Wall, were located on a municipal garbage dump and behind a public cemetery, respectively. All three settlements consisted of shabby, makeshift dwellings; ramshackle buildings constructed out of every conceivable material—sturdy wood and zinc shacks stood alongside flimsier ones made out of discarded fruit crates and cardboard.

All three shantytown communities were populated by those colloquially known in Jamaica as sufferers: destitute, uneducated, unemployed (which includes in its ranks the underemployed and unemployable) black city dwellers living in overcrowded and unhygienic conditions. As Leonard Barrett so starkly puts it, sufferers are those black Jamaicans who have "known only a life of emptiness, poverty and lack of opportunity."[12] They were in Marley's youth, as they continue to be now, a constituency embattled and hard-pressed to secure even the most basic resources such as water, latrines, and cooking facilities. Poor as the Trenchtown inhabitants were, they were constantly joined by even more indigent Jamaicans migrating from the economically strapped hinterland, exacerbating conditions even further. For decades it has been a pattern of Jamaican life: a vicious cycle of poverty leading to deracination, the further destruction of rural communities, the growth of urban ghettoes, which in turn fuel the internecine violence in Trenchtown and the Dungle. When Marley and his mother arrived in the capital, the most recognizable manifestation of this phenomenon was youth gangs, known as "rude boys," who roamed the alleys and backyards of the settlements. In the post–World War II era these small-time gangsters were armed with knives (Okapi was the brand of choice in Marley's day), and given—in equal measure—to swagger, braggadocio, and flashy clothes as to robbery, rape, and assault. The most publicly resistant members of those that Rex Nettleford has dubbed the "perpetual poor," apart from the Rastafarians, the rude boys tried to overcome their externally imposed structural disenfranchisement through horizontal violence.[13] The rude boys used the authorities' indifference to the settlements and fear of them to intimidate and physically harm their equally destitute neighbors.

Not long after Marley arrived from Nine Miles he took on the mannerisms of the rude boys. Like Bunny Livingston (later Bunny Wailer) and Peter Tosh (born Peter MacIntosh), his original fellow Wailers and Trenchtown residents, Bob was associated with the

> youthful anarchists who celebrated the criminal life and hatred of authority as the only freedom left open to them under the racist structures of the colonial system. The term "rude" applied equally to the anarchic and revolutionary youth of the slums, the young gunmen, gangsters and mercenaries who were pressed into shantytown goon squads by the two political parties ... The rudies redefined Kingston street life into a phantasmagoria of insolence, trolley-hopping and purse-snatching.[14]

Bob, Bunny, and Peter, who adopted the haunting, painful, and hungry cries of the ghetto as their musical identity, were familiar with the violence that pervaded the communal yards of Trenchtown. In fact, they were not averse to adopting some of the rude-boy behavior—such as smoking ganja, hanging out in a yard, or carrying knives. After all, the Wailers met each other and started practicing together as a group in exactly such a setting. That yard was located on Third Street in Trenchtown and it belonged to Joe Higgs, one of Jamaica's earliest recording stars and the Wailers' first singing coach. The embryonic Wailers were cultural rude boys more than they were "gunmen, gangsters and mercenaries." (Peter Tosh, particularly in his post-Wailers day, is somewhat of an exception. Even during their Wailer days, unlike the political Bob and the profoundly spiritual Bunny, Peter adopted the confrontational stance of the Trenchtown rude boys. He did not shirk physical altercations, often becoming the ratchet-wielding persona of "Steppin Razor," his rude-boy anthem. Tosh was especially aggressive with the Jamaican authorities, who were well known in their dislike for him.[15]) The nascent Wailers immersed themselves in the Trenchtown youths' defiance of mainstream social norms and their resistance to the colonial structures dominated by white colonials and the light-skinned Jamaican middle class.

Rude-boy culture was but one face of Trenchtown, the more overtly aggressive expression of the west Kingston ghetto. The other visage, that of Rastafarianism, was no less offensive to mainstream society; to black, white, and "high brown" Jamaicans alike. (The "adoption of the Rastafarian faith was to the orthodox Jamaican Christians blasphemous and anti-Christian."[16])The Rastas presented as much of a challenge, though on a completely different psychic level, to the island nation's ruling elite as their "trolley-hopping and purse-snatching" counterparts. While their religion made them a visible constituency within Trenchtown, they raised—in George Lamming's estimation—an issue far more crucial to Jamaican identity. "The Rastafari dramatised the question that had always been uncomfortable in Caribbean history," Lamming writes, "and the question is where you stand in relation to blackness."[17] Because of their faith, the Rastafarians foregrounded not only Jamaican society's "relation to blackness," but also, by extension the very source of that "blackness," Africa. Despite being the origin of over 90 percent of the country's population, the continent had no place in the official representation of the Jamaican nation. By publicly embracing Haile Selassie as God and Ethiopia as a biblical Zion, the Rastafarians provided a sharp rebuke to the state's denial of its African roots.

The St. Ann Story: From Marcus to Marley

The profile of the Rastafarian face was so distinct that its members stood out even within the ranks of the Kingston poor. Bearded, dreadlocked, boldly dressed in the Rasta colors of gold, green, and red, they spoke in a rich patois blended out of biblical connotation, spiced with African imagery and black Jamaican English. Carolyn Cooper's *Noises in the Blood*, her study of Jamaican popular culture, shows these tropes are central to Marley's lyrics. "Marley's skillful verbal play," Cooper argues, depends on his "use of biblical allusion, Rastafarian symbolism, proverb, riddle, aphorism and metaphor."[18] The relationship between Rastafarianism and Africa in Jamaica is a uniquely symbiotic one, deriving from Marcus Garvey and his vision of a black people liberated, prosperous, and united across the globe. Garvey is almost single-handedly responsible for the introduction of Rastafarianism into Jamaica in the first decades of the twentieth century. Through his Universal Negro Improvement Association (UNIA) Garvey not only popularized Pan-Africanism, but also encouraged black people to reject traditional (white) Christianity and pay homage to a god who more closely resembled them. "At the 1924 [UNIA] convention," Horace Campbell writes, Garvey "unveiled a large oil painting of a Black Madonna and child and the gathering implored blacks to worship God in their own image."[19] A scant six years after the 1924 convention, this Garveyite "image" of God would find physical manifestation in the coronation of Haile Selassie as emperor of Ethiopia. The fledgling Rastafarian movement in Jamaica, led by ex-Garveyites such as Leonard Howell, Joseph Hibbert, Archibald Dunkley and Robert Hinds, took the African event of 1930 as the fulfillment of both the UNIA leader's prophecy and the Bible.[20] Psalms 68:31 pronounces, "Princes will come out of Egypt, Ethiopia stretches forth her hands unto God."

Translating this biblical phrase into 1920s Pan-Africanism, Garvey intoned like an Old Testament prophet during his now-famous speech at the UNIA's 1924 meeting in New York City: "Look to Africa, where a black king shall be crowned. For the day of deliverance is here." The most resonant phrase of his career, "Look to Africa," had been coined and it was to become synonymous with the movement's leader and the Rastafarians (particularly that of the faith's repatriationist tendencies) in Jamaica. Through his political campaigns, his journalistic endeavors (he founded the *Negro World* in New York in 1918), and his (unsuccessful) economic schemes, Garvey consecrated Selassie and Ethiopia for a Caribbean Rastafarianism just starting to find its spiritual feet in the late 1920s. In his work on Jamaican religion, Barry Chevannes maps the historical trajectory that links Selassie to Garvey and Rastafarianism: "Early Rastafari, leaders and followers alike, all considered themselves Garveyites. To them he was John the Baptist, leading them to one who would be greater than himself."[21]

Chevannes's biblical analogy is apt. Born in St. Ann's Bay in 1887 (d. 1940), Marcus Garvey was a man of many and varied guises. He was a turn-of-the-century champion of black self-determination, a black nationalist, repatriationist, and entrepreneur. He used the UNIA as a platform from which to prophesy the coming of a glorious African dawn, predicting a day in which diasporic Africans would be reunited with their continental cousins. Garvey held that it was the wish of every black person to "lay down our burden and rest our weary backs and feet by the banks of the Niger, and sing our songs and chant our hymns to the God of Ethiopia."[22] The "God of Ethiopia," so pivotal to Garvey's nationalist and Pan-Africanist vision, was anointed in August 1930. Haile Selassie, a black man, was crowned "Negus Negast"—King of Kings, Conquering Lion of the Tribe of Judah—at an elaborate ceremony in the capital city of Addis Ababa. To Selassie's Jesus Christ, Garvey had played a militant, committed, dynamic, deeply flawed, and, finally, suitably tragic John the Baptist.

Garvey's prophetic skills were beyond question; he had foretold the coming of the king. But some of his financial ventures (such as the founding of the Black Star Line to repatriate blacks) were politically disastrous for the leader and brought economic ruin to several thousand black people who invested in his scheme. By the time Selassie became the latest emperor the oldest royal African lineage, one that dated back to the biblical King Solomon and Queen Sheba, Garvey was in disrepute. In February 1925 he was found guilty, under highly dubious circumstances, of mail fraud and sentenced to five years in prison in the United States. He served almost three years in an Atlanta prison before being pardoned by President Calvin Coolidge in December 1927. Upon his release Garvey became critical of Selassie's autocratic tendencies—especially after the 1935 invasion by Mussolini's forces when Garvey adroitly distinguished between support for the Ethiopian people and endorsement of the monarch—but his diminished public stature meant that his denunciations went largely unheeded. History proved Garvey's judgment of the emperor to be correct. Garvey's later position is, however, easily overshadowed by his early endorsement of Selassie. The UNIA leader is best remembered for his role as the emperor's champion and the original spokesperson for a Pan-Africanism that made Rastafarianism an integral part of black identity in the Caribbean.

The UNIA, which Garvey founded in Kingston in 1914, was instrumental in providing the groundwork for a black Jamaican cultural nationalism. With characteristic hubris (but no small amount of truth), Garvey outlines his mission in a 1923 autobiographical essay, "A Journey of Self-Discovery." Committed to black liberation, Garvey situates himself and the UNIA's goals within the framework of a highly raced, color- and caste-conscious Jamaican society in the second decade of the twentieth century. In a declaration of ideological intent, Garvey says, "I had to decide whether to please my friends and be one of the 'black-whites' of Jamaica, and be reasonably prosperous, or come out openly and defend and improve and protect the integrity of the black millions and suffer. I decided to do the latter ..."[23] Clearly evident here is Garvey's conception of the black struggle both as a local and a global phenomenon: against colonialism, against the internal caste system, racism, and the economic exploitation. Through the UNIA Garvey assailed the racist depictions of black people and posited the radical possibilities for an internationally emancipated black polity. Within this struggle, Garvey assigned a privileged place for West Indians. "I make no apology for prophesying that there will soon be a turning point in the history of the West Indies," he declared confidently, "and that the people who inhabit that portion of the Western Hemisphere will be the instruments of uniting a scattered race . . ."[24] Characteristically, Garvey was too optimistic about his hopes for a quick "turning point in the history of the West Indies." It would take some four decades of intense political campaigning before Anglo-Caribbean independence—for Trinidad and Tobago and Jamaica—became a reality. But politically his vision of a greater Pan-Africanism motivated many of the Anglo- and Francophone Caribbean intellectuals who succeeded him, among them C. L. R. James, Aimé Césaire, and Frantz Fanon, to pursue his cause of black unity in their own ways.

However, none of these venerated Caribbean intellectuals sought to fulfill Garvey's grandest dream, that of "uniting a scattered race," more seriously than his fellow parishioner from St. Ann. Symbolically, at the very least, Marley stepped into the historical breach Garvey had vacated almost forty years earlier. As a figurehead for and visionary of Pan-Africanism and as a spokesperson around whom political ambitions accumulated, Garvey was Marley's precursor. (While Marley's investment in the Pan-Africanist project was immense, he was not the only prominent Caribbean figure of that moment who represented the spirit of Garvey in and for Trenchtown. Marley was joined, metaphorically and ideologically, in this venture by University of the West Indies history lecturer Walter Rodney—the Wailers' Garveyite contemporary. Marley and Rodney were both deeply committed, in their own ways and through vastly different discourses, to the cause of the Trenchtown sufferers. And, like Garvey, they wanted to situate the Caribbean within the Pan-Africanist experience. Marley's and Rodney's paths did not cross in any substantive way, but they both represented a new generation of thinkers molded in the UNIA leader's image.) Through his music, the reggae star took up the cultural and ideological cudgels that Garvey had laid down decades ago. Possessed of a Garveyite charisma, endowed with the proletarian version of the radical UNIA leader's rhetorical skill, Marley sought to give international expression to Garvey's vision, a struggle that started right in the backyards of Trenchtown and extended to capitals in both the metropolis and postcolonial Africa.

Despite their Garveyite lineage, their status as champions of black pride, their organizational structure, and their growing numbers (by 1934, "under the leadership of Howell, Dunkley and Hinds a solid nucleus of Rastafarians had been established in Kingston"), Rastafarians were accepted neither in the shantytowns of West Kingston nor in the more fashionable quarters—the high-brown sector—of Jamaican society. This internal alienation meant that Rastafarians who had lived in ghettoes in and around the capital since the 1930s were not only unacceptable and largely invisible to the middle-class and elite residents in the hills overlooking Kingston, but also were being ridiculed by their neighbors in Trenchtown and Back O'Wall—a settlement especially renowned as a Rasta stronghold—after they had been there for decades. Father Joseph Owens, a Catholic priest and scholar of the movement, describes the different subjugations Rastas confronted: "The lowly position of the Rastafarians in Jamaican societies is accompanied by persecution at the hands of the government, brutality from the batons of the police, and taunts from the mouths of the common people."[5]

Trenchtown Rock

In "No Woman No Cry," at once his elegy for Trenchtown and one of his most poignant love songs, Marley addresses—and tries to redress—the problem of this denigrated and stereotypical perception of the Rastas in West Kingston:

> No woman no cry
> 'Cause I remember when we used to sit
> In the government yard in Trenchtown
> Oba, ob-serving the hypocrites
> Mingle with the good people we meet;

> Good friends we have had, Oh good
> friends we've lost along the way.
> In this bright future you can't forget
> your past,
> So dry your tears, I say.[26]

In her reading of the track, Carolyn Cooper argues that the song is both "an expression of [a woman's] personal grief" and a "more general lamentation for an irretrievable past."[27] In addition to its deeply felt nostalgia, "No Woman No Cry" also stands as the imaginary reconstruction of Trenchtown life. In this song West Kingston is figured as an ideologically embattled space: the ghetto is depicted as a moral arena being struggled over by the righteous Rastafarians—the "good people / Good friends"—and the "hypocrites"—those opposed to Marley and his religious community. Marley's dislike for the hypocrites is twofold: he is intolerant of their lack of faith, and he despises their surreptitiousness.

Marley cannot abide the hypocrites' ability to insinuate themselves—"mingle"—into the fabric of Rasta Trenchtown life. This is a strategic lyrical move by Marley, one that enables him to reduce Trenchtown to a set of polarized moral oppositions; it also allows him to exaggerate the role played and influence exerted by the Rastas in the ghetto. In "No Woman No Cry" anyone and everyone opposed to the Rastafarians is morally deficient. Within this song, *hypocrites* functions as a composite term of critique, embracing inter alia rudies, orthodox Christians, and other religious groupings; the song represents the "government yard in Trenchtown" as metonymic of a larger, more international spiritual struggle the Rastafarians are engaging. (The opposition between Rastas and hypocrites is a recurring trope in Marley's songwriting, but "No Woman No Cry" is salient in that these tensions are seldom staged in Trenchtown itself; more often, of course, Marley recasts this antagonism as Zion versus Babylon.)

However, for all its lyrical hubris and disingenuousness (Trenchtown was a more variegated community, composed of many more constituencies than the song allows, including other religious groups who would not consider themselves morally lacking), "No Woman No Cry" lyrically registers the depth of Marley's commitment to Rastafarianism. The song articulates the ways in which the "dreads" provided a rare source of moral and material sustenance and resilience in ghetto life:

> And then Georgie would make the fire light,
> Log wood burnin' through the night.
> Then we would cook corn meal porridge
> Of which I'll share with you.[28]

In this verse, Marley celebrates the sufferers' "share-pot" culture. Described by former prime minister Michael Manley as an arrangement in which "families whose providers are in jobs share their food with their less fortunate neighbours," "No Woman No Cry" records the ways in which Trenchtownians bond together to overcome the scarcity of food.[29] The "fire light" and the "log wood" convey a warmth and the shared "corn meal porridge" evokes a spirit of communality—as well as communal concern for the lives of other sufferers.

The 1974 song "Belly Full," also called "Them Belly Full (But We Hungry)," reiterates the theme of Trenchtown resourcefulness and collectivity. Documenting the poverty Trenchtownians endured on a daily basis, the track is propelled by the same kind of binary logic as "No Woman No Cry"; except that here the Rasta-hypocrite polarity is replaced by a class-based oppositionality—the rich "them" versus the massively impoverished "we." But the outstanding feature of "Belly Full" is, like that of many Marley songs, the crucial way in which the experience of the sufferers is informed by the ethos and the culture of the Rastas.

> Them belly full but we hungry.
> A hungry mob is an angry mob.
> A rain a-fall but the dirt it tough;
> A pot a-cook but the food no 'nough.
> We're gonna dance to Jah music, dance.
> We're gonna dance to Jah music, dance.

. . .

> Cost of living get so high
> Rich and poor they start to cry
> Now the weak must get strong.[30]

Destitute to the point of starvation, the sufferers find even their customary strategies for survival, the share-pot culture, insufficient. This song is an indictment of "them's full bellies," a track that marks the real limits of share-pot culture. The sufferers are a community without adequate resources, victims of living conditions that are harsh to the point of being insurmountable: "A pot a-cook but the food no 'nough." The sufferers' plight is so dire that despite their tradition of sharing with their neighbors, there is simply not enough food to go around. Even nature is impervious to the best intentions of the sufferers. The "dirt," at once an obvious metaphor for ghetto poverty and a critique of the unfeelingness of the country's elite, is so resilient that it cannot be penetrated (or softened) by the "rain."

The Dark Keys of the Lyrical Rasta

Girding "Belly Full" is an ominous set of warnings. Structurally disenfranchised as they are, the Trenchtown poor maintain a latent capacity for effecting a major upheaval in Jamaican society. Invoking the specter of Marie Antoinette and Toussaint's *sans culottes*, Marley summons the image of an insurrection—"A hungry mob is an angry mob," he announces incendiarily. The prospect of violent resistance emerges again, though this time with a biblical inflection ("The meek shall inherit the earth"), when Marley urges the "weak" to "get strong." The dark undertones of Marley's injunction to the "weak" betrays the scorn motivating his economic analysis—"Cost of living get so high / Rich and poor they start to cry." The rigors of inflation, especially within a traditionally fragile Jamaican economy, affect the rich and poor very differently—for the former it represents a loss of profits, while it imperils the latter's very existence. Within this bleak and foreboding context, the promise of

"Belly Full," that "we're gonna dance to Jah music, dance," assumes the aspect of a threat rather than the prospect of a Rastafarian religious ceremony. "Belly Full" represents an image rare in the Marley musical canon: a moment when the "dark keys," to use jazz musician Branford Marsalis's metaphor for brooding musical contemplations, dominate Marley's music. In the case of "Belly Full" the chords and the lyrics both are particularly "dark" because it marks an occasion when Rastafarian symbols, in fact its very deity, is used as a harbinger of violence—as opposed to its usually peaceful and spiritual deployment in his lyrics.

The dark keys have a salience in the Marley oeuvre, particularly because his music is more often than not read simply as a celebration of Africa and its causes. Marley's reggae turns on the deliberate and lyrical forging of links between diasporic blacks in the Caribbean and their cousins in the motherland. But while Marley's esteem for Africa was not unusual, black American artists such as James Brown and other soul artists (inter alia) regarded it as central to their cultural experience, the Jamaican approached the continent from a unique ideological locale: as an autochthonous, vernacular Trenchtownian. The reggae artist is a cultural figure who reflects his constituency in his personal attire and political outlook, as well as being a musician who consciously fashions himself as a public spokesperson for the struggles of the sufferers. Marley's was at once intensely local, the iconographic Trenchtown Rasta, and gloriously international, the dreadlocked shaman who represented universal black aspirations for freedom. Linking the Caribbean to Africa, his music mediated between the histories of Kingston and Addis Ababa; his post-1977 critiques of postcolonial Africa were steeped in Rastafarian metaphors and linguistic tropes he had invoked when commenting on his native Caribbean; and he reinscribed and symbolically strengthened the bonds between the diaspora and the continent through his variously expressed distrust of political leaders, local and foreign.

Marley's Trenchtownian situatedness is of the expanded, postcolonial variety. He integrates himself into and speaks for the cause of an imagined black Atlantic constituency, a body politic bound and symbolically unified by the common experience of colonial rule and neoimperial exploitation. The reggae artist's articulations on postcolonial situations the Third World over were informed by and contingent on the struggles against poverty and inadequate housing, the patois, the self-representation, and the religious beliefs of his Trenchtown minority. Marley's rootedness within the Trenchtown experience is always expressed in the vernacular. For Marley, political and economic history—slavery, deracination, repatriation to Africa, and caste-based racism and linguistic patterns—the peculiar patois of Jamaican Rastas—are of especial importance. Through his music, the reggae artist represented Trenchtown as a global experience, translating Jamaican particularity into an internationally understandable, recognizable, and resonant discourse.

Inspired by a faith in both the pre- and post-Babylonian possibilities of a liberated black Africa, Marley fundamentally recast the postcolonial paradigm. The postcolonial experience is refracted through Rastafarianism, an unusual (and unusually) religious lens. Like Ali, Marley is an "essentialist" vernacular intellectual, and like Ali's faith in the Nation of Islam, so Marley's religion forms the basis of his vernacularity: both these figures view the world, Marley more so than Ali, from a locale that is not wholly secular. While Ali and Marley lived "in the world," practiced a secular faith and vernacularity rooted in the material, popular experiences of their respective communities, Islam and Rastafarianism distinguish them as "nonmodernist" intellectuals; theirs is not intellectuality rooted solely in rationality. Unlike the Marxists James and Hall (though Marley, and even Ali, are not without their Marxist tendencies), and countless other post-Renaissance/Reformation intellectuals, Ali and Marley intervened from positions informed by spirituality: their faiths ameliorated, complicated, and inflected how they viewed and acted in the world. They are vernacular thinkers grounded in the subaltern popular but who also act with a sense of transcendence, a belief that Louisville and Kingston may be deeply racist and impoverished places, but that there is world beyond America and the Caribbean, a universe where Allah and Jah offer a different, just dispensation.

Marley maps African and Caribbean independence through the tenets of Rastafarianism, in the course of which his faith underwrites and complicates postcolonialism, all the while coexisting creatively with Marxist critiques of class—an approach that takes primarily the form of attacks on property and proletarian exploitation. Marley conceived of the postcolonial world as insistently and self-reliantly black, fashioning himself as the spokesperson for a small, tightly knit but geographically dispersed community of Bible-quoting, bearded, dreadlocked adherents of Emperor Haile Selassie. Marley is, however, not simply a vernacular intellectual who internationalizes a single, idiosyncratic organic constituency. This is not simply the local organic gone transnational (or the Jamaican local translated into the Euro-American metropolitan with multiple resonances in the postcolonial periphery). Rather, it is the reconceptualization of the organic intellectual into the vernacular intellectual. (The conversion from small-time gangster to shaman/spiritual leader and public intellectual has been made before, most notably by Malcolm X. Islam, however, included a much larger constituency, consisting of adherents all across the globe. Marley's transition from rude boy—"bwoy"—to a worshiper of Jah was rendered unique by the religious and cultural means—Rastafarianism and reggae—through which the Jamaican musician took as his pulpit the international stage.)

Through his music, the structural disenfranchisements of Trenchtown function both literally and symbolically, becoming synonymous with, say, the injustices of Portuguese colonial rule in Mozambique and Angola or the peculiarities of white minority rule in UDI Rhodesia. Marley concurrently emphasized, metaphorized, and exceeded his primary community; he globalized, in much the same way that Ali internationalized the 1960s African-American experience, the Caribbean vernacular. Within the Marley oeuvre, Trenchtown is a vivid (and overdetermined) representation of the shantytowns all over the postcolonial (and colonized) world; remaining all the while, of course, metonymic of Marley's critiques of the conditions that existed in the slums of West Kingston. The metaphoric Trenchtown enabled Marley to transform Jamaica's national self-representation both at home and abroad. The protagonists and narratives of Marley's music constitutes a rejection of the Anglophone-U.S. culture of the high browns or the Afro-Saxons, as the country's ruling class is colloquially known (or the black-whites, as Garvey called them), in favor of the sufferer.[31] Marley's music represented Jamaica as black, poor, alternately angry and humble, but almost always Rastafarian. It was through his depiction of Trenchtown life that Marley, and reggae culture in general, reconfigured Jamaican national identity and produced out of those experiences a new international culture. The message's resonance—the affirmation of blackness—was international, but it was rooted in, and so always echoed, its Trenchtown origins.

By popularizing and ensconcing Trenchtown within his music, Marley elevated it to the status of the familiar. The Kingston shantytown became not only a recognizable postcolonial site, but also a powerful emblem of black destitution, exploitation, and impoverishment common throughout the third and first worlds. Through the local vernacular the postcolonial was transformed, reconfigured, provided with a new language, a new set of metaphors, animated by an ancient but unheralded religious practice, all of which Marley invigorated and popularized in ways previously unimaginable for unexpected audiences. Through his music, and that of his contemporaries such as Third World, Jimmy Cliff, and Burning Spear, Marley gave postcolonial subalterns an entirely new vocabulary (as diasporic and metropolitan audiences added terms such as *Jah* and *Trenchtown* to their everyday exchanges), new forms of self-styling and self-representation (as dreadlocks, Rastacolored beanie hats and beads, and untrimmed beards became fashionable from London to Lagos), and a new way to express their oppositionality and resistance to the unwelcome ubiquity of Babylon. Jamaica's most dynamic cultural expression, born in the 1920s fervor of Garvey's UNIA movement, nourished by the deprivations of the ghettoes, and inflected by Marley with the anger, raw energy, and joie de vivre of the Trenchtown rude boys, Marley converted reggae into the vernacular of the postcolonial project from the mid-1970s until years after his death in 1981.

Manley and Marley

In so many significant ways, it is entirely appropriate that the Rufaro Stadium performance should stand as the apogee of Marley's entire musical career. His performance there stands as an emotionally charged and exceptional historical event. Zimbabwe 1980, more than "Zimbabwe" of the album *Survival,* was a moment of optimism. That April night was an expression of faith in the continent and its postliberation possibilities. Zimbabwean independence represented a cause for rejoicing in the postcolonial world because it marked the triumph of a black people's will to self-determination. Moreover, for a Rastafarian who held the continent sacred, Zimbabwean independence symbolized a crucial step in the complete liberation of black Africa. With Zimbabwean sovereignty, only Namibia (still South-West Africa in 1980, ruled as a province in the mid- to late 1970s by the apartheid regime) and South Africa remained oppressed by white minorities. These struggles had been at the forefront of Marley's consciousness when he scripted "War":

> Until the ignoble and unhappy regime
> That holds our brothers in Angola, in Mozambique
> South Africa
> Suffer human bondage
> Have been toppled
> Totally destroyed
> Well, everywhere is war.[32]

True to the spirit of Selassie's speech, this track balanced the desire for "lasting peace/world citizenship" with a poetic cry for justice and morality, and was scripted, of course, with an eye to its true motivation: the total destruction of colonialism and racism, as the refrain from the song reminds the audience. Performing "War" in the heady atmosphere of African nationalism lent Marley's clarion call an especially strong ideological reverberation.

Although "War" is clearly indebted to Selassie and Garvey, deriving its lyrics from the former and its Pan-African sensibility from the latter, the song cannot be fully understood without acknowledging the importance of another key Jamaican political personality. "War" invokes a third philosophical source, an influence that is seldom recognized (and even less frequently acknowledged) because his thinking is so embedded in the traditionally violent, expedient, and entangled fabric of the island nation's political life. For all this, however, he did serve as a source that facilitated Marley's ideological development domestically: Michael Manley, prime minister of Jamaica. In addition to the ideological space Manley created for Marley and the Rastas (a move that of course had electoral benefits for him), however, are the many ways in which the musical and political careers of Marley and Manley in the early and mid-1970s intersected, paralleled, echoed, and even amplified each other. So neatly do these phases of their careers mirror each other that Manley's ascension to national leadership in 1972 coincides with the release of Marley's first (and indeed the first ever reggae) album—*Catch a Fire*. (This LP was released only a year later in both the UK and the United States.)

As leader of the PNP, Manley's 1972 election victory over Hugh Shearer's JLP signaled a major change in the society's politics. Coming to power on a platform he dubbed the "politics of change" ("Jamaican society is disfigured by inequities too deep for tinkering. Our concern, therefore, must be with the politics of change"), Manley sought to produce a coalition that did more than just—as was customary PNP and JLP policy up to that point—exploit and co-opt the sufferers' vote. In the 1972 election, Manley used terms from the Old Testament that reflected Rastafarian speech and sensitivity toward the sufferers. According to a Manley scholar, songs such as "Beat Down Babylon," "Small Axe," and "Must Get a Beating" expressed the outrage of many poor people toward the "oppressors," loosely identified as the JLP and associated groups such as "capitalists."[33]

Deeply immersed in the Rastafarian ethic, Manley drew liberally from all its cultural texts—its religious vocabulary, its political critiques, and its music.[34] It is no surprise that Marley's "Small Axe" constituted one of the anthems for Manley's groundbreaking 1972 campaign. The song is nothing if not a critique of Jamaican capitalism and social inequity underscored by that most ennobling of biblical parables, the triumph of David over Goliath, lent a contemporary threatening edge by Marley's (ominous) lyrics: "If you are the big tree, / We are the small axe / Sharpened to cut you down." The Jamaican state, in all its power, is being put on notice in this incendiary song: Rastafarian retribution, biblical vengeance, is explicitly threatened in "Small Axe." The track also has a nascent anti-imperialism undertone that is more global in its scope, speaking as Marley was from a Caribbean routinely exploited by imperialist America—the title's *small* is a mobile metaphor.

Relying only on the portentous desire for justice in this song, Manley saw it as his opportunity to represent the sufferers while maintaining the PNP's colored ruling- and middle-class basis. In his "ideal of an egalitarian society," Manley wanted to "incorporate the poor, the starving and the homeless."[35] The new prime minister's commitment to an "egalitarian society" arose, in part, from his ability to understand how the Jamaican political landscape was shifting, what those changes were, what social forces motivated the changes, identifying what new voices were speaking for and from the ghettoes (and increasingly, in the coming years, echoing beyond Trenchtown and transforming Jamaica's international image because of reggae and Rastafarianism), the vocabulary and inscriptions of those voices, and how the transitions required a different engagement with the country's black majority. All these positions emanated from Manley's newly acquired Pan-Africanism, his recently discovered commitment to black Jamaican culture, and his long-held opposition to U.S. hegemony, especially as it applied to the Caribbean and the Third World: "By linking up with roots and Rasta reggae, Manley was also linking Jamaica's future with the Third World rather than with white America."[36] Manley's vision of Jamaica's future coincided precisely with Marley's, and reggae's. The high-brown politician, this well-educated son of the Jamaican elite, and the barely schooled mixed-race sufferer from Trenchtown were set on parallel, and sometimes overlapping, political paths. Between, and because of, their two different projects, Jamaica would become, racially, a radically altered society.

The events that encapsulated all these issues, in the course of which it also dramatically transformed Jamaica's politics of race, were the Rodney riots of October 16, 1968. Marley's contemporary (he was the organic intellectual to Marley's vernacular figure) the black Guyanese historian Walter Rodney was based at the Mona campus of the University of the West Indies, in Kingston. Rodney was an articulate advocate of Black Power who had strong links with the Trenchtown poor, about whom the young Wailers were beginning to sing:

> I have spoken in what people call "dungle," rubbish dumps, for that is where people live in Jamaica … I have sat on a little oil drum, rusty and in the midst of garbage, and some Black Brothers and I have grounded together.[37]

Having taught at the University of Dar-Es-Salaam in Tanzania (after completing his doctoral work on the slave trade on the upper Guinea coast in the seventeenth and eighteenth centuries), Rodney was deeply immersed in the Pan-African experience. Rodney's was a message that found a ready reception with the Rastafarians, especially since, as is evident from this quotation, he understood the Rastafarian vocabulary in which *groundation* signifies not simply a meeting, but a gathering of Rastas (as equals, with special status afforded older men) discussing matters of biblical and political significance. His reference to the Dungle indicates that Rodney knew West Kingston's urban geography (not only who the poor were, but where they lived), and he was situating himself within the most denigrated, and oppositional, element in Jamaican society. Rodney's description of Trenchtown life was Marley's experience of the capital until he succeeded as a reggae star. Deeming Rodney a subversive, the Jamaican authorities refused to grant him reentry to the country after he returned from a writers' conference in Canada. The reactionary response of Shearer's JLP government not only sparked a day and a half of riots in Kingston, but also marked a watershed event in Jamaica's brief independent history: it "denot[ed] the proper beginning of the postcolonial era" because that was the definitive moment of racial crisis in the society.[38]

The Rodney riots were a clash between the black sufferers and the high-brown elites, a battle that the Afro-Saxons won by virtue of controlling the state's repressive apparatus. The saga, however, was lost ideologically by the Jamaican ruling class, because this was the historic moment in which Jamaican society began to conceive of itself as a black "African" nation. The Rodney riots represent a rejection and replacement of the white, British-identified minority, high-brown culture. The black voices that Rodney, and later Marley, spoke for led the protests against the Guyanese scholar's extradition, because the sufferer's recognized how the groundation view of black history, culture, and tradition was at odds with the dominant, minority-imposed one. While blacks were a majority in Jamaican society, their African heritage and culture found no articulation in the nation's international (self-)representation. Because of the Black Power movement in the United States and the anticolonial struggles in Africa, black Jamaicans recognized the disjuncture between their numerical superiority and their effective political disenfranchisement (national leaders were invariably drawn from the high-brown ranks) and their cultural debasement. Rodney's message, which would find its fullest enunciation in Marley's music, resonated sufficiently with the sufferers for the Trenchtownians to take to the streets of Kingston in protest. (Marley spent some time in the United States in the tumultuous 1960s, working at a DuPont plant in Wilmington, Delaware, so he would have had some firsthand exposure to this phenomenon.)

In *The Politics of Change*, which should be read as Manley's political manifesto-cum-moral treatise on Jamaican life (hence the subtitle *A Jamaican Testament*), the new leader acknowledges the importance of the concerns raised by Rodney's activism, and, more crucially within the context of ghetto constituencies, the criticisms contained in the tracks of Marley's *Catch a Fire*. Manley's manifesto is, among the writings of his nation's leaders, a work groundbreaking in its commitment to forging a political discourse that blended a striking morality (again aligning him, surprisingly for so scholarly and occasionally Marxist a leader, with Marley) with the demands of Jamaican realpolitik. Here was a man, a highly trained member of the Jamaican ruling class, who thought "unemployment" both a "reproach to human conscience" and a "total failure of the economic processes to meet social needs."[39] But nowhere is Manley's critical acumen more astute than in his reading of reggae as a vigorous popular cultural commentary. In an appropriately poetic moment, he says of the artists and their music, "These are the singers who bespeak the tragedy and the pain, the hopes and the aspirations of the ghetto. In their music, the reggae, there is eloquently foreshadowed the concept of a just society as they protest its absence."[40] The "absence" of social justice echoes from the very core of *Catch a Fire*, especially in the album's moral pillars—"Slave Driver" and "Concrete Jungle." Animated by the history of black Jamaicans' suffering, "Slave Driver" shares Manley's political concerns and brims with a *Politics of Change*–like morality:

> I remember on the slave ship
> How they brutalize our very souls
> Today they say that you're free
> Only to be chained in poverty
> Good God I think its illiteracy.[41]

Both Marley and Manley clearly understood the limitations of the enfranchisement of blacks in postcolonial Jamaica. It was an abstract, constitutionally guaranteed "freedom" that did not translate into any basic rights for those who lived in the ghettoes. None of the fundamental restructuring imagined by the anticolonialists, the right to employment, decent housing, running water, or education, materialized in the wake of postcolonial independence. The incarceration of the "slave ship" and the plantation has been replaced by the postcolonial "chains" of "poverty" and "illiteracy." In "Concrete Jungle" Marley employs the same imagery to reiterate this theme: "No chains around my feet / But I'm not free." (Manley went so far as to put a fairly precise number on the nation's illiteracy: "By the start of the 1970s exactly one quarter of the total Jamaican population were functionally illiterate").[42] Both Marley's and Manley's critiques are motivated by a desire for sociopolitical restructuring. *The Politics of Change* is Manley's program of action for his fellow Jamaicans and "people in all developing countries"; "Slave Driver" expresses its commitment to social transformation in the form of a warning—not a dire one, but strangely ominous nonetheless:

> Slave driver
> The table is turned
> Catch a fire
> So you can get burned.[43]

"The table is turned" is clearly a metaphor for political change, but the real caution to the "slave driver" (which may be read as a description of the JLP government, in office for the decade since formal independence) is contained in the more threatening images of immolation—"fire" and "burned." "Catch a fire," the Jamaican equivalent of the colloquial "you're gonna catch hell," is clearly the more incendiary of these lines and again intended as a warning, however ineffective, for the high-brown authorities. Manley and Marley are, in this instance, clearly—almost literally—on the same ideological page.

In retrospect, the album title's real salience resides elsewhere. This 1972 LP announced that a whole new political and spiritual philosophy was "catching fire" in Jamaican society. On the secular front the JLP had been defeated and replaced by a Manley government ostensibly committed to a revised, more anticolonially recognizable social contract: "A stirring of popular excitement and anticipation, a renewal of faith, a light in the eye of the disinherited who sense that their claim to a place in national life is dominant consideration in governmental and political action."[44] Spiritually, a once-denigrated cultural formation had found its first full-length public articulation in the person of three sufferers from Trenchtown. Marley, Peter Tosh, and Bunny Wailer had given voice to the "wailin'" of the ghetto. Rastafarianism was the spiritual "fire" and, following Marley's lyrical lead, it was poised to set Jamaica and the rest of the world alight. Manley understood not only the domestic—he had long since identified the Rastas as the ghetto community that championed the symbolic and ideological centrality of blackness in Jamaica, but the Pan-Africanist dimension of Rastafarianism—he also, in an effort to align himself with this movement and integrate himself and his political party Trenchtown life (which contained a set of crucial constituencies within the Jamaican electorate), visited Ethiopia in 1971 and met with Selassie—the occasion on which the Jamaican politician was given the wooden staff, a gift quickly christened "the Rod of Correction" by the local press.

Through the Rod of Correction Selassie symbolically invested Manley with a moral authority and implicitly made him the candidate of choice for Trenchtown Rastas such as Marley and the Wailers. Moreover, because of Selassie's putative endorsement, there was a massive shift in Jamaican Rastafarian ideology. Pre-Manley (and Marley, since the latter was actively responsible for this ideological transition), Rastafarians eschewed participation in Jamaican politics: Jamaica belonged to the Babylonian construct and Rastafarians did not want to be contaminated by exercising their franchise rights. Attaining Zion, returning to their African home, was their aim in life. Before 1972, Rastas rarely voted in the Jamaican elections, much less stood for political office. With Selassie's metaphoric intervention, Manley's Third Worldist appeals to the Trenchtown communities, and Marley's growing interest in Jamaican politics because he recognized that the Rastas needed to take a hand in determining their own (national if not spiritual) future, Rastafarians became actively involved in the Jamaican electoral process for the first time. In the process, they were indeed "contaminated" and sullied by their participation (so violent and disruptive were those events), but they also entered the political mainstream, marked themselves as national citizens who made claims on the state, and symbolically—some might argue permanently—postponed their return to Zion. In the same (extended) moment that Manley visited Ethiopia and Marley and the Wailers released *Catch a Fire*, Rastafarians became enfranchised Jamaicans: Babylon became, not (only) a temporary location, but a site of ideological and spiritual struggle, a dystopic home, to be sure, but still a place where Rastas now demanded that they be represented, that their voices be heard. Either through the ballot box or, more lyrically, in the music Marley, Tosh, Bunny Wailer, Burning Spear, and other reggae artists were making. Sometimes, as in the 1976 concert (to which we turn shortly), Marley's involvement in the Jamaican elections proved nearly fatal. After 1972, however, the Rastas could retreat into neither the ghetto nor spiritual righteousness. For better and worse, Marley, Manley, and Selassie made "Jamaicans" of the Rastafarians in the 1972 election and through the release of the Wailers' LP. It is paradoxical that it was not a "black" Rastafarian who integrated their nation's electoral fabric. It was, rather, the collective efforts of a symbolic black deity (the absent presence), a mixed-race sufferer, and a high-brown PNP leader who drew the anti-Babylonian Rastafarian community into Jamaica's political system.

Manley's courtship of Selassie marked, for all its domestic electoral benefits, less a gesture of expedience than the beginning of a substantive and politically unprecedented engagement with the African continent and the Third World. Manley was committed both to rethinking the self-perception and self-representation of the Jamaican body politic and to resituating his country within a postcolonial world. Manley made his position on this issue clear in one of his first speeches to the Jamaican House of Representatives after taking office in 1972: "I say it quite bluntly, Jamaica is part of the third World."[45] Unlike any Jamaican leader, including his father, Norman Washington Manley, whom he replaced as head of the PNP, Michael Manley was committed to the ideological transformation of his society. He wanted not only to foreground the experiences of black Jamaicans, but also to elevate their African background and affiliations from the status of public nonrecognition, or deliberate exclusion, to definitive within the nation's post-1972 history. "I am satisfied," he asserted, "that the citizen of the Black Caribbean will never be at peace with himself until he makes his peace with Africa."[46]

"Making peace with Africa" required a break with the metropolitan identification of the ruling class—the replacement of Europe with Africa—and the acknowledgment by the white and high-brown minority that Jamaica was indeed a black (majority) society and that their origins deserved national prominence. "Making peace with Africa" demanded that Rastafarianism, outwardly the most visible expression of Jamaica's link to the continent, be recognized as a bona fide faith, that it be respected and protected from ridicule and denigration, and that its adherents take their place as full-fledged members of the national community. Metonymically, Selassie and the Rastas constituted the African presence in the Jamaican body politic.

Manley's investment in Africa and the Third World, and his commitment to making Jamaica a significant member of the Non-Aligned Movement (an organization at whose founding in 1961 Jamaica had been present), provided the basis for a dynamic—if not always amicable— relationship between the PNP prime minister and the reggae community. Artists such as Marley supported the PNP over the JLP, becoming spokespersons for the Manley government and drawing their fans into the political process as PNP voters. This kind of cultural endorsement was especially crucial for Manley in the fractious and violent election of 1976.

The Parting of the Ways

Over the course of Manley's four years in office, Marley's position on the Jamaican political landscape changed considerably—from local reggae artist to international black icon, an invaluable election asset for the PNP. Marley had been electorally neutral in 1972 (though he is widely believed to have voted for Manley and his music interpellated him into the PNP camp), but by the time the 1976 election came around Marley was closely identified with "Joshua" and the PNP. Caught in an uncomfortable space, between wariness of the ways in which he was being deployed as political capital by a Manley government and a distaste for the partisan election strife that turned the ghettoes into war zones, Marley agreed to participate in the now famous Peace Concert in December 1976. A free public event, with Marley headlining and supported by acts such as the ex-Wailer Peter Tosh and Third World, it was an (unsuccessful) attempt to cool the political temperature in Trenchtown. On the day preceding the concert Marley barely survived an assassination attempt on his life (and, collaterally, that of his manager, his wife, and some of his band members) by unknown men—suspected, of course, of being JLP hitmen, so seriously was Marley's endorsement of the PNP regarded, so politically transformative to the electoral system was the decision by Rastafarians such as Marley to participate in Jamaican democracy. Through the *Catch a Fire* moment, Marley—and the Wailers—integrated Rastas into, and identified them as, not to put too fine a point on it, the mainstream of the Trenchtown vernacular. In becoming politically active, Rastafarians became more than situated within ghetto life: they became a key (moral) constituency, especially for the Manley government. Marley's 1976 injuries, the price of (full) Trenchtownian vernacularity, bore testimony to the extent to which the Rasta bloc (in the Gramscian sense) altered the capital's electoral landscape.

Courageously, Marley played the event (with a makeshift band and with Rita still in her hospital gown) and then interrupted it at a key moment: he made Manley and the opposition leader Seaga come onto the stage and shake hands, a symbolic PNP-JLP "peace" agreement signed in the presence of the Jamaican public. Even as a symbolic gesture, both men were reluctant to commit themselves to ending the factional, party-inspired disputes. In a triumph of the vernacular intellectual over the political leadership (which derived from the nation's traditional intellectual strata), Marley understood at once the significance of the Peace Concert moment and his own status in Jamaican society. In the absence of postcolonial leadership, the society's cultural figurehead intervened in the national debate and used his elevated standing to produce a brief (and symbolic) truce in the internecine ghetto war. Marley showed that he was, unlike Manley and Seaga, capable of stepping outside and above the strictures and vested interests of Jamaican politics and acting in the cause of the vernacular: "his" Trenchtownians, the constituency that hosted many of the most violent PNP-JLP exchanges. In the Peace Concert moment Marley foreswore his own political affiliation (and suspended his support for Manley) in an effort to change Jamaica's electoral habits. Written especially for the Peace

Concert, "One Love" was Marley's attempt to lyrically substantiate the event's supposed ambitions:

> One Love, One Heart
> Let's get together and feel all right.
> Hear the children crying. (One Love.)
> Hear the children crying. (One Heart.)[47]

Marley's call for national unity and peace was heard but not heeded by Manley and Seaga. Despite his effort at strategic neutrality, Manley used the concert as a PNP endorsement and went on to win the elections. (Fearing for his life, Marley fled Jamaica after the concert and went into exile.) The PNP electoral victory served to undermine the reggae star's intervention into the national discourse and worked mainly to affirm the Marley-Manley links in the Jamaican political imaginary—the unlikely, though ideologically firmly girded, symbiosis of the Trenchtown sufferer and the uptown Kingstonian. (By this time, of course, Marley had moved to his famous 56 Hope Road house and had himself become an "uptowner.") It is a perception not without validity. In some instances Manley functioned as more than the (formal institutional) political corollary for the agenda of Marley and the reggae artists. Manley's Third World vision was such that, through his socialist leanings and his involvement in the Non-Aligned Movement, he gave Jamaica's symbolic and technical support to the anticolonial struggles in southern Africa into which Marley would later write himself, Trenchtown, and his Caribbean nation:

> Jamaica must be totally dedicated to the active support of all those measures that can lead to the overthrow of the apartheid regime in South Africa, the Smith regime in Rhodesia and Portuguese tyranny in Angola and Mozambique. In other words, where wars of liberation for the purpose of establishing national freedom are being fought, the objective of freedom legitimises them and commands our unswerving support.[48]

In this 1974 essay, published before Marley moved into his own postcolonial phase, Manley anticipated several of the causes that the reggae artist would later champion—his antiapartheid stance, his critiques of Portuguese tyranny, and his commitment to the African revolution. Most important is how Manley's Third World policy statement foreshadows Zimbabwe, Marley's signal achievement, a historic moment that coincided—paradoxically—with the demise of the Jamaican leader's experiment in "democratic socialism" in his own country.

Manley's PNP lost the 1980 elections to Seaga's party, but he bequeathed Jamaica a rare accomplishment. Manley had enabled, more than any political figure of his (and many other) day(s), a salient ideological moment: the triumphant conjuncture of cultural and electoral politics, of the vernacular and the traditional. Rastafarianism and "democratic socialism," a blend first imagined as a national politics by Manley, was distilled—with the accoutrements of Marley's faith—into the person of the reggae artist in Zimbabwe. Jamaica's commitment to the Third World, which first found international articulation through Manley, was produced as a unique manifestation of the (Caribbean) national and the (Rastafarian) diasporic in April 1980. Marley acted on that independence night both in his own capacity as postcolonial vernacular intellectual and as the fulfillment—though not the official representative—of Manley's postcolonial visions. A leading figure in the Non-Aligned Movement in his first four years as prime minister, during which he established Jamaica's global and postcolonial profile and cooperated closely with his Caribbean neighbor Fidel Castro, the precipitous decline in the Jamaican economy (a condition for which he held the United States directly responsible) during his second term in office compelled him to attend almost exclusively to domestic affairs—significantly lowering his international cachet, if not his commitment to the Third World. The failure of the ironically named Peace Concert proved generative for Marley. Forced into exile by interparty violence, Marley, through his work, began to grapple with a series of issues—violence, the role of the Rasta in Babylonian politics, the responsibility of the reggae artist to the community, including and beyond the Rastafarians—that his residence in Jamaica had not required of him. After being shot at, Marley used his all-too-intimate experience of violence to rethink the content and the criticisms contained in his music. Marley's exile, devoid as it is of a nostalgic rendering of Rasta (or subaltern) life in the Jamaican ghettoes, compelled a more scrupulous contemplation on Caribbean society, including a symbolic disassociation with Manley.

Ironically, at the very moment (circa 1976) Manley was forced to become a "local" political figure, Marley's music started to expand its conceptual framework. The 1976 LP *Rastaman Vibration* marks the last instance when Marley's subject matter can be said to be primarily Jamaican. With the exception of "War" and "Rat Race," the 1976 album is narrowly concerned with the experience of Jamaica's Rastafarians; songs such as "Crazy Baldhead," "Who the Cap Fit," and "Roots, Rock, Reggae" represent the last occasion when Marley's domestic Rastafarian-phase tracks would dominate a project; these songs are, despite the ways in which they can (legitimately) be read as universal expressions of the dreads' condition, concerned with and grounded in a narrow context. The title of the next LP in and of itself signaled a major paradigmatic shift in Marley's music: *Exodus, "Movement of Jah People."* Marley himself was, literally, on the "move"; paradigmatically he was moving away from Jamaica and physically, a development made necessary by the violence of the Peace Concert, his exiles—like James's and, to a lesser extent, Hall's—would prove conceptually productive. His time in the metropolises, mainly in England and then the United States (where he died), provided him with the opportunity to rethink his Rastafarianism, his loyalty to the Jamaican nation, and his investment in the postcolonial project. Exile from Jamaica gave his work not only a new impetus but also a completely new conceptual framework that resulted in a carefully distilled, and sometimes too-well-hidden, critique of postcolonialism.

Borrowing from the Old Testament story of the Jews' expulsion from their homeland, *Exodus* is the beginning of the process through which the then-exiled Marley sought to explore issues that were more diasporic than simply Jamaican, though the spirit of his native land remained formative and influential within the work. Driven out of Jamaica by political violence, but also increasingly attracted to the international music scene, Marley had to rethink his relationship to Jamaica and how it figured in his Rastafarian cultural imaginary; in this phase, his music assumes a new, more global perspective. A bluesy album, a tone evident in "Jamming" and "Waiting in Vain," *Exodus* is reflective commentary on domestic life and an exploration of the philosophical boundaries of reggae and Rastafarianism. In "So Much Things to Say" these two strands of *Exodus* come together:

> They got so much things to say
> But I'll never forget no way
> They crucified Jesus Christ
> I'll never forget no way
> They stole Marcus Garvey's rights
> I'll never forget no way
> They turn their back on Paul Bogle
> So don't you forget who you are
> And where you stand in the struggle[49]

"So Much Things to Say" constructs a transhistorical pantheon of heroes in which Marley positions Jesus as the universal revolutionary figure, Paul Bogle (a Baptist deacon hung by the British for his leading role in the abortive 1865 rebellion) as the Jamaican counterpart, and Garvey as the Pan-Africanist (whose rights were "stolen" not in the Caribbean but in the United States) who bridges the experiences of Rastafarian righteousness (the crucified Christ) and nationalist insurrection. Inasmuch as the song is about the importance of keeping a radical tradition alive ("I'll never forget no way," Marley repeats), it is also about the current historical obligations with which black people are charged. They are required to maintain their identity and an ongoing commitment to their particular struggle—remembering, as he said, "who you are" and "where you stand in the struggle." Prefiguring the articulations of *Survival*, in which he critiqued postcolonial elites, "So Much Things to Say" charges

Jamaicans, Rastafarians, Christians, and black people generally with personal political responsibility for their (Pan-Africanist) community's struggle—all the *you*'s stand in personal relation to Christ, Garvey, and Bogle. If there is, as he says in the song, "spiritual wickedness in high and low places," then his imagined black community bears a collective responsibility for its eradication. If Marley was going to fight this "wickedness" on a Pan-Africanist platform, then he was going to have to distance himself from Manley's domestic strategies and embark on an international campaign.

The Postcolonial Era

The period 1977 to 1980 was one in which the reggae musician produced his most incisive critiques and his most outstanding work. The albums, *Exodus, Survival,* and *Uprising* constitute a musically and politically brilliant trio of works. The salient feature of these LPs, produced in the final period of Marley's career, is songwriting at once lyrically rich, politically suggestive, and ideologically sharp. It is also the most genuinely transatlantic postcolonial work that he ever did. In these four short years Marley moved from automatic support for all things African to a position in which his music represented the motherland in terms that ameliorate celebration with a sense of ideological unease. That is not to say that the songs and the albums are uniformly critical; they are not. There are tracks unqualified in their nationalist, Pan-Africanist, and Rastafarian celebration, as well as songs that contain only an underlying caution—*Exodus*'s "The Heathen," *Survival*'s "Wake Up and Live," and *Uprising*'s "We and Dem" fit this description. Superficially endorsing cooperation between "we and dem," the song cannot overcome the threat (of violence) aimed at "dem":

> But we have no friends in a high society
> We have no friends, Oh mark my identity
> We have no friends
> We no know how we and dem a go work this out
> We no know how we and dem a go work it out[50]

Alienated and without access to "high society," "we" still presents itself as a danger to the ruling group. The caution is contained ominously in the refrain not because of what it says, but because of Marley's ability to use "ignorance" and an ostensible lack of strategy as a fear-inducing mechanism—"We no know how we and dem a go work this out."

There are also tracks, such as "Jamming" and "Could You Be Loved" (later covered by fellow Kingstonians Third World), which attained commercial success because of their ability to blend the thematics of reggae with a bouncy dance beat, or because they were catchy slower dance numbers. This popularization of reggae enabled Marley and other artists to reach a wider audience that identified with the musicians culturally, if not always ideologically. Eddie Grant is one of the artists who understood the demand for this brand of reggae and successfully tailored his music for this mainstream niche. The predominantly white British group, UB40, with almost no original work, made almost a career out of covering reggae standards. (UB40 was, in a small way, emulating a tradition established by fellow Brit and renowned blues guitarist Eric Clapton. One of Clapton's most famous recordings was "I Shot the Sheriff," a hugely successful cover of a Marley original. There is also, however, a very different tradition of white reggae and ska in Britain. Groups such as the Police and the Clash immersed themselves in the politics of reggae and produced a whole new form of critique of the white metropolis.) But Marley, and to a lesser extent Third World, made reggae both politically salient and commercially viable. "Jamming"' (the act of praising Jah), the Babylonian indictment "Pimper's Paradise," and the hauntingly beautiful account of the Middle Passage "Redemption Song," were all successful singles.

However, the dominant mood and mode on the Marley trilogy is political reflection couched in narrative sophistication. On these tracks the original Wailers' reservations about the Babylonian nation-state are not lyrically prominent, which is to say that they are not found in the catchy choruses. Cleverly hidden and ideologically inconspicuous, the critiques reside in the body of the lyrics and almost imperceptibly convey his ambivalence about the continent. In this phase Marley's lyrics started to take on, though in much more subtle textures, the overtones of his critiques of the Jamaican government that first brought his work popular and critical attention. "Small Axe" encapsulates the tone and content of Marley's early anticolonial and antipostcolonial work:

> Why boasteth thyself, oh evil men
> Playing smart and not being clever?
> I say you're working iniquity to achieve
> Vanity
> But the goodness of Jah Jah endureth
> Forever
> If you are the big tree,
> We are the small axe
> Sharpened to cut you down
> Ready to cut you down[51]

Invoking the phrasing and relying on the retributive tone ("An eye for an eye . . .") of the Old Testament, "Small Axe" is boldly confrontational. First recorded in 1969, "Small Axe" is a metaphor for the structurally disenfranchised in Jamaica—a threat that though they are disempowered, they are still capable of not only challenging but overthrowing the status quo. A power gained, ironically, in no small measure from the ways in which poverty, anger, and hunger "sharpen" the appetite for change. Unlike the layered and nuanced postcolonial critiques of the mature Marley phase, "Small Axe" throws down the gauntlet aggressively—it is an unambiguous warning to the Jamaican state. However, for all the stylistic differences, "Small Axe" provided the germ for later songs such as "Africa Unite" and "Zimbabwe"—tracks with a much broader canvas but with the same misgivings about postcolonial leadership.

The clearest demonstration of Marley's postlapsarian approach to Africa can be located in songs such as "Zimbabwe," "Redemption Song," and "Real Situation." Here Zion is the dominant ideological and spiritual trope, but Africa is tactfully stripped of its mythical purity—if not its allure. During this period Marley's work becomes much more engaged with Africa; as a result he subtly investigates, reconceptualizes, and represents the continent as an imperfect Promised Land—as opposed to the flawless Zion of his early music. While still a potential paradise for blacks in the diaspora, Africa is also depicted as both politically and spiritually deficient. Engaging this dilemma, Marley establishes a contrast between Zion and its depraved counterpart, Babylon. Through producing this exchange, he has to confront and overcome his own predispositions and deep investments in a symbolic Africa. The antecedents of this struggle can be traced directly to Marley's experiences of and in the continent in the period 1977 to 1980.

Marley in Africa

During these years Marley made three quick visits to a continent that his music had, prior to *Survival*, routinely deified. These trips were all made within the space of less than two years, after never having been to Africa before. While the final trip, Zimbabwe, was undoubtedly the highlight, the first trip was by far the most instructive and illuminating; because of this visit Marley composed *Survival*, the middle album of the trilogy and arguably the politically sharpest of his entire oeuvre. Coming as it did while he was in exile from Jamaica, the first journey to Africa was to Ethiopia, by way of Kenya, a deeply moving personal experience for Marley. In late 1978, the world's most famous reggae musician and Rastafarian was visiting not only the motherland, but Ethiopia itself. Marley, the Rasta from Trenchtown, was in Zion. Historically, this northeastern African state was afforded—as James, Amy Garvey, and George Padmore's work in the International African Service Bureau attests—a hallowed place by blacks in both the diaspora and the continent. Black people the world over regarded it as the cradle of civilization, Marcus Garvey and the Rastafarians prominent among them.

As the most famous follower of Emperor Haile Selassie, Marley had considerable trouble obtaining a visa from the new Marxist government of General Mengistu Selassie Mariam. After an oligarchical rule of more than forty years, Selassie was overthrown by Mariam's Marxist regime in 1974. Disgraced, the monarch was buried in an unmarked grave after spending the last few months of his life in internal exile. Selassie's elevated standing within the international Rastafarian community, however, was barely diminished, in no small measure because of Marley's continued loyalty and veneration in his music. The Jamaican continued to praise Selassie, no more so than in the immediate aftermath of his death. In response to the ridicule heaped on the Rastas because of Selassie's passing, Marley released a single defiantly, if unimaginatively, entitled "Jah Lives." "It's a foolish dog who barks at a flying bird," the lyrics mocked those who chanted, "Rasta, your God is dead." After a couple of years the Mariam government relented and granted Marley a visa, a delay that made his eventual visit there all the more special. Marley toured sites associated with Selassie and emerged awed and inspired by his African experience. Against this backdrop the aftermath of the military coup that had displaced Haile Selassie seemed insignificant.

What Selassie was to Marley, Elijah Muhammad's relationship to Ali can only approximate. The Nation of Islam leader was only the messenger; Selassie was a "living god." However, the relationship of these vernacular intellectuals to their spiritual father figures was in both cases marked by a problematic silence. While Ali could, and has, never indicted the messenger, Marley remained equally unable to critique Selassie for the selfsame postcolonial excesses committed by Caribbean and other African leaders. However, whereas Ali never offered any criticism, subtle or forthright, of postcolonial Africa, Marley undertook this task with craft and ingenuity. He found, unlike Ali, a lyrical way to make his point, to register his dissent from his spiritual and physical homeland. If Marley drew the line of critique at Selassie, he was still able to metonymically—if not explicitly—(slyly, implicitly) inveigh against the emperor. So adept was Marley's criticisms in his postcolonial phase that, as he was presciently indicting Mugabe, distancing himself from Manley, and making clear his dislike for Gabon's bankrupt leadership, Selassie was charged—if not indicted—by association if not by name. Finally, however, both Marley and Ali, who had—respectively—no or difficult relationships with their biological fathers, were not able to critically slay the symbolic father. And so, much like the ghost of Hamlet's father,

Selassie and Elijah Muhammad remain as unspeakable specters, remind-
ers of the limitations of their critical projects, hovering ominously over
their careers—casting shadows, sometimes longer and more portentous
than others: the ghost, of postcolonial or radical black alterity, whose
name cannot be spoken.

Nothing made the recent history of Ethiopia's civil strife pale into
insignificance more than the commitment of Mariam's (and Selassie's)
people to the struggle of their fellow Africans in Zimbabwe—black Africans engaged in a bloody war of liberation against the minority white
government of Prime Minister Ian Smith. The strong advocacy for
the Zimbabwean cause was borne as much out of support for African fraternity as it was for ideological common cause. Like Mengistu Mariam,
Robert Mugabe then still favored a Marxist state; from the Angolan and
Mozambican experience, brutally crushed by the apartheid regime (often
proxy sponsors for the United States) because of their links to Moscow, the Ethiopians had learned of the vulnerability of the Marxist
cause in Africa, and their enthusiastic promotion of the Zimbabwean
struggle attests to both an ideological displacement and wish fulfillment
of sorts. The ethnographer David Lan provides a succinct description of
the events that led up to the war for Zimbabwean independence: "In
1965, as an act of defiance of the government of Britain, the Rhodesian
parliament issued an Unilateral Declaration of Independence (UDI)
together with a clutch of promises that power would remain in the hands
of the tiny white minority for all time to come."[52] Within a year of the
UDI, black Zimbabweans had organized the first armed response to
Smith's government; when Marley was in Ethiopia the Lancaster House
agreement, a British-brokered deal that transferred power to the country's black majority, was only months away. Marley was so impressed by
the Ethiopians' Pan-African spirit that upon leaving the country he
immediately started to write and produce *Survival*. This album, produced together with the rest of the Wailers and Alex Sadkin, inspired the
most Africa-centered (but not Afro-centric) of the Wailers' albums.

Survival was Marley's considered, articulate, ambivalent (an ideological balancing evident in the discrepant views espoused in tracks such

as "Africa Unite" and "Babylon System"), and unexpected response to the second crisis—the first of the postcolonial African variety, though—in his career as vernacular intellectual. On the one hand, having gone to Ethiopia to pay homage to Selassie, he found instead a political system (a variant of Marxism that recalled Manley's) that was expansive and comradely. For a brief moment during that visit it seemed to Marley that Africa could indeed "unite," without the beneficence or the authorship of the black man he deemed god. On the other, however, he encountered in Gabon a Babylonianism that evacuated Africa of its Rastafarian mythology and its spiritual purity.

However, while black Zimbabweans of all ethnic backgrounds were uniting to defeat Smith's UDI government, the "internal power struggles" Marley was to sing about on "Zimbabwe" were wreaking havoc among two of their neighbors in southern Africa; states, moreover, who had only just attained national sovereignty. In the western and eastern corners of the subcontinent, Portugal's ex-colonies Angola and Mozambique were engaged in the first chapters of bloody and protracted civil wars. These wars, while not ignited, were certainly sponsored by the apartheid regime in South Africa—with the ideological and technical support of the United States. Opposed to the Marxist governments of Angusto Neto in Angola and Samora Machel in Mozambique, the South Africans and the Americans funded their opponents. UNITA (Angola) and Renamo (Mozambique) were patronized as convenient anti-Marxist vehicles in the southern African edition of the Cold War. Today those wars rage on even as South Africa has left behind the formal mechanisms of apartheid and the United States has long since abandoned the region.

Marley's second visit, which followed hard on the heels of the first, was the one for which he had the greatest expectations. Invited by President Omar Bongo, Marley and the Wailers flew out of Kingston with immense anticipation for a two-week sojourn in the relatively prosperous West African nation of Gabon, which was celebrating its twentieth year of independence. It was to be the Wailers' first performance on African soil, but it proved to be an anticlimactic experience. Expecting to perform for the country's general populace, Marley found the Wailers entertaining only members of the young Gabonais ruling class in a couple of concerts at a tennis stadium. "Bob tried to hide his disappointment when he learned he would not be performing in a concert for the general population," Roger Steffens writes of the event, "but would be playing in a small tennis stadium for the royal family and their friends."[53] The audiences for each of the 1979 concerts in the capital of Libreville did not exceed two thousand. It may have been the disillusionment with the lack of liberties in Gabon, on a trip taken by the Wailers at the very beginning of 1979, that counterbalances the optimism of Ethiopia on "Zimbabwe," *Survival*'s pivotal track. In the few months that separated Gabon from Ethiopia, Marley was given two starkly contrasting views of the African continent, both of which found articulation in *Survival*.

The ideological solidarity and Pan-African spirit Marley experienced in Ethiopia provided a sharp counterpoint to the elitism and self-indulgence of his visit to Gabon. The incommensurability of these two African encounters explains why Marley undercuts the celebratory tones of "Zimbabwe" with a dire warning:

No more internal power struggle
We come together to overcome
The little trouble
Soon we'll find out who is
The real revolutionaries
'Cause I don't want my people to be
Tricked by mercenaries[54]

Marley's is a prophetic view of the world, one that redeems and invokes a noble and egalitarian African past. "Zimbabwe" demonstrates how his vision is solidly grounded in the workings of contemporary history and amends itself to the conditions of the motherland as he finds them. Political optimism is never far removed from political caution. Housed in the luxurious beachfront Ikoume Palace Inter-Continental Hotel on a visit during which the group dismissed their manager Don Taylor for misappropriating funds, Marley and the Wailers did not encounter any "real revolutionaries." All he and the Wailers witnessed were the excesses of an indigenous African elite. Here was a group of black "mercenaries" who behaved in a supremely "Babylonian" fashion, antidemocratic, indulgent, and unwilling to expand freedom or improve the material conditions of life for the populace. Marley's Zion-Babylon binary, constructed on the basis of racial and caste differences, is reconfigured here. Here class—control of the nation's political and economic institutions and access to resources such as education—distinguishes the Gabonais tennis-court elite from the employees at the Inter-Continental Hotel. "Zimbabwe" is Marley's rejoinder to this particular crisis. The song reveals the ways in which Marley's critical paradigm has shifted from his earlier, optimistic mode to his mature, critical one. Though still a crucial dimension of his argument, his concern about "spiritual wickedness" is supplanted by his attacks on the disturbing ways in which Zion and Babylon resemble each other. The differences between the two conceptual spaces can no longer be reduced to a racial marker; *Zion* may denote a black African nation, but it does not inevitably follow that this is a democratic society without "spiritual wickedness," corruption, and the oppression and exploitation of blacks by blacks. At this postcolonial conjuncture, Marley recognizes how his vernacularity has to account for the failures of Zion as a black political project.

On these trips to Africa Marley finds that Zion has, to coin an awkward phrase, been "Babylonized" by the black postcolonial elite. Developing this insight, Marley critiques the black postcolonial state from a new vantage point: black Africa must be read in its own, neo-Babylonian terms. *Survival* marks both the end of Marley's "innocence" about Africa and the point in his trajectory at which race is deessentialized. A compromised Zion is filtered through a lyrical prism in which a complicated notion of race melds with his arguments about politics, ideology, class, history, and the failures of (postcolonial) nationhood and leadership. For the first time, Marley comprehends Africa critically: he sees it as a flawed and contradictory project, a collection of nation-states as capable of rhetorical support for southern Africa's struggles as it is of exploiting its masses. His affinity for Pan-Africanism does not waver, but his music displays a subtle new attribute—deftly disguised qualification and reservation.

Marley's newly nuanced understanding of the black postcolonial and diasporic condition finds a striking articulation in a single track not about blacks in Africa, but about those on the other side of the Atlantic, the United States. Posthumously released, though recorded in at least two versions near the beginning of his creatively dynamic period (1978), "Buffalo Soldier" is a rich cultural artifact. "Buffalo soldiers," as the native Americans named them, comprised black privates and noncommissioned officers who made up four post–Civil War regiments of the United States Army—the 9th and 10th Cavalry and 24th and 25th Infantry. A song about the contentious role of late-nineteenth-century African-American soldiers in the war against Native American communities such as the Cheyenne, the Commanche, and the Sioux, "Buffalo Soldiers" is a signal achievement. It demonstrates not only an application of Marley's new critical approach, but also an expansion of his lyrical landscape, a song in which issues usually pertinent in his oeuvre to Africa and the black Caribbean diaspora are investigated in a new site—and not without a controversial approach. As an ideological meditation, which is its foremost mode, "Buffalo Soldiers" is about balancing arguments and temporarily—but not indefinitely—suspending historical judgment. Marley never explicitly, or even implicitly, for that matter, denounces the black regiments. Instead, in its own muted way the song wavers between political affiliation ("Buffalo soldier, Dreadlock Rasta") and political enquiry. The song's refrain, "Buffalo soldier, Dreadlock Rasta / The heart of America," suggests the hallmarks of a Rasta tribute; Marley, it would seem, is making common cause between his own religious community and that of the African-American privates.

However, in other telling lines the Jamaican artist undercuts the communal resonance of the chorus. In these extracts Marley presents his critiques of the role of people of African descent in committing violence and atrocities against other marginal communities as a question of history. "If you know your history," he charges, "You will know where you coming from." Understanding one's origins is crucial because it determines the appropriate actions and responses in other historically pivotal situations. These lines emphasize a theme dominant in his music and a subject of key significance to his faith. Familiarity with black history, with both the minutiae of the topic and its grand accomplishments, is central to Rastafarians, a constituency that depends on its ability to craft a counternarrative with a minimum of resources. Attention to factual detail and black historical accountability echoes throughout his work. In "No Woman No Cry" he warns us, "In this great future / You can't forget your past" and, as we have already seen, in "So Much Things to Say" he crafts a minipantheon of Jamaican heroes—Garvey and Paul Bogle, victims of an unjust American legal system and British colonial violence. Their lives and their battles are an injunction across the many decades that separate their historical campaigns from the contemporary moment: "Don't forget who you are / And where you stand in the struggle." History has determined identity and charged black subjects with an unending, always critical, political responsibility.

As the bard of the Rasta experience, Marley relied on affirmative and honorable accounts of black experience with which to challenge the hegemony of white European historical, religious, and cultural narratives. The capacity to remember their struggles, to not "forget the past," is fundamental to black identity—"knowing who you are." "Knowing black history" is a cherished and much-debated subject among Rastafarian brethren. Their regular groundations, as Rodney so well knew, revolve around biblically based debates about philosophy, theology, and, most importantly, history. Rastafarians expect its adherents, and indeed black people the world over, to be aware of their past; the past gives black people cause for pride and self-worth; knowledge of past experiences shapes the black present and future. The African-American Buffalo soldiers, fourteen of whom were decorated with the Medal of Honor, were either insufficiently conscious of their own history of enslavement or disrespectful of it. Either way, their ignorance of or disregard for black history made them complicitous in the genocide of Native Americans. The Buffalo soldiers, like the postcolonial elite, had forgotten where they came from and to whom they were accountable. Consequently, neither grouping could have any conception of how they were, the Buffalo soldiers less so than the Gabonais or Zimbabwean leadership, making themselves part of a Babylonian present and future. Historically removed but ideologically analogous, the Buffalo soldiers served as an apt metaphor for Marley's critiques of postcolonial Africa.

Buffalo Africa

"Buffalo Soldier" and "Zimbabwe" are texts, both of which speak of the ways in which Marley's visits to Africa enabled him to complicate and refine his own sense of the continent's history, that undo Africa as an idealized black space. Through these songs Marley was rethinking the relationship between where he came from geographically and his symbolic and spiritual home. The Africa-Caribbean link was being reconsidered, the similarities between the two contexts explored, and the differences accounted for; in the process, Marley discovered that the antiestablishment critiques that motivated his early work in the Caribbean had found a new, though no less worthy, target. In delivering these sociopolitical commentaries, he had available a stock of images and metaphors that he—more than any other reggae artist—had created and internationalized, and to which he had only recently added a new lyrical sophistication. *Survival*, even more than the later *Uprising*, shows that Marley had made the imaginary and ideological trek (and transition) from Trenchtown to Harare—with all the valuable political lessons and songwriting tools in hand. *Survival* announced, in the most dexterous and poetic terms, that Marley had exceeded his own symbolic characterization of Africa, that he was capable of utilizing crisis to creative ends. "Privation," or loss of faith, in Marley's case, showed itself to be crucial to providing his lyrics with its critical edge. Conceptually, crises were of "great profit" to Marley.

Released in 1979, *Survival* takes as its overarching theme the condition of late-twentieth-century Africa. Many of the album's tracks address the issue of Africa's current struggles and the bleak future possibilities for the continent in a Babylonian world system. "So Much Trouble in the World," "Top Rankin'," and even the title track, relying on biblical allusion ("We're the survivors / The black survivors / Like Daniel in the lion's den"), make these points amply. But no track is quite as forceful or ideologically charged in its condemnation of postcolonial Africa's plight as "Babylon System":

> Babylon system is the vampire
> Sucking the children day by day.
> Babylon system is the vampire
> Sucking the blood of the sufferers.
> Building church and university
> Deceiving the people continually.
> Me say them graduating
> Thieves and murderers,
> Look out now
> Sucking the blood of the sufferers.
> Tell the children the truth.[55]

Marley's attack on the ruthless "Babylon" spares no institution of the "system." The "church" and the "universities" are failing in their social responsibility, behaving neither charitably nor educating the population. Marley accuses them directly of acting like pernicious and nefarious institutional state apparatuses (of Althusser's paradigm): "Me say them graduating / Thieves and murderers." The Babylonian state, which figures now as the "system" and not simply the anti-Zion state, has turned misanthropically and violently against its own. "Babylon System" is a grim portrait of parasitism, in which the postcolonial state has become transfigured as a "vampire," where the national leadership has no regard for the living conditions of the black poor. The system practices a merciless exploitation and drains the very lifeblood of its populace—"sucking the blood of the sufferers," the one moment when the song's metaphors reveal its Jamaican antecedents though *sufferers* functions as a description of a global black condition. More reprehensible than anything, however, is the system's capacity for structural deception. Not only do the religious and educational institutional state apparatus deliberately produce a false consciousness, against which the song tries to warn the citizens ("Look out now"), but the state hides its real intentions from its most vulnerable members—"Tell the children the truth," he urges. To no avail, of course, because the system is bent on indiscriminate exploitation and not accountability to the nation's variegated constituencies.

In contradistinction to this bleak portrayal of the postcolonial state in *Survival* is Marley's vision of black unity. The solidarity of black people is, in his view, the only force capable of withstanding and redressing the horrendous conditions that exist in Africa and the Caribbean. "Africa Unite," the second song on *Survival,* stands as the counterpoint to "Babylon System" and establishes the tone for this theme:

> Africa, Unite,
> 'Cause we're moving right out of Babylon,
> And we're going to our Father's land.
> . . .
> How good and how pleasant it would be,
> Before God and Man, yeah.
> To see the unification of all Africans, yeah.
> As it's been said already
> Let it be done, yeah.
> We are the children of the Rastaman.
> We are the children of the Higher Man.[56]

This gentle and hauntingly melodic tune is scored less like a protest anthem than a Marley love song. "Africa Unite" derives its force from the ways in which Marley's vocals dominate the song. His voice is soft but strong, overriding a muted beat and not thrown into relief against the choppy, insistent one that drives so many of Marley's other anthems. As the Wailers' lead singer, Marley is complemented in key moments by the harmonies of the I-Threes, the backing group—an all-female trio comprising Rita Marley, Bob's wife, Judy Mowatt, and Marcia Griffith. Like many reggae songs, "Africa Unite" draws on biblical imagery and in this instance Marley's songwriting echoes the Lord's Prayer. Giving himself over to a higher authority ("Higher Man"), Marley converts the prayer's obedience—"Let thy will be done"—into a prophetic inevitability—"As its been said already / Let it be done."

The higher authority Marley appeals to here is implicitly Selassie or "Jah," the Rastafarian abbreviation for Jehovah. It also implies a greater political cause: the unification of diasporic blacks and Africans for the "benefit" of the continent. Marley conjures up a splendid vision in his heartfelt plea for global black unity:

> How good and how pleasant it would be
> Before God and man
> To see the unification of all Africans.[57]

In later verses "Rastaman" and "Zion Man" substitute for "African," showing at once the breadth of Marley's political canvass and serving also to reinforce the continental-diasporic alliance. This conception of a seamless transatlantic black unity is a consistent feature of Marley's songwriting. Against this backdrop, where Marley's plea that blacks "unite for the benefit of your people / Unite for the benefit of the children" registers with melancholic conviction. The call for black unity acquires a special poignancy because of the physical and moral devastation visited upon children in "Babylon System." Here the children are not owed the "truth," but are the catalyst for an imagined African unity. "Zimbabwe," the most powerful track on the album, also invokes the trope of unity:

> Arm in arm
> We'll fight this little struggle
> Because that's the only way
> We come together to overcome
> This little trouble
> We're gonna fight
> We're gonna fight for our rights

Africans a liberate a Zimbabwe

I-n-I a liberate Zimbabwe[58]

Penned as a dedication to the battle Robert Mugabe and Joshua Nkomo's Patriotic Front forces were fighting against Ian Smith's Rhodesian army, it echoes the African-diasporic connection so strongly as to render the two black constituencies so united as to be interchangeable. In the patois of Jamaican Rastafarians, where "I-n-I" functions as the plural "we," the Wailers' lead vocalist proclaims that "I-n-I a liberate Zimbabwe." In this momentous historical instance the *I-n-I* of "Zimbabwe" could stand as an expression of a genuinely transatlantic, postcolonial synergy.

In this regard Marley's participation in the Zimbabwean independence celebrations was signal: it indelibly stamped his identity as a black revolutionary and authorized his standing as a postcolonial intellectual who articulated the struggles of disenfranchised and marginal communities from the Caribbean to Africa to Europe and the United States. Marley had now officially assumed, as Timothy White (author of the second biography on Marley) suggests, Marcus Garvey's mantle. Zimbabwe 1980 summarily ordained Marley as the "most charismatic emissary of modern Pan-Africanism."[59] Marley's appearance in Harare marked an occasion when his Rastafarian faith, the radical political undergirding with which he had inscribed reggae, and his ability to fuse "charismatically" these tendencies, came together in the most spectacular fashion. Through reggae, Marley had long sought to demonstrate the similarities between the struggles of black, proletarian postcolonials in sites as diverse as Gabon, Jamaica, and Zimbabwe. "Peace will come to Zimbabwe," African-American soul star Stevie Wonder had predicted (Wonder played a famous concert in Jamaica in 1975 and was one of the Americans most deeply influenced by reggae, still a relatively new phenomenon then). When "Zimbabwe" was released in 1979 it would be just a year before Marley would have the honor of leading the new nation in its first song—a prophetic compilation he had penned from across the Atlantic, an album conceived, written, and produced in exile, a condition he shared with the black Zimbabwean guerrilla leadership. Unlike Marley, however, Mugabe would prove himself blind to the lessons of African postcoloniality acquired while in exile.

"It was perhaps the single greatest moment of Bob Marley's life," writes his original biographer Stephen Davis. "He felt that he had influenced history with his music, and now was part of the solution."[60] Even more than being "part of the solution," Marley had actually aided the business of African "liberation." Just over a year later, in May 1981, the thirty-six-year-old reggae star would succumb to cancer (again in exile) in Miami, so it is appropriate that the highlight of his life should have been his role as a key cultural agent in the achievement of an African freedom. Ironically, while violence engulfed his native Jamaica, Marley was there to celebrate peace in Zimbabwe. Through reggae the cultural revolutionary from the Caribbean had combined with the guerrilla fighters in Robert Mugabe and Joshua Nkomo's armies to defeat a racist neocolonial regime.

With the Rufaro performance, the subtle critiques of postcolonialism and the revolutionary impulses that motivated and sustained reggae music were grandly displayed in the presence of the international media. Zimbabwe marks the transatlantic, Pan-African success that Garvey had dreamed of but never come close to achieving. Rufaro 1980 is the expansively Rastafarian, Jamaica-derived reinscription of Manley's Third World vision. At a moment when Muhammad Ali was turning to the right, about to endorse Reagan, Marley showed himself to be the "real, vernacular, cultural revolutionary." Marley may have been unable to take Selassie to task, but unlike Ali, he demonstrated a surer, more incisive, and astutely critical grasp of postcolonial Africa. Even when asked to come and praise, he was deft enough to dissent lyrically without giving offense. Having learned the lessons of the abortive Peace Concert in 1976, he knew how, in a foreign environment where the room for ideological maneuver was slight, to register disagreement in frequencies not low but detectable only to the wary, attentive postcolonial ear.

Marley's prescience, his instinctive unease about Mugabe, would prove accurate, but mainly because (unlike James who was unable to translate Dessalines into Nkrumah and Kenyatta) he had lived (a possibility not available to James) the failed promise of Manley; and he foresaw the grim future that Seaga would mean for the Jamaican people. While James's work on postcolonialism had fallen largely into disuse as the Trinidadian grappled with other ideological issues, stung by his inability to successfully affect political events in his native Caribbean, Marley became the antipostcolonial critic; responding energetically to the various crises he faced, Marley gave the role of vernacular antipostcolonial intellectual a substance and adroitness perhaps matched only poetically, in that moment, by the biting criticism of Kenyan novelist Ngugi wa Thiongo's work *Petals of Blood*. Published in 1978, postmodernist in feel (with the same narrative being told four times, albeit from the position of four different protagonists), *Petals of Blood* is a stinging indictment of sub-Saharan corruption, betrayal, and failure, produced by a novelist whose earlier work had formed the bulwark in the anticolonial project.

While Hall was coming to and confronting race seriously for the first time in the mid- to late 1970s, Marley already moved toward a critically different position, a product of his remaining—despite his exiles—symbolically rooted in Jamaica. Marley developed a profound dissatisfaction with, and skepticism for, black—or high-brown—postcolonial leadership. Marley had made out of popular culture a critical tool that Hall would, a decade later, recognize as the most viable weapon in the struggle against hegemony. When Bob Marley inaugurated the Zimbabwean nation, he demonstrated clearly that he had made Garvey, Selassie, and Manley's project uniquely, vernacularly, his own, inflected with nuances none of his intellectual and spiritual predecessors could have imagined. When Marley took the Rufaro stage he showed himself to be, when set alongside Ali, James, and Hall, arguably the most adept reader of the postcolonial condition: more aware of the "profit" that attends to crisis, more willing to critique, account, and apportion responsibility for its failures, less tolerant of its excesses, and in no way—

with the exception of Selassie—reluctant to lyrically indict its leadership. While Ali may stand as the prototypical, most popular, and well-known vernacular intellectual, Marley is a uniquely, poetically potent vernacular intellectual who has no postcolonial equal. Especially not as a lyrical thinker.

Notes

Introduction

1. See Houston Baker's *Blues, Ideology, and Afro-American Literature,* for a discussion of vernacularity in African-American culture (Chicago: University of Chicago Press, 1987).

2. Antonio Gramsci, *Selections from the Prison Notebooks of Antonio Gramsci,* ed. Quintin Hoare and Geoffrey Nowell Smith (New York: International Publishers, 1989), 9.

3. For a discussion of Hall's belated integration into the Caribbean intellectual tradition, see Grant Farred, "You Can Go Home Again, You Just Can't Stay," *Research in African Literatures* 27.4 (Fall 1996): 28–48.

4. The issue of transgression, of what kind of work is appropriate for black scholars to do in the academy, reached a crescendo in 2001–2002 with the very public disagreement prominent between African-American philosopher and cultural critic Cornel West and Harvard University president Lawrence Summers. According to Summers, West was spending too much time on his extracurricular pursuits, which included campaigning for the Reverend Al Sharpton and Senator Bill Bradley and making a rap album. Summers did not deem this appropriate work for a Harvard professor.

5. Jacques Derrida, *On the Name,* ed. Thomas Dutoit, trans. David Wood, John P. Levy Jr., and Ian McLeod (Stanford: Stanford University Press, 1995), 109.

6. See Stuart Hall's "Son of Margaret?" *New Statesman and Society,* October 6, 1995, for his critique of Blair. In this essay, written before Labour defeated the Tories to gain office, Hall offers an engaging account of Blair's accomplishments and, more importantly, a fairly dire warning about the consequences of

his potential ascension to power. For a further discussion of Hall's critique, see a three-part discussion between Hall and Martin Jacques: "The Great Moving Centre Show," *New Statesman*, November 21, 1997, 26–28; "Les enfants de Marx et de Coca-Cola," *New Statesman*, November 28, 1997, 34–36; and "Cultural Revolutions," *New Statesman*, December 5, 1997, 24–26.

7. For more on a critique of James's postcolonial limitations, see Grant Farred, "A Thriving Postcolonialism," *Nepantla: Views from South* 2.2 (2001): 229–46.

8. *The Oxford English Dictionary*, vol. 19, 2d ed. (Oxford: Clarendon Press, 1989).

9. Michael Hanchard, "Cultural Politics and Black Public Intellectuals," *Social Text* 48, 14.3 (Fall 1996): 95.

10. Ibid.

1. Muhammad Ali, Third World Contender

1. "Applied Derrida: An Interview," online at www.hydra.umn.edu/derrida/applied.html (August 12, 2002).

2. Robert Lipsyte, "Chicagoan's Eyes Cut and Swollen," *The New York Times*, February 7, 1967.

3. Ibid.

4. Jeffrey T. Sammons, "Rebel with a Cause: Muhammad Ali As Sixties Protest Symbol," in *Muhammad Ali: The People's Champ*, ed. Elliot J. Gorn (Chicago: University of Illinois Press, 1995), 161.

5. Muhammad Ali with Richard Durham, *The Greatest: My Own Story* (New York: Random House, 1975), 105.

6. Lipsyte, "Chicagoan's Eyes."

7. Jack Olsen, "A Case of Conscience: Learning Elijah's Advanced Lessons in Hate," *Sports Illustrated*, May 2, 1966, 37.

8. Joe Louis (as told to George Whiting), *The Ring*, February 1967, 6.

9. "White man's nigger" is, to Budd Schulberg's mind, the "most despicable of black epithets" (Schulberg, *Loser and Still Champion: Muhammad Ali* [New York: Doubleday, 1972], 48). It is burdened with the suggestions of race treachery, disloyalty, and automatic submission to whites—in short, an Uncle Tom, which is what Ali called him during the fight. For a fuller discussion of the distinction between the "white man's nigger" and the "bad nigger" see Al-Tony Gilmore's biography of Jack Johnson, *Bad Nigger! The National Impact of Jack Johnson* (Secaucus, NJ: Castle Books, 1995).

10. The desire for a White Hope reached epic and mythically victorious proportions in the 1970s with Sylvester Stallone's *Rocky* movies. In these movies whiteness is ameliorated, but not necessarily complicated, by ethnicity. Rocky— clearly intended to invoke if not emulate the great heavyweight champ Rocky Marciano—is an Italian American, a run-of-the-mill white boxer who beats the stronger, but not smarter, black champion; this black boxer, a fighter who in no way resembles Ali, is the *Rocky* movie's—or movies'—pugilistic repressed: the immensely intelligent, verbally adroit black boxer who disdains white, and black, journeyman fighters. However, if the real Ali could not be beaten by the white fighters of his day, at least he could be intellectually reduced to a Frazier-like champion, combative, tough, but not as ring-savvy as Ali, and defeated by white grit.

11. Tex Maule, "Showdown with a Punching Bag," *Sports Illustrated*, March 28, 1966, 37.

12. Eldridge Cleaver, *Soul on Ice* (New York: Bantam Doubleday, 1991), 91.

13. Floyd Patterson, "Cassius Clay Must Be Beaten," *Sports Illustrated*, October 11, 1964, 80.

14. Floyd Patterson as quoted in Gerald Early's *The Culture of Bruising: Essays on Prizefighting, Literature, and Modern American Culture* (Hopewell, NJ: Ecco Press, 1994), 36.

15. Jose Torres, . . . *Sting Like a Bee: The Muhammad Ali Story* (New York: Ableard-Schumann, 1971), 143.

16. Robert Lipsyte, "Clay Knocks Out Patterson in the 12th," *The New York Times*, November 23, 1965.

17. Ibid.

18. Floyd Patterson and Milton Gross, "I Want to Destroy Clay," *Sports Illustrated*, October 19, 1964, 43.

19. "Alas, Poor Cassius," *Ebony*, July 1965, 144.

20. No organization reflected this radicalization more than the Student Non-Violent Coordinating Committee (SNCC). A bastion of the Civil Rights brigade in the early years of the decade with its historic sit-ins and the Summer of 1964, the movement changed character dramatically in its 1966 election of office bearers—a process that saw Trinidadian-born Stokely Carmichael inducted as its chairperson. However unfair or shortsighted Carmichael's dismissal of civil rights as the "posture of . . . the dependent, the suppliant," his elevation to national leadership signaled a major break with the policies of the past (Stokely Carmichael, "Toward Black Liberation," in *An Anthology of Afro-American*

Writing, ed. Leroi Jones and Larry Neal [New York: William Morrow, 1968], 126). In "Toward Black Liberation" he clearly outlined this position: "SNCC proposes that it is now time for the black freedom movement to stop pandering to the fears and anxieties of the white middle class in the attempt to earn its 'goodwill,' and to return to the ghetto to organize these communities to control themselves" (129). Carmichael's appeal to political nationalism was a kind of rhetoric with which Ali and the Nation of Islam had more in common than the integrationist strands of the Civil Rights era.

The widespread turbulence of the 1960s found a different, though no less confrontational, articulation in white left politics of this period. The growing antiwar movement, which quickly claimed Ali as a spokesperson (and enabled him to make a living giving speeches at college campuses such as Harvard, MIT, and Princeton during his banishment from the ring), the radicalization of the university itself, the growth of underground political movements, and events such as the 1968 Siege of Chicago, were all instances of this explosive new form of white politics.

21. Jeffrey Sammons, *Beyond the Ring* (Champaign: University of Illinois Press, 1990), 200.

22. Ali, *The Greatest*, 219.

23. It is often forgotten that Patterson (b. 1935) was only a scant seven years older than Ali. The two men fought twice, first in 1965 and then again in 1972. However, in the period in which they met in the ring even the slight age difference meant considerable generational and ideological shifts. Patterson, a reformed juvenile delinquent (an "overreformed" one, as Budd Schulberg put it), could not grasp Ali's proclivities toward Islam or the nationalist impulses of the Nation. Neither, for that matter, could Patterson comprehend Liston's "disrespect"—as he perceived it—for the heavyweight crown.

24. The symbolism and political import that accrued to the Ali-Patterson bout was such that the fight recalled the intensity of the 1910 "ideological encounter," as Budd Schulberg puts it, between black champion Jack Johnson and white ex-champ Jim Jeffries (Schulberg, *Loser and Still Champion*, 47). Johnson won that July 4 fight in Reno, Nevada, convincingly, sparking outrage and anxiety in white (and black) America. White America's social Darwinism was rudely invalidated, its physical basis for supremacy seriously questioned; black America relished the triumph of a black man over a white one, but feared retribution by local whites. See Gilmore's *Bad Nigger!*, especially chapter 3, which deals with the postfight reactions.

25. Robert Lipsyte, "Clay Refuses Army Oath; Stripped of Boxing Crown," *The New York Times*, April 29, 1967.

26. Lipsyte, "Clay Refuses Army Oath."

27. Nat Fleischer, "Nat Fleischer Speaks Out," *The Ring*, June 1964, 5.

28. Jacques Derrida, *On the Name*, ed. Thomas Dutoit, trans. David Wood, John P. Levy Jr., and Ian McLeod (Stanford: Stanford University Press, 1995), 13.

29. Steve Cady, "Clay, on 2-Hour Tour of U.N., Tells of Plans to Visit Mecca," *The New York Times*, March 4, 1964.

30. "Champ's African 'Love Affair,'" *Ebony*, September 1964, 85.

31. The domestic entanglement in Indo-China also gave Ho Chi Minh's Vietnamese forces a special cachet. Panther Minister of Defense Huey Newton compared the "Negro struggle in America" to the "world revolution and to the example of the people of Vietnam. 'There were only 30 million of them,' says Newton, 'but they threw out the Japanese, then they drove out the French and now they are kicking the hell out of the Americans'" (Sol Stern, "The Call of the Black Panthers," in *Black Protest in the Sixties*, ed. August Meier and Elliot Rudwick [Chicago: Quadrangle Books, 1970], 234).

32. Carmichael, "Toward Black Liberation," 124.

33. Stern, "Call of the Black Panthers," 239.

34. Gene Roberts, "The Story of Snick," in Meier and Rudwick, *Black Protest in the Sixties*, 145; Stern, "Call of the Black Panthers," 230.

35. See C. Eric Lincoln's *The Black Muslims in America* (Boston: Beacon Press, 1961) for a history of this movement. Lincoln provides a useful account of the Nation of Islam's background, its future prospects, the kind of influence it could expect to exert in the black community, internecine struggles, as well as a discussion of how the Nation's Islamic practices diverged from that of orthodox Muslims.

36. "Decision Is Made after Long Study: Clay Says He Is Convinced That Movement Is 'the Truth and the Light,'" *The New York Times*, February 28, 1964.

37. Ali, *The Greatest*, 125.

38. Derrida, *On the Name*, 7.

39. William Nack, "The Fight's Over, Joe," *Sports Illustrated*, September 30, 1996, 60.

40. Ibid.

41. Ibid., 56.

42. Stuart Hall, "Negotiating Caribbean Identities," *New Left Review*, no. 209 (January–February 1995): 4.

43. Carmichael, "Toward Black Liberation," 119.

44. See, for example, Gilmore's *Bad Nigger!*, Jeffrey Sammons's *Beyond the Ring*, and Gerald Early's *Tuxedo Junction*.

45. Schulberg, *Loser and Still Champion*, 128.

46. Al Buck, "Clay-Johnson Parallels Warn Cassius Beware," *The Ring*, June 1966, 12.

47. Early, *The Culture of Bruising*, 61.

48. Thomas Conklin, *Muhammad Ali: The Fight for Respect* (Brookfield, CT: New Directions, Milbrook Press, 1992), 41.

49. Ali was, however, invited by Gerald Ford after he won the title from George Foreman in Zaire.

50. See Gilmore's account of the Johnson-Willard fight, "The Road to Cuba, 1915," in his *Bad Nigger!* Gilmore discusses several aspects of the bout—whether or not Johnson "threw" the fight in order to return to the United States, the champion's physical condition, the effects of exile, and the consequences of Johnson's defeat for black heavyweight contenders.

51. Buck, "Clay-Johnson Parallels Warn Cassius Beware," 12.

52. Lipsyte, "Clay Refuses Army Oath."

53. Robert Lipsyte, "Clay Discusses His Future, Liston and Black Muslims," *The New York Times*, February 27, 1964.

54. Schulberg, *Loser and Still Champion*, 48.

55. Lipsyte, "Chicagoan's Eyes Shut and Swollen."

56. For Ernie Terrell's account of the fight and how he came to call Ali "Clay," see Thomas Hauser, *Muhammad Ali: His Life and Times* (New York: Touchstone, 1991), esp. 162–63.

57. Ali, *The Greatest*, 167.

58. Othello Harris, "Muhammad Ali and the Revolt of the Black Athlete," in Gorn, *Muhammad Ali*, 66.

59. Ali, *The Greatest*, 144.

60. Ibid., 143.

61. "Alas, Poor Cassius," 144.

62. Schulberg, *Loser and Still Champion*, 47.

63. Steve Cady, "Winner by Decision," *The New York Times*, June 29, 1971.

64. See Grant Farred, "The Prettiest Postcolonial," in *Boys*, ed. Paul Smith (Boulder, CO: Westview, 1997).

65. Gilbert Rogin, "Man in the Champ's Corner," *Sports Illustrated*, May 24, 1965, 36.

66. C. L. R. James, "Garfield Sobers," in Anna Grimshaw, *The C. L. R. James Reader* (New York: Blackwell Publishers, 1992), 379.

67. Angelo Dundee as quoted in Hauser, *Muhammad Ali*, 39.

68. Gilbert Rogin, "The Giant They Love to Hate," *Sports Illustrated*, December 6, 1965, 107.

69. Budd Schulberg, epilogue to Torres, . . . *Sting Like a Bee*, 221.

70. Michael Oriard, "Muhammad Ali: Hero in the Age of Mass Media," in Gorn, *Muhammad Ali*, 9.

71. Ferdie Pacheco, *Muhammad Ali: A View from the Corner* (New York: Birch Lane Press, 1992), 16.

72. See Ali, *The Greatest*, particularly the chapters "Resurrection" and "For the Victims," in which Ali describes how he and Bundini came to coin this phrase. An important part of that process was Ali's sense of his own place in boxing history and how he drew on the legacy of, among others, Johnson, Louis, Archie Moore, and Sugar Ray Robinson.

73. As quoted in Ali, *The Greatest*, 64.

74. Thomas Hietala, "Muhammad Ali and the Age of Bare-Knuckle Politics," in Gorn, *Muhammad Ali*, 132.

75. Ali, *The Greatest*, 64.

76. Ibid.

77. Ibid.

78. "S. Africa Wants Ali for Lectures," *The New York Times*, July 29, 1972.

79. Sammons, *Beyond the Ring*, 231.

80. Ibid., 233.

81. Cheo Taylor Tyehimba, "Heavy, Ain't He," *Vibe*, March 1997.

82. Foreman recently spoke about this incident in an interview with *60 Minutes* correspondent Lesley Stahl (April 16, 1995). His explanation of his flag-waving actions was interesting but always girded by a certain patriotism. Foreman accounted for his decision in terms of his East Houston ghetto background and the way in which boxing ameliorated that experience—providing him with a rare sense of achievement; he discerned in the Olympic crowd a decided anti-Americanism and felt compelled to respond to it pugilistically; finally, however, he asked very simply how he could not do it.

83. Pacheco, *Muhammad Ali*, 136.

84. Grant Farred, "Feasting on Foreman: The Problematics of Postcolonial Identification," *Camera Obscura* 39 (September 1996): 63.

85. Ibid., 67.

86. Schulberg, *Loser and Still Champion*, 50.

2. C. L. R. James, Marginal Intellectual

1. C. L. R. James, *Beyond a Boundary* (New York: Pantheon Books, 1983), 55. All further references are to this edition and will be cited in the text.

2. Stuart Hall, "C. L. R. James: A Portrait," in *C. L. R. James's Caribbean*, ed. Paget Henry and Paul Buhle (Durham: Duke University Press, 1992), 3. In recent years James's work has been the focus of increased critical attention, as evidenced by the Henry and Buhle collection. Paul Buhle has also produced a biography, and Anna Grimshaw's *The C. L. R. James Reader* (Worcester: SUNY Press, 1995), which has been widely and favorably reviewed, provides an excellent sweep of the James oeuvre; there is also a forthcoming biography by Kent Worcester. Grimshaw and Jim Murray of the C. L. R. James Institute in New York have made significant efforts to widen the distribution of James material by putting out several pamphlets on and by James, which indicates that work is being done to redress the situation and make him available to new readers and to those who know his writing only superficially.

3. See Martin Glaberman's essay "The Marxism of C. L. R. James," *The CLR James Journal* 3.1 (Winter 1992), for a brief but effective account of the history of the Johnson-Forest tendency in the United States. The Johnsonites, as the tendency became known, was a movement that split from the main U.S. Trotskyist party, the Socialist Workers Party, primarily because of two issues: Stalinism, and their refusal to support the Soviet Union in World War II. James and Trotsky's ex-secretary Raya Dunayevskaya, respectively, adopted the pseudonyms Johnson and Forest because of James's problems with the U.S. immigration authorities. The Johnson-Forest tendency functioned as an intellectual think tank for this particular group of Trotskyists, with an accent on study groups and the publication of pamphlets by group members. James, Dunayevskaya, and the African-American philosophy Ph.D. Gracie Lee were the most prolific writers in the group, which also included Glaberman.

4. Hall, "C. L. R. James," 8.

5. Michel Foucault, "Intellectuals and Power," in *Language, Counter-Memory, Practice: Selected Essays and Interviews* (Oxford: Blackwell, 1977), 206.

6. This condition ranges from repressed and not-so-repressed anti–Eric

Williams Indian sentiment to the potentially explosive racial politics of the Basdeo Panday regime in late-twentieth-century Trinidad and Tobago.

7. This same sense of distance from the life of the Trinidadian masses is expressed by the narrator of James's first published short story, "La Divina Pastora." The story opens with what amounts to a disavowal, though not a lack of investment, by the narrator: "Of my own belief in the story I shall say nothing. What I have done is to put it down as far as possible just as it was told to me, in my own style, but with no addition to or subtraction from the substantial facts" ("La Divina Pastora," in Grimshaw, *C. L. R. James Reader*, 25). His determination to achieve authenticity reduced him to the function of social conduit rather than local historian.

8. C. L. R. James, *Minty Alley* (London: New Beacon Books, 1971), 21.

9. *The Concise Oxford Dictionary*, 5th ed. (Oxford: Clarendon Press, 1964).

10. Edward Said, *Culture and Imperialism* (New York: Alfred A. Knopf, 1993), 245.

11. Julien Benda, *The Treason of the Intellectuals [La trahison des clercs]*, trans. Richard Aldington (New York: W. W. Norton, 1969), 45.

12. Antonio Gramsci, "The Formation of Intellectuals," in *The Modern Prince and Other Writings*, trans. Louis Marks (New York: International Publishers, 1959), 118.

13. R. Radhakrishnan, "Toward an Effective Intellectual: Foucault or Gramsci?" in *Intellectuals: Aesthetics, Politics, Academics*, ed. Bruce Robbins (Minneapolis: University of Minnesota Press, 1990), 63.

14. Gramsci, "The Formation of Intellectuals," 89.

15. Radhakrishnan, "Toward an Effective Intellectual," 88.

16. The *Chambers Twentieth-Century Dictionary* defines *organic* as "pertaining to, derived from, like, of the nature of, an organ (in any sense)."

17. "C. L. R. James: West Indian George Lamming interviewed by Paul Buhle," in Henry and Buhle, *C. L. R. James's Caribbean*, 34.

18. In his introduction to *Intellectuals*, Robbins provides a careful working through of the "grounding of intellectuals" (Robbins, *Intellectuals*, xi–xii), particularly in relation to Gramsci's and Foucault's work on intellectuals.

19. Gayatri Chakravorty Spivak, "Criticism, Feminism, and the Institution," in Robbins, *Intellectuals*, 170.

20. I want to make it clear that I am using Spivak's phrase, articulated in an interview with Elizabeth Gross, mainly as a point of departure to think through the issue of how James comes to commit himself to the concept of a

working-class revolution. Spivak herself says nothing further in the interview to develop or amend the point, but her brief comments offered an entree into this vital aspect of James's intellectual life. The denseness of Spivak's phrase, and the kind of unpacking it required, served as catalysts for engaging this task.

21. Salman Rushdie's *Satanic Verses* of course shows how, over the course of successive generations, the migrant communities from the erstwhile colonies impact culturally on the life of the metropolis. In the postcolonial moment, where the migrant communities have secured a place for themselves, they can now move beyond the confines of that space and transform the metropolis itself in terms that Gibreel Farishta proposes: "No more British reserve; hot water bottles to be banished forever, replaced in the foetid nights by the making of slow and odorous love. Emergence of new social values: friends to commence dropping in on one another without making appointments, closure of old folks' homes, emphasis on the extended family" (Rushdie, *The Satanic Verses* [New York: Viking Penguin, 1989], 354).

22. See, in this regard, the work of authors as different as Sam Selvon *(The Lonely Londoners)* and Buchi Emecheta *(Second Class Citizen)*, inter alia, who deal with the experience of first-generation Caribbean and sub-Saharan African immigrants, respectively, through markedly difference prisms—race and gender. The work of the Trinidadian-born Selvon is especially resonant here because it applies both to James and Hall, writing as he does from the location of a post–*Empire Windrush* experience that recalls earlier moments in the Caribbean migration to Britain.

23. Robbins, introduction to *Intellectuals*, xix.

24. James, *The Black Jacobins*, 198.

25. Ibid., 120.

26. Michel Foucault, "On Popular Justice: A Discussion with Maoists," in Michel Foucault, *Power/Knowledge: Selected Interviews and Other Writings 1972–1977*, ed. Colin Gordon, trans. Colin Gordon, Leo Marshall, John Mepham, and Kate Soper (New York: Pantheon Books, 1980), 3.

27. James, *The Black Jacobins*, 60.

28. C. L. R. James, *American Civilization* (Oxford: Basil Blackwell, 1993), 297.

29. Grimshaw, *C. L. R. James Reader*, 7. All further references to this work will be cited in the text.

30. See the essay "The Revolutionary Answer to the Negro Problem in the USA," in which James develops this point more fully; see also "Black People

in the Urban Areas of the United States," both of which are in Grimshaw, *C. L. R. James Reader*.

31. It is interesting to note that in the 1938 reception of *The Black Jacobins*, reviewers often gestured toward the connections between James's critique of late-eighteenth-century colonialism and contemporary colonial conditions without ever investigating these links more fully. The review in *The Keys* is representative in this regard: "But still the clearest warnings are the lessons in revolution, for to the end we are faced with many of the symptoms that exist today, and the writer strikes many parallels in today's imperial world, leaving the reader to draw the moral" (*The Keys* 6.2 [October–December 1938]: 3). See also Said, *Culture and Imperialism*, 245–61.

32. James, "The Case for West Indian Self Government," in Grimshaw, *C. L. R. James Reader*, 62.

33. In only one of the reviews of the first publication of *The Black Jacobins* (London: Purnell and Sons, 1938) have I been able to find any commentary on the analogy between the Haitian insurrection and the broader project of the International African Service Bureau. In the very last paragraph of *The Keys* review, "K. A." writes, "This period in West Indian history provides many invaluable lessons in de-imperialisation, and demonstrates the arguments in favour of such a step" (review in *The Keys*, 3).

34. The preceding three paragraphs comprise a transcription, with some adjustments, omissions, and rewritings, from my essay "A Thriving Postcolonialism: Toward an Anti-Postcolonial Discourse" (*Nepantla* 2.2 [2001]: 236).

35. C. L. R. James, *Modern Politics: A Series of Lectures on the Subject Given at the Trinidad Public Library, in Its Adult Education Programme* (Detroit: Bewick Editions, 1973), i.

36. C. L. R. James, *Party Politics in the West Indies* (San Juan, Trinidad: Imprint Caribbean, 1962), 11.

37. See the foreword and "Part I: The Report of June 1958" in James, *Party Politics*. In one of his more savage attacks on the PNM leadership, James accuses the party of political bankruptcy and intransigence: "In many cases the Party does not exist except in name and the most urgent and repeated efforts to correct this meet with the indifference, carelessness, ignorance and now the obstinacy and hostility of the Party leadership" (5).

38. Unlike St. Hill, who remained in Trinidad all his life, Constantine would not tolerate the disjuncture between his limited cultural enfranchisement and political disenfranchisement: "Constantine, the heir-apparent, the happy

warrior, the darling of the crowd, prize pupil of the [white] captain of the West Indies, had revolted against the revolting contrast between his first-class status as a cricketer and his third-class status as a man. The restraints imposed upon him by social conditions in the West Indies had become intolerable and he decided to stand them no longer" (James, *Beyond a Boundary*, 110). Constantine left for England, where he played professional cricket for Nelson in the Lancashire League. In fact, Constantine sponsored James's first trip to England and he also underwrote the expenses for the publication of *The Case for West Indian Self-Government*.

39. See "Garfield Sobers," in Grimshaw, *C. L. R. James Reader*, 378–89, and "Kanhai: A Study in Confidence," in C. L. R. James, *At the Rendezvous of Victory: Selected Writings* (London: Allison and Busby, 1984), 166–71. See also *Cricket*, ed. Anna Grimshaw (London: Allison and Busby, 1986).

40. From the pamphlet by Anna Grimshaw and Keith Hart, "C. L. R. James and *The Struggle for Happiness*" (New York: The C. L. R. James Institute, 1991), 49.

3. Stuart Hall, the Scholarship Boy

1. "The Formation of a Diasporic Intellectual: An Interview with Stuart Hall by Kuan-Hsing Chen," in *Stuart Hall: Critical Dialogues in Cultural Studies*, ed. David Morley and Kuan-Hsing Chen (New York: Routledge, 1996), 487.

2. Ruth Glass (assisted by Harold Pollins), *London's Newcomers: The West Indian Migrants* (Cambridge: Harvard University Press, 1961), 94.

3. Tom Nairn, *The Break-Up of Britain: Crisis and Neo-Nationalism* (London: Verso, 1981), 75.

4. England, rather than Britain, is the national project in which Hall is invested. Even as he is identified as a member of the British left, for him that is an Anglo-centered political institution that hegemonically includes in its ranks the Scots, Welsh, and Irish. England, be it London, Oxford, or Birmingham, is the ideological configuration from which Hall engages not only the rest of the world, but also the other nation-states that compose Britain. The phrase *Anglo-British* that Nairn, a Scot who was heavily involved in the New Left, coined enunciates the split between how "England," the political base from which the Rhodes scholar works, and his critiques of "Britain," the larger sociopolitical entity that is affected by developments in London, functions for Hall. This distinction simultaneously enables a situation of Hall within the British left and a full recognition that a discussion of that political bloc infers an English center,

a (neo)imperial site that draws on and interpellates a Scot such as Nairn, a working-class Welshman such as Raymond Williams, and a brown middle-class Jamaican such as Hall.

5. E. P. Thompson, "Outside the Whale," in *Out of Apathy*, ed. E. P. Thompson (Kenneth Alexander, Stuart Hall, Alasdair MacIntyre, Samuel Ralph, Peter Worsley) (London: New Left Books, Steven and Sons Limited, 1960), 188.

6. Michael Kenny, *The First New Left: British Intellectuals after Stalin* (London: Lawrence and Wishart, 1995), 4.

7. As a description of the New Left's ideological basis, "socialist humanism" is not only apt but clearly articulated in the subtitle of the *New Reasoner: A Journal of Socialist Humanism*, one of the two journals out of which the *New Left Review* was borne. (The other journal was, of course, the *Universities and Left Review*.) The *New Reasoner* was edited by the two Yorkshire historians John Saville and E. P. Thompson from 1957 to 1959. Thompson's contribution to the development of socialist humanism was particularly important, nowhere more so than in his work *William Morris: Romantic to Revolutionary* in which he claims the poet as both a radical and thinker with a strong sense of political conscience and morality.

8. Lin Chun, *The British New Left* (Edinburgh: Edinburgh University Press, 1993), 7.

9. Founded in the early 1930s by a group of first-generation middle-class intellectuals in Cambridge's recently established English School (led by F. R. and Q. D. Leavis), the *Scrutiny* collective positioned itself as an "anti-[Bloomsbury] *salon*" (Francis Mulhern, *The Moment of "Scrutiny"* [London: New Left Books, 1979], 34).

10. Ibid., 95.

11. Chun, *The British New Left*, 27.

12. Raymond Williams, *Culture and Society: 1780–1950* (New York: Columbia University Press, 1983), 319.

13. In tracing the trajectory and lineage of the New Left, David Harris measures the historic import of the cultural impact of the movement's intellectual progenitors. Approaching Hoggart's, Williams's, and Thompson's writings as an heir of the New Left's cultural politics, Harris recognizes how these figures "opened our eyes to our own [working-class] traditions and cultures, restored our history, raised our consciousness, and rattled the confidence of the middle classes by destroying the old myths about an inferior, passive and ignorant proletariat" (David Harris, *From Class Struggle to the Politics of Pleasure: The Effects of*

Gramscianism on Cultural Studies [New York: Routledge, 1992], xiv). Though one could take issue with Harris about the "passivity" of the working class (a hundred years of class warfare had certainly done a great deal to dispense with that notion, one would have presumed), he nevertheless provides a sense of the importance of Williams, Thompson, and Hoggart to later generations of cultural critics.

14. Alasdair MacIntyre, "Breaking the Chains of Reason," in Thompson, *Out of Apathy*, 239.

15. Stuart Hall produced the CND manifesto, *Steps Toward Peace*. See Peter Sedgwick's introduction to *The Left in Britain, 1956–68* for a historicization and critique of CND. Sedgwick is particularly useful on the "international" aspect of CND (*The Left in Britain, 1956–68*, ed. David Widgery [Harmondsworth: Penguin, 1976], 24–26).

16. Edward Thompson and John Saville, "Beyond the Bomb," in Widgery, *The Left in Britain*, 124.

17. The other members of the editorial board were Gabriel Pearson, a graduate student in English at Balliol College; Charles Taylor, a Canadian Christian socialist; and Ralph Samuel, a Jewish historian at Oxford. Samuel and Pearson were from Communist Party backgrounds while Hall and Taylor represented the independent left tradition in Britain. See also Chun, *British New Left*, 13.

18. See Peter Sedgwick, "The Two New Lefts," in which he dates the "first New Left" from the "spring of 1957 until around the summer of 1961" (in Widgery, *The Left in Britain*, 131).

19. Stuart Hall, "Introduction," *New Left Review*, no.1 (January–February 1960): 1.

20. In the inaugural issues of the *New Left Review*, culture, economics, class, and the role of Cold War intellectuals were debated regularly. In the very first issue, Ralph Miliband critiqued the Labour Party's economic policies ("The Sickness of Labourism"), Ralph Samuel cast a skeptical eye on the "prosperity" of the welfare state ("The Deference Voter"), Michael Barratt Brown investigated Soviet imperialism ("Yugoslavia Revisited"), and Hoggart and Williams coauthored an essay on trends in working-class culture ("Working Class Attitudes"). Together with these authors, Thompson and Hall (who did a few pieces on literature in addition to editorial work) formed the core of the *New Left Review*'s contributors.

21. C. Wright Mills, "Letter to the New Left," *New Left Review*, no. 5 (September–October 1960): 22.

22. David Harris's *From Class Struggle to the Politics of Pleasure* is highly, and in places unfairly, critical of the first New Left's cultural concerns and the formation of cultural studies in particular. Harris, however, is useful in explaining the difference between the early and the second New Left. Under the editorial leadership of Anderson and Nairn, Harris argues, the *New Left Review* came into its own with its critiques of the "sad state of British political culture"; in lieu of a "native radical tradition due to [Britain's] peculiar history," the journal took on the task of appointing intellectuals to "investigate and popularise serious academic Marxist theory found in other (mostly European) countries" (Harris, *From Class Struggle to the Politics of Pleasure*, xv).

23. Antonio Gramsci and Louis Althusser are among the most influential European theorists who were introduced to and taken up by the British left. Much of the work of the European theorists, Althusser's in particular, was focused on a rethinking of Marx. Toward the end of the 1960s and the early 1970s the French structuralists, feminism, and the linguistic theories of Sassure also entered the critical vocabulary of the New Left. In that period theorists such as the sociologist Karl Mannheim were teaching at British institutions, the London School of Economics in his case.

24. The Anderson-Nairn/Thompson debates started in 1964 with Anderson's "The Origins of the Present Crisis" and continued for a couple of years. See particularly the *New Left Review* 1964 through 1966, especially Thompson's 1965 essay "The Peculiarities of the English"; also, Chun devotes a section of her chapter "Society and Politics" in *The British New Left* to these exchanges.

25. Nairn, *The Break-Up of Britain*, 367.

26. See note 13 for a discussion on the influence of European theory on the British New Left. See also Harris's *From Class Struggle to the Politics of Pleasure*, chapters 2 through 4, for an engagement with the compartmentalization of history (the "attempt to periodise history into phases of settlement and crisis is characteristically gramscian"); the construction of youth as a political category ("'youth' as a significant new social grouping"); and women (the importance of the Women's Study Group for Birmingham University's Centre for Contemporary Cultural Studies).

27. Seth Moglen, introduction to *Out of Apathy: Voices of the New Left Thirty Years On*, ed. Robin Archer et al. (London: Verso, 1989), 5.

28. Chun, *British New Left*, 147.

29. Nairn, *The Break-Up of Britain*, 277.

30. The first of these figures was obtained from Paul B. Rich's *Race and Empire in British Politics* (New York: Cambridge University Press, 1990, 167), a work that demonstrates the link between black immigration and British industrial needs; the later number is cited in Francois Bedarida's *A Social History of England, 1851–1990* (New York: Routledge, 1991, 278). Bedarida argues that by 1971 immigrants, of whom the greater majority is from the Caribbean and south Asia, constituted 2.5 percent of the British population.

31. Glass, *London's Newcomers*, 27.

32. Richard Hoggart, *The Uses of Literacy* (London: Penguin, 1958), 292.

33. Rex Nettleford, leading scholar of black Jamaican culture, is one Caribbean intellectual whose trajectory from Oxbridge provides a perfect counterpoint to Hall's. Black in Jamaican terms, and invested in working-class culture from a much earlier moment than Hall, Nettleford returned to Kingston after finishing his studies in England and within a year he had embarked on his crusade to promote and critically engage Afro-Caribbean cultural practices. Nettleford's commitment to black culture was, until that moment, unprecedented in Jamaican history.

34. Stuart Hall and Paddy Whannel, *The Popular Arts: A Critical Guide to the Mass Media* (Boston: Beacon Press, 1964), 13. All further references to this work will be cited in the text.

35. I use "Birmingham scholars" to suggest that while the CCCS represented a common project, a multiplicity of positions existed among the intellectuals who worked there. As Hall has said, "There is no such thing as the Birmingham school. (To hear 'the Birmingham School' evoked is, for me, to confront a model of alienation in which something one took part in producing returns to greet one as thing, in all its inevitable facticity)" (Hall, "The Emergence of Cultural Studies and the Crisis of the Humanities," *October*, no. 53 [1990]: 11–23; quotation from 11).

36. Ibid.

37. Ibid. Among the graduate students who emerged out of the Birmingham program are Paul Gilroy, Angela McRobbie, Simon Frith, and Hazel Carby, all of whom have continued to work in the cultural studies project in some form or another.

38. See Albert K. Cohen's work on deviancy, especially *Deviance and Social Control* (Englewood Cliffs, NJ: Prentice Hall, 1966) and *Delinquent Boys: The Culture of the Gang* (Glencoe, IL: Free Press, 1964). See also *Deviance and Social Control*, ed. Paul Rock and Mary McIntosh (London: Tavistock, 1974). This collection features an essay by Hall, "Deviance, Politics and the Media."

39. Stuart Hall and Tony Jefferson, eds., *Resistance through Rituals: Youth Subcultures in Post-War Britain* (Cambridge: Cambridge University Press, 1976), 12.

40. Hall, *The Hard Road to Renewal: Thatcherism and the Crisis of the Left* (London: Verso, 1988), 36.

41. Kenny, *The First New Left*, 159.

42. Hall, *Hard Road to Renewal*, 7.

43. Antonio Gramsci, *Selections from the Prison Notebooks of Antonio Gramsci*, ed. Quintin Hoare and Geoffrey Nowell Smith (New York: International Publishers, 1989), 14.

44. Karl Marx, "The Eighteenth Brumaire of Louis Bonaparte," in *The Marx-Engels Reader*, ed. Robert C. Tucker (New York: W. W. Norton, 1978), 595.

45. Stuart Hall belongs to a generation of Caribbean intellectuals who came to Britain in the late 1940s and early 1950s, a generation that included the Trinidadian-born novelist V. S. Naipaul. Like Hall, Naipaul attended Oxford after arriving in England a year before the Jamaican, but their ideological trajectories—their relationship to blackness and the politics of race in the metropolis and their places of origin—could not have been more divergent.

46. Stuart Hall, Chas Critcher, Tony Jefferson, John Clarke, Brian Roberts, *Policing the Crisis: Mugging, the State, and Law and Order* (London: Macmillan, 1978), 245.

47. Morley and Chen, "Formation of a Diasporic Intellectual," 502.

48. Stuart Hall, "Minimal Selves," in *Identity: The Real Me, ICA Documents 6* (London: Institute of Contemporary Arts), 44.

49. Ibid.

50. Morley and Chen, "Formation of a Diasporic Intellectual," 488.

51. Ibid., 485.

52. Stuart Hall, "Black Britons," in E. Butterworth and D. Weir, eds., *Social Problems of Modern Britain* (London: Fontana, 1972), 324. Hall's essay was first published in 1970 in the journal *Community* (April 1970), the quarterly journal of the Community Relations Commission.

53. Morley and Chen, "Formation of a Diasporic Intellectual," 501.

54. Stuart Hall, "Racism and Reaction," in *Five Views of Multi-Racial Britain: Talks on Race Relations Broadcast by BBC-TV* (London: Commission for Racial Equality, 1978), 24.

55. Immediately after the Great War, "in the early summer of 1919, there

were dramatic race riots in Cardiff and Liverpool" and "disturbances in most dock areas which had coloured 'colonies'—in Newport, on Tyneside, in Glasgow and in the East End of London" (Glass, *London's Newcomers*, 127).

56. At the start of the 1950s, the West Indian population in Britain stood at 74,500; by 1959 that figure grew to some 336,000.

57. Rich, *Race and Empire in British Politics*, 175.

58. Ibid., 164.

59. Glass, *London's Newcomers*, 130.

60. Ibid., 153.

61. See Stuart Hall's essay "A Torpedo Aimed at the Boiler-room of Consensus," *New Statesman*, April 17, 1998, for Hall's reflection thirty years later on the ways in which Enoch Powell's rhetoric reconstituted the discourse of race in postcolonial Britain.

62. Glass, *London's Newcomers*, 244.

63. Rich, *Race and Empire in British Politics*, 186.

64. This information was obtained in an interview of Paul Gilroy in London, June 1993, in a discussion about Stuart Hall.

65. Hall, "Racism and Reaction," 25.

66. See David Widgery's *The Left in Britain, 1956–68* for a critique of the New Left in its fullest national and international perspective. The crises of Suez and Hungary are discussed along with commentary on the Campaign for Nuclear Disarmament, arguably the most successful New Left political movement. Notting Hill and Kelso Cochrane, however, are glossed over and not represented as crucial political moments.

67. Hall, *Policing the Crisis*.

68. Edward Said, *Representations of the Intellectuals* (New York: Pantheon Books, 1994), 11.

69. Hall, *Policing the Crisis*, 100.

70. Ibid., vii; emphasis in original.

71. Ibid., 29.

72. Paul Gilroy has addressed this issue consistently in his work and it finds succinct, eloquent expression in *Small Acts: Thoughts on the Politics of Black Cultures*, a collection of essays. In "Wearing Your Art on Your Sleeve," Gilroy historicizes the defensive posture of the first generation in terms of cultural familiarity. "The proximity of Britain's black settlers to the experience of migration," he holds, "also means that the cultures of the Caribbean have provided important resources which enabled people to retain and re-create links with the

cultures from which they came" (Gilroy, *Small Acts* [London: Serpent's Tail, 1993], 251). See also Sam Selvon's novel *The Lonely Londoners*, which narrativizes the experience of first-generation immigrant alienation.

73. Hall, *Policing the Crisis*, 245.

74. Ibid., 101.

75. Gilroy, *Small Acts*, 249.

76. Ibid., 251.

77. Hall, *Policing the Crisis*, 351.

78. Hall, *Hard Road to Renewal*, 32.

79. Ibid., 75, 55.

80. See Hall's essay "The Great Moving Right Show" in *The Hard Road to Renewal* for a discussion of this phenomenon.

81. Ibid., 68.

82. Ibid., 299.

83. Ibid., 80.

84. Hall, *Hard Road to Renewal*, 79.

85. Hall, "Black Britons," 324.

86. Hall, *Policing the Crisis*, 351.

87. Hall, "Minimal Selves," 44.

88. Hall, *Hard Road to Renewal*, 4.

89. Ibid., 2, 262.

90. Ibid., 68, 44.

91. Ibid., 272, 7.

92. Ibid., 235, 253.

93. Ibid., 12, 13, 178, 250.

94. Stuart Hall, "Son of Margaret?" in *New Statesman and Society*, October 6, 1995, 28.

95. Ibid., 29.

96. Hall, *Hard Road to Renewal*, 83. 2.

97. Ibid., 19.

98. Ibid., 77, 78.

4. Bob Marley, Postcolonial Sufferer

1. The early Wailers music was deeply influenced by New Orleans–based soul artists such as Fats Domino, Louis Jordan, Alvin Robinson, and Huey "Piano" Smith. Marley and Bunny Wailer also modeled their first harmonies on the work of the Drifters (songs such as "There Goes My Baby" and "This Magic

Moment" were especially popular on Jamaican radio) and, more importantly, the Impressions, a trio hailing from Chicago. The two lead singers, Jerry Butler and Curtis Mayfield, were vocalists on whom the nascent Wailers modeled themselves.

2. Horace Campbell, *Rasta and Resistance: From Marcus Garvey to Walter Rodney* (Dar Es Salaam: Tanzania Publishing House, 1985), 95.

3. Eusi Kwayama, preface to Campbell, *Rasta and Resistance*, ix.

4. This quote is from my notes on Roger Steffens's presentation on Bob Marley at the Rock 'n' Roll Hall of Fame and Museum in Cleveland, Ohio, on February 4, 1996; used with Steffens's permission.

5. Bob Marley, "Natural Mystic," in *Bob Marley: Songs of Freedom* (Milwaukee, WI: Hal Leonard Publishing, 1992), 117.

6. *Bob Marley: Songs of Freedom*, comp. Trevor Wyatt and Neville Garrick (Birmingham, England: Island Records, 1992), 44.

7. These lyrics have been transcribed by the author.

8. Stephen Davis, *Bob Marley* (Rochester, VT: Schenkman Books, 1990), 228.

9. Davis, *Bob Marley*, 1. Davis provides a useful definition of *custos*, which distinguishes between the state-sanctioned understanding and the local interpretation of the position. "Officially," he writes, "the title of custos referred to the chief magistrate of the parish who presided over the courthouse at St. Ann's Bay, fifteen miles away on the north coast of the island. But in the speech of the Jamaican country people, the custos is a man who, though short of stature, still commands enormous respect" (Davis, *Bob Marley*, 1).

10. Anthony Payne, *Politics in Jamaica* (New York: St. Martin's Press, 1994), 18.

11. Davis, *Bob Marley*, 25.

12. Leonard E. Barrett Sr., *The Rastafarians: Sounds of Cultural Dissonance* (Boston: Beacon Press, 1988), ix.

13. Rex Nettleford, *Mirror, Mirror: Identity, Race, and Protest in Jamaica* (London: Collins Clear-Type Press, 1970), 139.

14. Davis, *Bob Marley*, 49.

15. During his performance at the 1976 Peace Concert, Tosh used the occasion to berate the Jamaican authorities and to call for the legalization of ganja. The police responded by arresting him at a roadblock and beating him severely.

16. Nettleford, *Mirror, Mirror*, 45.

17. George Lamming, untitled article, *Daily News*, September 28, 1980.

18. Carolyn Cooper, *Noises in the Blood: Orality, Gender, and the "Vulgar" Body of Jamaican Popular Culture* (Durham: Duke University Press, 1995), 118.

19. Campbell, *Rasta and Resistance*, 89.

20. In his essay "Introducing the Native Religions of Jamaica," Barry Chevannes makes the point about how Garvey created an interest in events in Africa. "The Afrocentricity of Garveyism," he claims, "would of itself have made his followers in Jamaica turn their attention to the momentous events in Ethiopia" (*Rastafari and Other African-Caribbean Worldviews*, ed. Barry Chevannes [London: Macmillan, 1995], 10.)

21. Barry Chevannes, "New Approach to Rastafari," in Chevannes, *Rastafari and Other African-Caribbean Worldviews*, 29.

22. Marcus Garvey's speech delivered at Madison Square Garden, March 1924, quoted in John Henrik Clarke, "Marcus Garvey: The Harlem Years," *Transition*, no. 46 (1974): 14–19.

23. Marcus Garvey, "A Journey of Self-Discovery," in *Marcus Garvey and the Vision of Africa*, ed. John Henrik Clarke with the assistance of Amy Jacques Garvey (New York: Vintage Books, 1974), 75.

24. Marcus Garvey, "The British West Indies in the Mirror of Civilization," in Clarke, *Marcus Garvey and the Vision of Africa*, 82.

25. Joseph Owens, *Dread: The Rastafarians of Jamaica* (London: Heinemann, 1979), 243.

26. Marley, *Bob Marley: Songs of Freedom*, 131.

27. Cooper, *Noises in the Blood*, 130.

28. Marley, *Bob Marley: Songs of Freedom*, 131.

29. Manley, *The Politics of Change* (Kingston, Jamaica: Heinemann, 1990), 154.

30. Marley, *Bob Marley: Songs of Freedom*, 14.

31. The term *Afro-Saxon*, which has pejorative implications in the Caribbean, is used more affirmatively in the British metropolis. There it functions both as an instance of clever wordplay (a racialized, postcolonial punning of *Anglo-Saxon*) and a marker of the ways in which sectors of the black Caribbean population have integrated themselves into the British experience—in the process of which they have of course considerably altered the British cultural and political landscape.

32. These lyrics have been transcribed by the author.

33. Manley, *Politics of Change*, 16; Darrel E. Levi, *Michael Manley: The Making of a Leader* (London: Andre Deutsch Limited, 1989), 126.

34. For a brief discussion of the relationship of Michael Manley and Edward Seaga to Jamaican popular music, see Dick Hebdige's *Cut 'N' Mix: Culture, Identity and Caribbean Music* (New York: Routledge, 1990; esp. chap. 14) and Stephen Davis and Peter Simon's *Reggae Bloodlines: In Search of the Music and Culture of Jamaica* (New York: Da Capo Press, 1992).

35. Payne, *Politics in Jamaica*, 45.

36. Hebdige, *Cut 'N' Mix*, 124.

37. Walter Rodney, *The Groundings with My Brothers* (London: Frontline Publishers, 1969), 64.

38. Payne, *Politics in Jamaica*, 15.

39. Manley, *Politics of Change*, 90.

40. Ibid., 156.

41. These lyrics have been transcribed by the author.

42. Manley, *Politics of Change*, 49.

43. These lyrics have been transcribed by the author.

44. Manley, *Politics of Change*, 203.

45. *Jamaica Hansard: Proceedings of the House of Representatives* 1.1 (1972–73): 313.

46. Manley, *Politics of Change*, 154.

47. Marley, *Songs of Freedom*, 147.

48. Manley, *Politics of Change*, 131.

49. These lyrics have been transcribed by the author.

50. Bob Marley, *Uprising*, sound recording (Tuff Gong Records, 1980).

51. Marley, *Songs of Freedom*, 151.

52. David Lan, *Guns and Rain: Guerrillas and Spirit Mediums in Zimbabwe* (Berkeley and Los Angeles: University of California Press, 1985), 3.

53. Roger Steffens, introduction to Bruce Talamon, *Bob Marley: Spirit Dancer* (Kingston: West Indies Publishing, 1994), 25.

54. These lyrics have been transcribed by the author.

55. As quoted in Cooper, *Noises in the Blood*, 123.

56. Marley, *Songs of Freedom*, 9.

57. Ibid.

58. The lyrics have been transcribed by the author.

59. Timothy White, *Catch a Fire: The Life of Bob Marley* (New York: Henry Holt, 1994), 2.

60. Davis, *Bob Marley*, 228.

Permissions

The University of Minnesota Press gratefully acknowledges permission to reprint the following song lyrics.

"Natural Mystic" (Bob Marley) copyright 1977 Fifty-Six Hope Road Music Ltd./ Odnil Music Ltd./Blue Mountain Music Ltd. (PRS). All rights for the United States controlled and administered by Rykomusic, Inc. (ASCAP). International copyright secured. All rights reserved.

"Slave Driver" (Bob Marley) copyright 1973 Fifty-Six Hope Road Music Ltd./ Odnil Music Ltd./Blue Mountain Music Ltd. (PRS). All rights for the United States controlled and administered by Rykomusic, Inc. (ASCAP). International copyright secured. All rights reserved.

"One Love" (Bob Marley) copyright 1968 Fifty-Six Hope Road Music Ltd./ Odnil Music Ltd./Blue Mountain Music Ltd. (PRS). All rights for the United States controlled and administered by Rykomusic, Inc. (ASCAP). International copyright secured. All rights reserved.

"So Much Things to Say" (Bob Marley) copyright 1977 Fifty-Six Hope Road Music Ltd./Odnil Music Ltd./Blue Mountain Music Ltd. (PRS). All rights for the United States controlled and administered by Rykomusic, Inc. (ASCAP). International copyright secured. All rights reserved.

"We and Dem" (Bob Marley) copyright 1980 Fifty-Six Hope Road Music Ltd./ Odnil Music Ltd./Blue Mountain Music Ltd. (PRS). All rights for the United States controlled and administered by Rykomusic, Inc. (ASCAP). International copyright secured. All rights reserved.

"Small Axe" (Bob Marley) copyright 1974 Fifty-Six Hope Road Music Ltd./Odnil Music Ltd./Blue Mountain Music Ltd. (PRS). All rights for the United States controlled and administered by Rykomusic, Inc. (ASCAP). International copyright secured. All rights reserved.

"Zimbabwe" (Bob Marley) copyright 1979 Fifty-Six Hope Road Music Ltd./Odnil Music Ltd./Blue Mountain Music Ltd. (PRS). All rights for the United States controlled and administered by Rykomusic, Inc. (ASCAP). International copyright secured. All rights reserved.

"Babylon System" (Bob Marley) copyright 1979 Fifty-Six Hope Road Music Ltd./Odnil Music Ltd./Blue Mountain Music Ltd. (PRS). All rights for the United States controlled and administered by Rykomusic, Inc. (ASCAP). International copyright secured. All rights reserved.

"No Woman No Cry" (Vincent Ford) copyright 1974 Fifty-Six Hope Road Music Ltd./Odnil Music Ltd./Blue Mountain Music Ltd. (PRS). All rights for the United States controlled and administered by Rykomusic, Inc. (ASCAP). International copyright secured. All rights reserved.

"War" (Allen Cole/Carlton Barrett) copyright 1976 Fifty-Six Hope Road Music Ltd./Odnil Music Ltd./Blue Mountain Music Ltd. (PRS). All rights for the United States controlled and administered by Rykomusic, Inc. (ASCAP). International copyright secured. All rights reserved.

"Belly Full" aka "Them Belly Full (But We Hungry)" (Bob Marley) copyright 1974 Fifty-Six Hope Road Music Ltd./Odnil Music Ltd./Blue Mountain Music Ltd. (PRS). All rights for the United States controlled and administered by Rykomusic, Inc. (ASCAP). International copyright secured. All rights reserved.

"Africa Unite" (Bob Marley) copyright 1979 Fifty-Six Hope Road Music Ltd./Odnil Music Ltd./Blue Mountain Music Ltd. (PRS). All rights for the United States controlled and administered by Rykomusic, Inc. (ASCAP). International copyright secured. All rights reserved.

Grant Farred is associate professor in the literature program at Duke University and the editor of the *South Atlantic Quarterly*. He is author of *Midfielder's Moment: Coloured Literature and Culture in Contemporary South Africa* and editor of the collection *Rethinking C. L. R. James*.